Be Amazing

Linda Sweeney, Eleanor Lewis, Traci Martin,
Michele Helms, Robin Rosebrough, and Pat Harley

BIG
DREAM
MINISTRIES

Second Edition
ISBN-13: 978-1-932199-84-0
ISBN-10: 1-932199-84-5

Cover design by Melissa Swanson

A special thank-you to Leigh Pennington and the 2013 Mt. Bethel retreat team for the title *Be Amazing*.

The anecdotal illustrations in this book are true to life and are included with the permission of the persons involved.

Printed in the United States of America

1 2 3 4 5 6 7 8 /18 17 16 15 14 13

Contents

Welcome to Be Amazing

Soon after I was married, the feminist movement began to take off. I was intrigued. I kept hearing words like *power, freedom, influence,* and *impact.* Well, who doesn't want those? I signed up for a class on feminism taught by two radical and enthusiastic single women. In the next few weeks I was indoctrinated into the feminist movement. Unfortunately, I embraced much of what they were teaching:

1. Men are oppressors. All of the problems women face are because of these oppressors. Now, for some reason it did not occur to me that I had a wonderful father, a loving husband, and a great and fair male boss.
2. Children are accessories. We can have them if we want, but they will slow us down in reaching our highest potential. They should be raised in day care.
3. Housework reduces women to slaves. We should not have to clean toilets, make meals, or perform other household duties. It is drudgery, and it is beneath us.
4. Our worth is determined only by what we achieve outside the home. If we want to prove our value, a career or a position of importance is a must.
5. Sex is recreation or entertainment. We can have it with anybody at any time. (Fortunately, this is one I never embraced!)

So I was elected to public office, became heavily involved in volunteerism, and sought power and freedom. I wanted to be an example, make an impact, and have influence. A few years later my marriage was disintegrating. I was angry, depressed, and miserable. This path had not led me where I wanted to go. It is interesting to note that today we no longer need to have classes on feminism. The culture has embraced it with enthusiasm. And yet the negative effects are all around us.

In that dark place, God began to draw me to Him. An acquaintance invited my husband and me to a Bible study on marriage. We went because we were desperate. And there I discovered that the Bible has quite a lot to say about my role as a woman, and it was in direct opposition to what I had been learning:

1. Men and women are coheirs of God's grace and created equal in His sight.
2. Children are a gift from God.
3. Homemaking is an honored profession, and a stable home and family are the foundation of a healthy and robust society.

4. My worth and my role are defined by God, not by a career.
5. Sex is for marriage only, is sacred and beautiful, and is given to a husband and wife for unity, pleasure, protection, and procreation.

As I read every verse I could find on the role of the woman, including Proverbs 31, I began to see something incredible. God wanted me to have what I longed for: to be an example to those around me, especially my daughters, to have an impact through the way I lived my life, and to be an influence in my community.

Titus 2:3-5 gives a clear command to women in the church. It is because of this command that Big Dream Ministries has produced *Be Amazing* to enable you to be amazing in today's world. There are twenty-four sessions: eight are about character, eight deal with relationships, and eight give practical, clear advice to help women in their home.

In your workbook there is a DVD outline to follow while watching the DVD if you desire. After you have watched the DVD there are some great discussion questions on the outline page. These are followed by three days of homework. The first day contains the lecture notes with some added details. We have included this because we learn both by hearing and by seeing. Days 2 and 3 of the homework will take you right to the Bible and give practical suggestions to help you in your role. There are also recipes, budgets, and other types of helps, plus great resources in the back of the workbook. This book is a wonderful resource manual. It is our desire that women will embrace their God-given roles and live them out in such a way that their homes will be refuges for their families and a blessing to their communities.

Some years ago, my husband's company employed a young man to do a particular job. He was intelligent, winsome, and very capable. But three months later, he was about to be fired. At the exit interview he was surprised to find he was being let go because though he was doing an awesome job, he was doing the wrong job! Corrections were made, he began to do the work he was supposed to do, and he became a good employee who was an asset to the company.

In the same way, I was doing a job, but not the job my Creator had given me. Fortunately I learned what my role was meant to be and was able to change directions before too much damage was done. I will be forever grateful.

God has a role for women, and it is a good one. In that role they will be wonderful examples, will make a great impact, and will influence many others for years to come. They will truly be amazing women!

Be Amazing

in Character

. . . .

Picture This: An Amazing Woman

Linda Sweeney

"That the word of God will not be dishonored."

TITUS 2:5

DVD Outline

I. **Pictures: A Woman's Portrait**
    A. What does a portrait of a Christian woman look like?
    B. Truth Versus Lies

II. **Every Woman a Theologian: Women Are Examples**
    A. A theologian is an expert in the knowledge of God.
    B. God's Command for Women: Titus 2:3-5
    C. Created for a Purpose

III. **Every Home a Refuge: Women Have Influence**
    A. We will have godly character.
    B. We will have godly relationships.
    C. We will have godly homes.

IV. **Every Community Blessed: Women Make an Impact**
    A. Character and conduct matter.
    B. Influencing Our World

Discussion Questions

1. What do you believe is the greatest challenge women face in the world today?
2. What do you personally hope to gain from this study?

Homework Day 1

What?

"Older women likewise are to be reverent in their behavior, not malicious gossips nor enslaved to much wine, teaching what is good, so that they may encourage the young women to love their husbands, to love their children, to be sensible, pure, workers at home, kind, being subject to their own husbands, so that the word of God will not be dishonored" (Titus 2:3-5).

So What?

Read the following notes from the DVD message "Picture This: An Amazing Woman" and answer the "Now What" question at the end.

I. Pictures: A Woman's Portrait

Have you ever taken a bad picture? I'd say lately most all of mine fit this category!

One time when I had to get my driver's license renewed, I learned a few things. First, they have no sense of humor at the Department of Motor Vehicles, and they will *not* take a second photo if you don't like the first one! Second, things aren't always what they seem. I was so upset because I initially thought I looked so cute in my denim jacket, but the result was terrible. I had forgotten about my neck. You know what I mean! I decided to remedy that by making myself a turtleneck using black electrical tape. It worked really well and I was quite proud of my creativity, but don't try this because I think it might be illegal!

Picture taking is agony for me. There are some interesting facts I've learned about photos:

- The older I get, the worse my pictures look (high definition cameras are not my friend).
- The pictures I hated years ago are looking better and better. I find myself saying, "Not so bad!"
- The way I see myself and the way a camera sees me are totally different. You probably have a "magic mirror" like mine that lets you see what you want to see. So when you see reality, it's pretty shocking.
- I find myself explaining the bad look: "It was a bad hair day." "I didn't get much sleep the night before." "I had grandkids all day." "That outfit makes me look big." You get the picture.

A. What does a portrait of a Christian woman look like?

As I've gotten older, I've come to realize that our picture is being taken all the time, from all angles, on good days or bad, in focus or out, ready or not! Others see our daily lives and have a picture to remember, and these are the pictures that really count because they reveal what's inside: the truth about us.

The question we should ask is this: What does our "portrait of a Christian woman" look like to others? According to God's Word, we can be amazing! He tells us how to do this because that is what He wants us to be. Whatever influence we have, for good or bad, is being remembered in the pictures people see and keep of us. Scary thought, right?

B. Truth Versus Lies

Today, women are under more pressure than ever. They believe lies and don't seriously consider the importance of their impact and influence as women. Ladies, our pictures need to be good, especially if we're representing Jesus! In order to be the amazing women God desires, there are two things we should consider. First, we should strive to be a theologian. Second, our goal should be to have a home that is a refuge so our community will be blessed.

II. Every Woman a Theologian: Women are Examples

A. A theologian is an expert in the knowledge of God.

God desires for every woman to be a theologian, which is an expert in the knowledge of God. She is not only to know God and His Word but also to live it out so she can be an example.

B. God's Command for Women: Titus 2:3-5

When we study God's Word, He reveals Himself to us and tells us what He requires. This study is based on God's command for women in Titus 2:3-5: "Older women likewise are to be reverent in their behavior, not malicious gossips nor enslaved to much wine, teaching what is good, so that they may encourage the young women to love their husbands, to love their children, to be sensible, pure, workers at home, kind, being subject to their own husbands, so that the word of God will not be dishonored."

In this passage older women are to teach (some translations say "encourage") the younger women in their character, relationships, and home. God not only gives the commands but also tells us why He is giving them: "that the word of God will not be dishonored" (some translations say "defiled" or "blasphemed"). The way His daughters live should bring honor to Him.

C. Created for a Purpose

God designed women for a purpose. Jesus is the Light of the World, and we are to reflect His light in this dark place. In addition to being our Creator and designer, He has given us His Holy Spirit to teach, empower, and help us in our role. It is encouraging to know the following:

- We were made for a purpose: to have a deep and intimate relationship with Him.
- We were created totally different from men for a completely different purpose.

In Genesis we read, "But for Adam there was not found a helper suitable for him. So the Lord God caused a deep sleep to fall upon the man, and he slept; then He took one of his ribs and closed up the flesh at that place. The Lord God fashioned into a woman the rib which He had taken from the man, and brought her to the man" (2:20-22). This Scripture presents a great principle: women are uniquely made to be uniquely used by God! God's plan calls for us to be amazing, and His Word tells us how.

My picture of an amazing woman is beautiful. The first older woman who was a picture of Jesus for me was my grandmother Katie. Words cannot begin to explain the picture I have of her in my mind because it is so lovely. I grew up in a dark place. Our home was pretty dysfunctional, and we all lived in fear of my dad. He was a really hard man. Mother spent her time trying to appease him, and I spent mine trying to stay as far from him as I could. But in that dark place of loneliness and fear I had a bright light of hope . . . my grandmother. I knew without question that she loved Jesus and me. It was because of her that I was taken to church and actually grew up going there and learning biblical truth. When I was with her I felt peace and love, and I so wanted her to be proud of me. We read the Bible together and watched Billy Graham's crusades on television. She was a great cook and often allowed me to help her in the kitchen, so it was from her I learned many skills of being a homemaker. I stayed with her as much as I possibly could. She lived to see my children born and to love on them as she had me. Her death was a great loss in my life. I will forever be grateful that she pointed me to Christ and that one day I will be with her again. She was truly my example of an amazing woman.

Sometimes I feel a tinge of envy when I hear others speak of their wonderful childhoods and loving parents. But then I remember how God protected me and set me apart to learn His truth and serve Him from a very early age, and I realize I am truly blessed!

By the way, because my grandmother's example started my life as a theologian and because I so desired not only to know but also to obey God's Word, I was able to forgive my father. Before he died he accepted Jesus and was changed. He became a sweet man the last year of his life, and that's an adjective I'd never have used to describe him prior to his decision to ask Jesus into his heart. One of the great things God did for me was to allow me to be at his bedside for the two days before he died. I was with him when Jesus took him away and consider that one of the greatest privileges of my life. I know I will be with him again, and it will be perfect.

III. Every Home a Refuge: Women Have Influence

As we live out God's Word our homes will be a refuge and we will be women of amazing influence. Because of my difficult childhood, I wanted my future home and the lives of any children I might have to be very different from how I was brought up. When I was young I didn't know God's Word that well, but when I grew older and left home, I began to see how studying, learning, and obeying it made a huge difference in every phase of my life. I saw families and lives changed when God's Word was revered and obeyed, when it was used as the filter and guideline for life in this world. Once I decided to obey its teachings and be trained by it and the Holy Spirit, I was able to break the cycle of darkness and fear I had learned to hate. Because I knew Jesus, things could and would be different. I wanted to be a Titus 2 woman, and I realized that God's Word told me how to do it.

This is the purpose of the *Be Amazing* study: to realize that *regardless of our past* we can be amazing women with God's help. In this study we will not only learn what God says but also get some practical help regarding how to live it out. Here is a short preview of what we will cover:

A. We will have godly character.

God tells us in Titus 2:5 that women are to have godly character by being pure, being kind, and having a sensible mind. As we set our minds on things above, not things here on the earth, we will think, act, and even dress in a different way.

B. We will have godly relationships.

1. **Wives** are to love and respect their husbands. My greatest regret is that it took me such a long time to understand what God was asking of me in my marriage. The word *love* used in the marriage relationship means "respect." So if I love Ed I'm to respect him. We will talk about this in depth later in the study, but in short, this means we're not to talk about him to others behind his back; we're not to share personal and/or private information about our marriage with friends and family; we aren't to ridicule him, correct him in front of others, ignore him, make fun of him, or knowingly make him uncomfortable with our words or actions. Did you know that love is a choice . . . an act of the will?

2. **Mothers** are to love their children. We may say "that's a given" (or maybe not), but this means we're to be their authority, not their friend. Today's thinking would not agree. The biggest part of loving our children should be training them in godliness so they will grow up to love and obey God and know the importance of His Word. We read in Deuteronomy, "These words, which I am commanding you today, shall be on your heart; and you shall teach them diligently to your sons and shall talk of them when you sit in your house and when you walk by the way and when you lie down and when you rise up" (6:6-7). In other words, we are to talk to our children about God's Word all the time, using every opportunity.

Howard Hendricks said, "God's fulcrum is always the family. . . . No society has ever survived after the breakdown of the family."[1] Being a wife and mother is the most important role there is for a woman.

3. **Older women** are to teach and encourage the younger women. God moved us to New Orleans, Louisiana, when both our children where quite young, and we soon settled into a wonderful church that became family to us. I was greatly influenced by a godly woman named Alice who was the picture of a beautiful southern Christian lady. Most of the young wives spent a lot of time learning from her and wanting to be like her. Alice was an amazing woman worth imitating.

I was also in a great Sunday school class with an outstanding teacher, Janet. She was talking to us one week about the bad habit of watching soap operas. I must admit I was guilty, but I didn't want Janet to know this. I had grown up watching them and had justified in my mind that they were harmless. Janet was also the director of the church's preschool and kindergarten, where my three-year-old son was enrolled. I was hired there to be a helper. Ryan was thrilled. One day he proudly presented me with a paper he had written about his mommy. Actually, his teacher wrote it from his dictation. I could hardly wait to read it, until I did! He said, "My mommy is really nice and a good cook. She even teaches at my school and comes into my room to help. She has a "zoom shirt" like me, and I get to ride to and from school with her each day. When we come home she makes me a hot dog and puts me down for a nap while she watches her soap show on TV." When I read that I wanted to crawl underneath the carpet. First, I knew Janet had read it, and second, I knew it was wrong. God used my child to convict me! Once I realized how my influence was affecting my children, who were watching, telling, and probably imitating what I did, I never watched another soap opera. God's Word teaches us that loving our children means we are to influence them toward Him, not toward the world in which we live. Older women who are godly examples are amazing women with great influence!

C. We will have godly homes.

Women are to be the CEO of the home. I had the blessing and privilege of being able to stay at home with my children after learning that being employed outside the home was not working for me or for them. Now when we travel down memory lane, which we often do on the occasions when we're all together, I smile at the things they remember—good *times*, not *things*. When I left my very good job, it cut our income by more than half, and I was miserable for about a week. After that there was no way I would substitute the income for the joy I saw in my children and felt in my heart. We didn't have much during that period of adjustment, but this was a really sweet time in our lives, and I thank God for it, especially when I see what fabulous adults and Christians they've become. God gives us the privilege of being amazing when we make our homes a refuge for Him.

Now I smile, realizing how blessed I am to have children and grandchildren who know, love, and serve the Lord. My daughter and I sometimes lead retreats together. She sings and I speak. Once she was asked to introduce me, and I cried so hard with joy at her words that I could barely pull myself together to do my part. Her picture of me was beautiful, and I saw I had been a pretty picture of influence for her. John put it this way: "I have no greater joy than this, to hear of my children walking in the truth" (3 John 4).

IV. Every Community Blessed: Women Make an Impact

A. Character and conduct matter.

When we do things God's way, we are examples influencing others, and the result is that we influence our community so it is blessed as well. All of us can be women who are theologians and great influencers, which results in blessings for many others.

One Mother's Day several years ago, I realized how much impact we women can have. I was very surprised to learn that the sermon for the day was not one of accolades for the mothers that we'd come to expect but rather was based on Isaiah 3:16-26 and entitled "Lose the Ladies, Lose the Land." It was about a sad time in Judah's history when the women helped bring about the captivity of the nation. The pastor said, "When the ladies lose it, all hope is gone! The women's behavior was the last straw for God." In this history lesson, God judged Judah, and it seems we could be there again. Many homes are in ruin, marriages are falling apart, and children are suffering. Christian women through their godly character and conduct can be part of healing the home and land. We can influence our culture and future generations by leading them toward God and not away from Him.

We can have great influence in our neighborhoods as our pictures are being taken by other families. As we live out God's Word we can influence those in organizations where we volunteer or work, those in our church and community, and even our nation. The truth is each of us will leave a legacy, either positive or negative. We know we can't change everything, but we can change some things.

B. Influencing Our World

The world is influenced when God moves His amazing women to "walk in a manner worthy of the calling with which you have been called" (Ephesians 4:1). Sometimes women are moved to pray, and sometimes they are moved to give so that others can move where God sends them. Sometimes they are moved to make an impact in the hard places of the world.

A good example of an amazing woman who did this is Corrie ten Boom. She knew God's Word and practiced it even in a very difficult place for a long period of time—a Nazi death camp in Germany. She even forgave her brutal jailer. Her life was a beautiful picture of Christ. I also think of A. Wetherell Johnson, the founder of Bible Study Fellowship, International, who sacrificed all her comforts of home to teach the Bible to those in China who did not know God. She ended up in a Japanese concentration camp. Both of these women used their knowledge and experience to influence others around the world.

You may not go to China, but an amazing woman can change her own world—her family and neighborhood—through her example and influence. Therefore, our goal for this study is for you to be a theologian, a student of God's Word, with a home that is a refuge so your community will be blessed. Remember, God Himself created women uniquely to be uniquely used by Him. In addition, He has given us commands to follow so we can make the best possible picture.

So smile, because someone is most likely taking your picture, and you want it to be amazing!

Now What?

What were the most important points for you personally in this message, "Picture This: An Amazing Woman"?

Homework Day 2

What?

"Older women likewise are to be reverent in their behavior, not malicious gossips nor enslaved to much wine, teaching what is good, so that they may encourage the young women to love their husbands, to love their children, to be sensible, pure, workers at home, kind, being subject to their own husbands, so that the word of God will not be dishonored" (Titus 2:3-5).

So What?

Reputation is what people think we are. Character is what God knows we are. D. L. Moody is known to have said, "If I take care of my character my reputation will take care of itself." God is concerned about our character because character determines conduct. Let's look at our own lives:

1. From Titus 2:3-5, list the seven areas in which God encourages women regarding their character and conduct.

2. In which of these areas do you need the most help personally?

3. Why is our obedience to these commands important to God (see Titus 2:5)?

A woman is to be a theologian, an expert in the knowledge of God, and her home is to be a refuge so her community can be blessed.

1. Example: What woman is or was a positive example in your life? What specific areas of her character and conduct do you want to emulate?

2. Influence: Who is in my arena of influence? How am I influencing them for God?

3. Impact: What three events have made the most positive impact on your life and who were the people involved? (Have you ever thanked them?)

4. What action are you to take to become the amazing woman God has called you to be?

Homework Day 3

What?

"Charm is deceitful and beauty is vain, but a woman who fears the LORD, she shall be praised" (Proverbs 31:30).

So What?

1. Read Lamentations 1:1-9. Although God was describing the destruction of Jerusalem in this passage, what does He encourage and warn women to do that the people of Jerusalem did not do (see verse 9)?

2. God's Word gives examples of women we can learn from. Ruth is one example of a woman who considered her future. What did society or her community say about her (see Ruth 3:11)?

3. Another amazing woman is found in Proverbs 31. List what she did that we can learn from to be an amazing woman. How was she viewed by her husband and children (see verses 25-29)?

4. Remember, by the way we live our lives, we can bring honor or dishonor to God's Word. How did Elizabeth bring honor to God (see Luke 1:5-6)?

PART ONE: Be Amazing in Character

Now What?

In our next lessons as we unpack Titus 2:3-5, we will be convicted and challenged and will have the wonderful opportunity through God's design to grow into truly amazing women.

1. How have you been challenged through this lesson?

2. How have you been inspired to "Be Amazing"?

Session 2

It's the Truth!

Student of the Word

"That the word of God will not be dishonored."
TITUS 2:5

DVD Outline

I. **Reasons to Study the Bible**
    A. The Word is inspired, or God-breathed.
    B. The Word is eternal and unchanging.
    C. The Word is truth.
    D. The Word is wisdom, giving skills for living.
    E. The Word gives hope.

II. **The Word of God is an extraordinary gift of hope.**
    A. God's Word points to salvation.
    B. God's Word reveals the work of the Holy Spirit.
    C. God's Word equips us in a trial.
    D. God's Word shows us how to be amazing!

III. **Hear God's Word.**
    A. The whole Bible is to be heard, read, and studied.
    B. Study tools can give us a greater understanding of God's Word.
        1. The Chronological Bible
        2. The Amazing Collection: The Bible, Book by Book
        3. Helpful charts of the Bible
        4. Atlases or maps
        5. Observing the text
        6. Marking repeated words or phrases
        7. Using a concordance
            a. Do a word study comparing Scripture with Scripture.
            b. Do a word study of the meaning of the original language.
        8. Using a commentary

IV. **Obey the Word.**
    A. It is so much easier to hear than obey!
    B. Obedience is unnatural.

V. **Persevere in the Word.**

VI. Experience life change by the Word.
A. God's Word in a trial will comfort and change us.
B. The Word of God will give us hope, or assurance.

VII. Conclusion

Discussion Questions

1. Share a time when God's Word changed your thinking or gave your life direction.
2. What hinders you from studying on your own? How will this lesson help you?

Chronological Relationship of the Old Testament Books

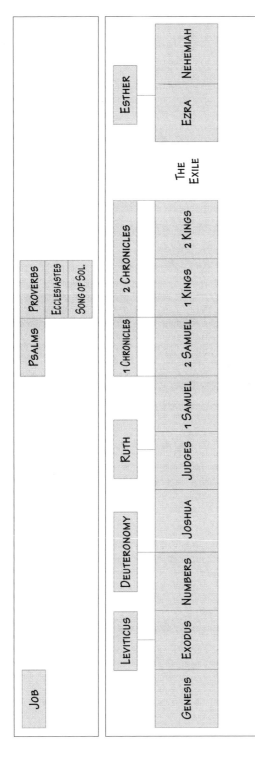

GENESIS	EXODUS	NUMBERS	JOSHUA	JUDGES	1 SAMUEL	2 SAMUEL	1 KINGS	2 KINGS

LEVITICUS   DEUTERONOMY   RUTH   1 CHRONICLES   2 CHRONICLES

THE EXILE

JOB

PSALMS   PROVERBS   ECCLESIASTES   SONG OF SOL.

ESTHER   EZRA   NEHEMIAH

ISAIAH	EZEKIEL	HAGGAI	MALACHI

JEREMIAH   DANIEL   ZECHARIAH

LAMENTATIONS
HOSEA
JOEL
AMOS
OBADIAH
JONAH
MICAH
NAHUM
HABAKKUK
ZEPHANIAH

NOTE:

The eleven books from Genesis through Nehemiah cover the Old Testament story from beginning to end. The other Historical, Poetical, and Prophetical books fit into this Old Testament story in various places, as shown by the vertical placement, and also provide additional information to the story.

Chronological Relationship of the New Testament Books

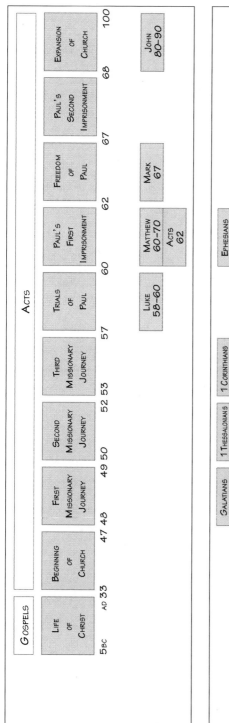

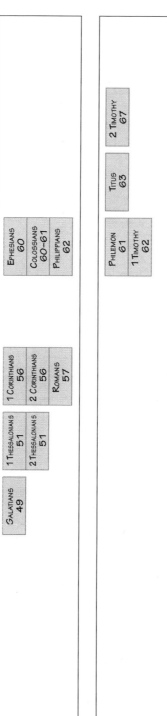

NOTE:
The timeline across the top of the chart shows the broad chronological story of the New Testament as told in the 5 Historical Books (Matthew–Acts). The individual 27 New Testament books are placed below the timeline indicating approximately when they were written.

Homework Day 1

What?

"Older women likewise are to be reverent in their behavior, not malicious gossips nor enslaved to much wine, teaching what is good, so that they may encourage the young women to love their husbands, to love their children, to be sensible, pure, workers at home, kind, being subject to their own husbands, so that the *word of God* will not be dishonored" (Titus 2:3-5).

So What?

Read the following notes from the DVD message "It's the Truth! Student of the Word" and answer the "Now What" question at the end.

Introduction

The Bible causes a lot of confusion. One little girl was asked what the first commandment was. She said it was when Eve told Adam to eat the fruit. She has a point. Another child was told that Solomon was the wisest man on earth, to which he replied, "But Solomon had three hundred wives and seven hundred porcupines, which doesn't seem very wise to me!" Even adults have a hard time with the Bible because we've heard lies such as, "It was written by men, so it's just man's opinion," "It is an old book that is not applicable to today," and "It has a bunch of errors in it." We have based this twenty-four-week course on this very old book because the Bible is not ordinary; rather, it is an extraordinary library of sixty-six books.

I. Reasons to Study the Bible

A. The Word is inspired, or God-breathed.

"No prophecy of Scripture is a matter of one's own interpretation, for no prophecy was ever made by an act of human will, but men moved by the Holy Spirit spoke from God" (2 Peter 1:20-21).

God wrote the Bible by using at least forty men on three continents—Asia, Africa, and Europe—in three languages: Hebrew, Greek, and Aramaic. It was written over a period of 1,500 to 1,600 years, and it all tells one story. Only God could do that!

B. The Word is eternal and unchanging.

"Heaven and earth will pass away, but My words will not pass away" (Matthew 24:35). "But the word of our God stands forever" (Isaiah 40:8; see also 1 Peter 1:25). "Jesus Christ is the same yesterday and today and forever" (Hebrews 13:8).

God wrote the Bible for us to live by and says it is applicable for today and tomorrow.

C. The Word is truth.

Jesus said, "Sanctify them in the truth; Your word is truth" (John 17:17). This is the only book that never needs to be revised because it is unchanging truth.

D. The Word is wisdom, giving skills for living.

"For the LORD gives wisdom; from His mouth come knowledge and understanding" (Proverbs 2:6). "Your word is a lamp to my feet and a light to my path" (Psalm 119:105). "How can a young man keep his way pure? By living according to your word" (Psalm 119:9, NIV).

The Word gives wisdom to know what to believe and therefore how to behave.

E. The Word gives hope.

The psalmist said, "And in His word do I hope" (Psalm 130:5).

II. The Word of God is an extraordinary gift of hope.

A. God's Word points to salvation.

When I use the word *hope* I mean "maybe." When God uses the word *hope* it means "something assured or promised"! Years ago someone asked me what assurance I had that I would go to heaven if I died right now. I had no assurance because being biblically illiterate I didn't know God's promises. However, when I heard His Word, I received God's gift of forgiveness by asking Jesus to be my Savior. He promises both forgiveness now and heaven someday.

B. God's Word reveals the work of the Holy Spirit.

For years I had a Bible on my dresser collecting dust, but I could not understand it. With forgiveness God gave another gift. God's Spirit came to live in me to be my teacher. "But the Helper, the Holy Spirit . . . will teach you all things" (John 14:26). "The Spirit of truth . . . will guide you into all the truth" (John 16:13). I needed Him to teach me. When I read the Bible with the Spirit in my life it was like a lightbulb had come on in my head!

C. God's Word equips us in a trial.

Receiving Jesus didn't mean I automatically had an interest in the Bible. I was not interested until my son was born with a severe birth defect. Thinking it was my fault, I picked up the

Bible looking for answers and found them in John 9:1-3. There God assured me this was not my fault and He would show His power. Problems can be gifts wrapped in a brown paper bag. This didn't look like a gift but caused me to seek God in His Word. "Before I was afflicted I went astray, but now I keep Your word" (Psalm 119:67).

D. God's Word shows us how to be amazing!

After receiving Jesus, I moved with my family to a new city where an older woman, Evie, taught and encouraged me by starting a Bible study in our neighborhood. Watching how she lived as a wife and mother and hearing God's Word for the first time caused my life to start changing. However, after one year we moved again, and this time there was no Evie. It was just the Lord and me. That, too, was a gift because to really learn, we need to know how to study the Bible for ourselves. What if you had no human teacher? Could you teach yourself?

Since the Word gives hope, or promises, we will use the acronym HOPE to help us be a student of God's Word and to live life at its best as amazing women.

III. Hear God's Word.

"Faith comes from hearing, and hearing by the word of Christ" (Romans 10:17).

A. The whole Bible is to be heard, read, and studied.

1. Jesus said, "Man shall not live on bread alone, but on every word that proceeds out of the mouth of God" (Matthew 4:4). Usually we don't begin a novel in the middle or read a chapter toward the end, because it is a story. So why do we do that with the Bible? It is God's story! The Old Testament covers four thousand years, and the New Testament covers ninety years of the story. We are now living it out, but we will never understand the Bible nor have an accurate picture of God without reading or studying it from beginning to end.

2. Hearing or studying the whole Bible helps avoid misconceptions. Many think the Old Testament shows God as angry and the New Testament as loving. Yet in the Old Testament we see a very patient God of tremendous love.

   a. He warned Noah of coming judgment and gave men 120 years to repent.

   b. In love He gave plans for an ark of safety to keep them from the judgment.

   c. He sent many prophets (sixteen of whom wrote books) over a number of years to warn the people of Israel to turn from their idolatry to be spared God's judgment.

In the New Testament God does show great love, but He also shows His anger.

a. We see God's anger at sin poured out on Jesus at the cross.

b. Ananias and Sapphira were struck dead by God for lying to Him.

c. Revelation shows the coming wrath of God on those who reject Jesus.

As we study the entire Bible we see God's love and His holiness in every book.

B. Study tools can give us a greater understanding of God's Word.

Those years without a teacher, I read through the Bible on my own, but I would get confused because I didn't understand that the Bible is not laid out in chronological order. Therefore, to help you understand the Bible I recommend the following resources and practices:

1. The Chronological Bible. Daily readings tell the story in chronological order with excellent notes to help explain more difficult passages.

2. *The Amazing Collection: The Bible, Book by Book* (DVD Bible study for women from Genesis to Revelation), www.theamazingcollection.org or 1-888-366-3460.

3. Helpful charts of the Bible

    a. **The Old Testament chart** on page 26 helps us understand the chronology. The books in the large boxes of the Historical Books section follow one another chronologically starting from Genesis to Nehemiah. The Historical Books in the smaller boxes above, such as Leviticus and Ruth, do not carry on the timeline but give additional information about what was happening during the book or time period below it. Ruth tells of God sending a Kinsman Redeemer during the wicked time of the Judges when "everyone was doing what was right in his own eyes." Though the prophets are placed last in the Old Testament, most of them were written during 2 Kings to lovingly warn God's people to come back to Him.

    b. **The New Testament chart** on page 27 again shows that the book order of the Bible is not the order in which the books were written. Though placed toward the end, James wrote the first letter. It also shows that Paul wrote Philippians, a book of joy, when he was imprisoned!

4. Atlases or maps. These give great insight and connect us to the land and locations of God's story. I wondered how far Mary traveled while pregnant to get to Bethlehem for Jesus' birth. The map shows it was about eighty miles directly to Bethlehem, but since Samaritans were enemies, they probably went around, adding even more miles!

5. Observing the text. It is important to read the Word in its context. There is an old saying, "text out of context is pretext." In other words, it's important to know the history—who it was written to and what was written before and after it. My father often jokingly quoted two verses of Scripture out of context: "Judas hung Himself . . . go and do thou likewise!" Obviously, verses taken out of context can lead to very dangerous beliefs. We want to *Observe* (*What* is it saying?), *Interpret* (*So what* does it mean?), and *Apply* (*Now what* am I going to do about it?).

6. Marking repeated words or phrases. When God repeats something He really means it, so marking repeated words or phrases shows what is important to God. You may be hesitant to mark up a Bible. If so, I encourage you to buy a paperback study Bible you can mark, for it will reveal much. For example, in Genesis 1 the phrases "then God said . . . and it was so" are repeated. From that we learn God spoke, and whatever He said happened. And that is still true!

7. Using a concordance. Do you speak Hebrew and Greek? I don't either. So we have to go to seminary, right? No, we just need a concordance, which contains the principle words in the Bible and where to find them. There are different concordances for different versions of the Bible; however, *Strong's Concordance* also tells the meanings of the words in the original language. You may use a hard copy, or you can find free websites offering the tools you need without the expense. Websites will change, but at this writing Gateway Bible and Blue Letter Bible are good ones. What are some of the things we can learn by using a concordance?

    a. **Do a word study comparing Scripture with Scripture.** Study a word you want to understand or are struggling with, such as *forgiveness*. To find every verse in the Bible that uses the word *forgive* (or any other word), go to your concordance and look up the word (hard copy or website).

        On the Blue Letter Bible website, as it works today, type the word into the search line. Scroll down to the version of the Bible you want to read. Click on the search button, and every Bible verse using that word will appear.

        Compare Scripture with Scripture, as one Scripture will explain another.

        Read the verses looking for *commands, principles,* or *consequences.* In my example of forgiveness, I quickly scanned through a number of verses but came to Matthew 6:12-15, where I found one of each:

- Command: I was to forgive as God had forgiven me.
- Principle: God would forgive me as I forgave others.
- Consequence: If I didn't forgive others, God wouldn't forgive me.

        After looking at every verse using the word *forgive, forgiven,* or *forgiveness,* you might be reminded of other Scriptures when God forgives, such as the following:

- He removes sin "as far as the east is from the west" (Psalm 103:12).
- He casts all our sins behind His back (so He can't see them) (see Isaiah 38:17).
- He casts all our sins into the depths of the sea (so we can't see them) (see Micah 7:19).

    b. **Do a word study of the meaning of the original language.**

        In *Strong's Concordance* (hardback), you will find a number beside most words. Go to the back of the concordance and find the number, and it will give you the complete Hebrew (if the word is in the Old Testament) or Greek (New

Testament) meaning for that word.

Using a website such as Blue Letter Bible, choose the KJV or NASB version and then check the "Strong's" box. The number will appear beside most words. Click on the number to see the meaning of the original word. *Forgive* in Matthew 6:14-15 was #863. The first line of the definition is "to send away." Therefore, to forgive is to send away a wrong. We are to send away others' wrongs just as God sent away ours "as far as the east is from the west."

8. Using a commentary. Commentaries are men's opinions and should be used after you have done research in the Word. However, most commentaries are written by excellent scholars and will give greater clarity. If possible, look at several. A few are listed on the Resources page at the end of this study and on Bible websites.

Once you have experienced God speaking directly to you, Bible study will become exciting. However, it is not always pleasant when God speaks. One time, He said I was stiff-necked!

IV. Obey the Word.

"Assemble the people . . . so that they may hear and learn and fear the LORD your God, and be careful to observe [to do or obey] all the words of this law" (Deuteronomy 31:12). (The NASB says "to observe," and the original meaning is "to do or obey.")

A. It is so much easier to hear than obey!
Our house was broken into and many items were stolen. Jesus said, "Love your enemies. . . . Whoever takes away your coat, do not withhold your shirt from him either" (Luke 6:27, 29). That's not what I wanted to give the thieves!

B. Obedience is unnatural.
We may hear God's Word, but obeying is the problem! That is another reason God gave us His Spirit. God says, "I will put My Spirit within you and cause you to . . . observe My ordinances" (Ezekiel 36:27). The Holy Spirit not only teaches us but also empowers us to obey God's plan.

V. Persevere in the Word.

"For whatever was written in earlier times was written for our instruction, so that through perseverance and the encouragement of the Scriptures we might have hope" (Romans 15:4). Paul was saying in the New Testament that the Old Testament (written in earlier times) was written for our instruction. An example is 1 Corinthians 10, where God gives warnings from

Israel's history so we won't fail as they did. What we call Old Testament stories God says were written to instruct us and give us hope.

We once lived in New York state, and I was doing radio and television commercials and cohosting a weekly television talk show. When my husband announced that his company was "promoting" us to another state, I didn't want to go. I cried, carried on, and then asked God, "Is this Your idea?" I was reading the Old Testament: "For promotion cometh neither from the east, nor from the west, nor from the south. But God is the judge: he putteth down one, and setteth up another" (Psalm 75:6-7, KJV). It sounded like God's idea! So I said, "I'd have to give up things here. What would I do there?" I read, "Do not remember the former things, nor consider the things of old. Behold, I will do a new thing" (Isaiah 43:18-19, NKJV). The Old and New Testaments are one story, and both instruct and encourage us. If we persevere in God's Word, He can direct our lives. In this case, we moved!

VI. Experience life change by the Word.

"We also exalt in our tribulations, knowing that tribulation brings about perseverance; and perseverance, proven [changed] character; and proven character, hope [assurance]" (Romans 5:3-4). The whole purpose of Bible study is to be changed into the likeness of Christ, into an amazing woman who beautifully represents God here on earth because she looks like Him.

A. God's Word in a trial will comfort and change us.

Remember, trials can be gifts. We usually don't say, "Yeah, I've got a trial!" But God says we can exalt in our troubles because God is changing our character and that gives us hope. In a short span of time, I experienced many troubles. My husband lost his job, which caused me great fear. I thought I trusted God, but really I had been trusting my bank account. I was hurt by someone I loved and trusted. My mom was dying of ovarian cancer and living with us. And to top it all off, I had a seizure and broke my nose. The blow to my head also caused a hole in my retina, requiring two nasty surgeries.

One day I lost it! There is a saying that goes, "What's in your well comes up in your bucket!" Times of trouble are not the time to start filling your well. God's Word in our mind before a trial comes gives us something to draw from. If we don't have God's Word, we will believe lies like I did. I said, "God, You don't love me anymore." But I remembered a verse: "I love you with an everlasting love." I said, "Then You have left me." I knew His Word said, "I will never leave you or forsake you." I said, "Then You don't care about me." He said, "Cast your care upon me because I care for you." We will all have tribulation; that's life. Is your well full of God's Word so He can speak truth to you when you need it?

I experienced a life change because the job loss and betrayal whittled off *self-righteousness* and humbled me. The sicknesses and surgeries whittled off *self-sufficiency* because I couldn't do it myself!

B. The Word of God will give us hope, or assurance.

Through God's Word I was given the hope, assurance, and promise of heaven someday, God's leading and strength for today, and God's promise that even trials will be used for good to make me like Him.

"It is good for me that I was afflicted, that I may learn Your statutes" (Psalm 119:71).

VII. Conclusion

Someone has said that many of us have a vacuum cleaner religion. We keep God in the closet until we make a mess; then we pull Him out to clean it up and put Him back in until we need Him again. How much better to be students of His Word with a full bucket of hope (assurances) because we have **H**eard, **O**beyed, **P**ersevered in, and **E**xperienced a changed life through God's Word. God has given us the extraordinary gift of His Word for our good and His glory to enable us to be amazing women!

Now What?

What were the most important points for you personally in this message, "It's the Truth! Student of the Word"?

Homework Day 2

What?

"Your word is a lamp to my feet and a light to my path" (Psalm 119:105).

So What?

For God's Word to lead us we need to spend time with Him. We have seen some of the great benefits of studying God's Word, but there are even more.

1. Hear the Word.

"So faith comes from hearing, and hearing by the word of Christ" (Romans 10:17).

In addition to giving faith, what is the Word to us (see Deuteronomy 32:46-47)?

2. Obey the Word.

"Assemble the people . . . so that they may hear and learn and fear the LORD your God, and be careful to observe [do or obey] all the words of this law" (Deuteronomy 31:12).

List the reasons or benefits for obeying God's Word given in each of these verses (see also James 1:22, 25).

Now What?

Since God's Word leads to faith, obedience to it brings blessing, and it is in fact our life, let's get started by doing a word study. Think of something you want to understand, such as faith, hope, love, peace, contentment, or trust.

1. Go to a concordance. There is a partial one in the back of most Bibles, but an exhaustive concordance has every verse in the Bible containing a particular word. Compare Scripture with Scripture by reading all the verses using that word.

PART ONE: Be Amazing in Character

Use an online concordance such as www.blueletterbible.org. (See the notes on III.B.7.a. "Do a word study comparing Scripture with Scripture" on page 32 for more detailed instructions.)

Ask, *What* is God saying? *So what* does it mean? *Now what* am I going to do about it?

2. Use *Strong's Exhaustive Concordance* to understand a word meaning in the original language. (See the notes on III.B.7.b. "Do a word study of the meaning of the original language" on pages 32–33 for more detailed instructions.) Find the number and read the meaning from the original Hebrew or Greek.

Record what God teaches you as you take this step in becoming a theologian, an expert in the knowledge of God, by becoming a student of His Word.

Homework Day 3

What?

"Blessed [happy] are those who hear the word of God and observe it" (Luke 11:28).

So What?

It is not enough to go to Bible studies or church and know what the Word of God says. God says blessings or happiness comes when we obey it. To have HOPE (assurances), we need to Hear God's Word and Obey it, but obedience requires perseverance.

1. Persevere in the Word.

"For whatever was written in earlier times was written for our instruction, so that through perseverance and the encouragement of the Scriptures we might have hope" (Romans 15:4).

What two things happen when you persevere (patiently endure) in God's promises (see 2 Peter 1:4)?

List qualities that are present in our life when we are diligent in our faith (see 2 Peter 1:5-7). Remember, "faith comes from hearing . . . the word of Christ" (Romans 10:17).

2. Experience life change by the Word.

"We exalt in our tribulations, knowing that tribulation brings about perseverance; and perseverance, proven [changed] character; and proven character, hope [assurance]" (Romans 5:3-4).

What must we do to experience a proven or changed life, and why (see Romans 5:3-4)?

Now What?

Not only can we study a word or concept such as anger or forgiveness, but we can also do a character study. The lives of men and women in the Bible teach us about God and His ways. We can learn lessons from their successes and failures. Let's look at a woman named Lydia.

1. Record what you learn about God and Lydia's character and conduct that you can apply to your life to become an amazing woman (see Acts 16:9-15, 40).

2. Now go to a commentary and record anything else you learn about her. You can find commentaries at websites such as www.blueletterbible.org/commentaries/ or www .biblegateway.com/resources/commentaries/.

Battle for the Mind

Be Sensible (Sound Mind)

Traci Martin

"That the word of God will not be dishonored."

TITUS 2:5

DVD Outline

I. **Introduction**

II. **The Enemy Attack: Three Common Battleground Areas**
  A. Appearance: Women must look perfect.
  B. Achievements: Women must do it all.
  C. Accumulation: Enough is never enough.

III. **Answers: Prepare for the Battle**
  A. Acknowledge the lie.
  B. Believe the truth.
  C. Combat lies with specific Scripture.

IV. **Action: Engage the Enemy**
  A. Battle of Appearance
  B. Battle of Achievement
  C. Battle of Accumulation

V. **Protecting the Thought Life**
  A. Combat inner thoughts.
    1. Cluttered minds: overextended and overwhelmed
    2. Runaway thoughts: anxiety and fear
  B. Pursue peace.

VI. **Conclusion**

Discussion Questions

1. What areas are battlegrounds for your mind?
2. In what ways have you been challenged to change your thought processes?
3. What is the next step you need to take to develop a sound mind?
4. Describe a time you experienced faulty thinking and how it was renewed.

Homework Day 1

What?

"Older women likewise are to be reverent in their behavior, not malicious gossips nor enslaved to much wine, teaching what is good, so that they may encourage the young women to love their husbands, to love their children, to be sensible, pure, workers at home, kind, being subject to their own husbands, so that the word of God will not be dishonored" (Titus 2:3-5).

So What?

Read the following notes from the DVD message "Battle for the Mind: Be Sensible: Sound Mind" and answer the "Now What" question at the end.

I. Introduction

Growing up, I did so many things I would now consider wrong. I dressed too provocatively, dated just about anyone who asked me out, and chased after worldly fun; yet for the culture I lived in, I was considered a good girl. The problem was my thinking was skewed because my view of life was muddled.

Coming to Jesus Christ was life-altering. The Holy Spirit moved into my heart. He allowed me to have the mind of Christ (see 1 Corinthians 2:16) and His perspective on life. As I began reading the Bible, I discovered that most of what I thought about life was not true. So now I was living in a way that was in direct opposition to the truth. That is what James 1:8 refers to as being double-minded. It is a restless and confused inner thought life with opposing thoughts. Which are we going to feed and grow, and which are we going to starve and remove? I had to choose between the truth of God's Word and my natural worldly thoughts.

There is a battle for the mind and an Enemy who does not want the mind of Christ to grow in us. Although Satan cannot read minds, he can send fiery darts disguised as thoughts to entice and ensnare. He uses temptations to allure us, accusations to cause false guilt, and deception to cause doubt.

The world is full of deception. The "world" is defined as a system of living, devised by man, that leaves God out. Satan is called the god of this world, and he is "a liar and the father of lies" (John 8:44). The constant bombardment of lies results in a battle within our minds. Satan knows if he can capture our minds, he has captured us.

However, Titus 2:5 commands us to be "sensible," that is, to have a sound or self-controlled mind. We need to recognize there is a battle for our mind from our Enemy and from our own skewed thinking.

II. The Enemy Attack: Three Common Battleground Areas

A. Appearance: Women must look perfect.

I was born completely cross-eyed; both of my eyes turned in toward my nose to the extent that my pupils were barely seen. By six months of age I had the first of four corrective surgeries and wore an eye patch much of my early childhood. I had years of vision therapy to strengthen my eye muscles, but I have always been conscious of this sensitive issue because I could never look perfect!

Before the writing of this study, Big Dream Ministries took a survey of several hundred young women. One woman stated that "the portrayal of women in the media continues to increase the pressures for women to be extremely thin. . . . I believed those portrayals were ideal and became anorexic." She went on to say, "Women are not encouraged enough to count on their inner beauty and love their bodies as they are, but are taught instead in our society that what we look like is most important." She was struggling with a mental battle over her appearance.

I have always had to watch my weight closely. I have lost and gained the same twenty pounds over and over again. I simply look at food and it goes right to my hips. I want to be healthy and strong, but instead I am tempted to think I must look like the fashion models. How easy it is to be deceived.

But even fashion models don't look like fashion models. Modern photographic tools can take a picture of a woman and use a computer to edit her into manmade perfection. To help us reach that perfection, we are offered beauty aids that go way beyond lipstick, such as eyelash extensions, Botox, chemical peels, teeth whitening, eye lifts, chin and cheek implants, and liposuction. The message is that there is nothing too excessive to reach a perfect appearance—as Hollywood or the fashion industry defines perfection! We all want to look our best, but how much is too much?

B. Achievements: Women must do it all.

A popular commercial played a jingle with the lyrics, "I can bring home the bacon, fry it up in a pan, and never ever let you forget you're a man. 'Cause I am woman," all the while depicting a beautiful woman going through all the different roles of her life. This ad reflected a growing movement in the world that a woman has to do it all and do it well. A woman's success is measured by her ability to climb the corporate ladder, keep the perfect home, be a perfect mother, and be passionate with her husband at all times. The battle within our mind convinces us of the need to try to accomplish everything while at the same time balancing our relationships around a packed schedule.

This ad resonated with me as a young woman. I grew up with a single mom. She worked very hard to keep a roof over our heads and food on the table. She wanted a different life for me and insisted on higher education. A career was expected so that when my man left me, I could take care of myself. I was not going to be left in a position of struggling to fend for myself. So I tried to create a perfect life by doing it all and trying to have it all.

So many women live overwhelmed because they are struggling with this battle of achievement in their mind. Additionally, there can be confusion about what is really needed in life, causing constant striving for more. This brings us to the next A of our battlegrounds—accumulation.

C. Accumulation: Enough is never enough.

A good friend of mine lives in a nice home, but every corner is filled to the brim with stuff. You have to turn sideways just to walk in the door. She is a hoarder.

Hoarding is a condition so prevalent that there have even been reality television shows depicting the lives of people who have more stuff than space. Although most of us do not live with that kind of extreme accumulation, we do replace our belongings often, not because items are broken or worn out, but because there is a new model available or styles have changed. This has also contributed to the rise in the use of self-storage units. According to the "Vital Statistics of the Self Storage Industry," "It has grown so fast that in the last twelve years the use has grown from one in every seventeen households to one in every ten."[2] So one in ten households have accumulated more stuff than they have room for!

We justify our ever-changing desires by storing our perfectly good items or donating them to charity. It is good to give, but not as an excuse to get more. The battle within our mind is that our lives won't be complete without _____ (you fill in the blank). Advertisers capitalize on this by bombarding us with marketing to evoke such feelings as:

- Pride—if you have more, you are on top.
- Fear—if you don't have more, you won't be on top.
- Inadequacy—if you don't have more, then you are not good enough.
- Coveting—if they have more, you must have more too.
- Greed—you need more, you need more, you need more.

The things we want, along with how we look and what we achieve, can become idols. Any thought process that leads us away from Christ has the potential to become a mental rut that skews reasoning and logic. These entrenched thoughts are to be "demolished" (2 Corinthians 10:4, NIV).

The three A's—achievement, accumulation, and appearance—are very common tactics the Enemy uses to attack our minds. So how do we strengthen our minds for battle?

Fortunately there is another A.

Battle for the Mind

III. Answers: Prepare for the Battle

First, put on the "helmet of salvation" (Ephesians 6:17), which protects us from the shrewd tactics of the Enemy. It keeps us from being confused by protecting our thinking because we understand that the world lies, but Jesus is the truth. We are able to use God's Word to discern truth as opposed to what the world communicates. A sound and sensible mind can be developed and provide the ammunition necessary to win the battle. It is wise to compare everything we believe, everything we know, and everything we learn to God's Word. Satan started with subtle twists of truth in the garden and now has developed a world accepting of bold and blatant opposition to God's truth.

If our thought process is rooted in the world, then our minds have been attacked. Romans 12:2 instructs us, "Do not be conformed to this world, but be transformed by the renewing of your mind, so that you may prove what the will of God is, that which is good and acceptable and perfect."

Renewing your mind is as simple as A, B, C.

A. Acknowledge the lie.

Start by acknowledging the lie. Things that are commonplace today were scandalous fifty years ago and would have resulted in stoning in Jesus' day. A good starting point is to ask if the attitude, action, or thought has stood the test of time in God's Word. Anything that goes against God's Word is not based on truth. We must see to it that no one takes us captive through philosophy and empty deception.

B. Believe the truth.

When we have a thought that is opposing God's truth, we have to choose truth. "[God's] word is truth" (John 17:17).

C. Combat lies with specific Scripture.

Finally, combat the lies with specific Scripture. It is not enough to simply believe the truth; we actually have to use it as the sword to fight the battle for our minds (see Hebrews 4:12).

IV. Action: Engage the Enemy

A. Battle of Appearance

The battle of appearance is thinking that if we perfect the outer package, we will be acceptable. There is nothing too excessive to achieve a perfect appearance, and anything less results in a sense of inferiority or failure. However, in the Bible, when Peter was teaching women, he told them external beauty that comes from styled hair, nice jewelry, and pretty clothes should not be their only effort. He was not telling them to disregard how they looked but rather to

PART ONE: Be Amazing in Character

focus on developing a beautiful heart (see 1 Peter 3:3-4). "Charm is deceitful and beauty is vain, but a woman who fears the LORD, she shall be praised" (Proverbs 31:30).

When our focus goes from the external to the internal, we focus on our relationship with God—exactly what a sound and sensible mind should do.

Over the last few years, my lazy eye has gotten progressively worse. I learned I could have another surgery that would likely make my eye straight; however, there is a risk that I would have double vision indefinitely and not be able to read. Although I would really like to have normal looking eyes, I came to my senses, put aside the pride, and made a decision against the surgery.

B. Battle of Achievement

The battle of achievement is thinking value comes from accomplishing something the world views as important, or even just something that pleases other people. However, God says in Isaiah 43:7, "Everyone who is called by My name . . . I have created for My glory."

We are not here to bring glory to ourselves but to God. Our obedience to God brings Him great glory—exactly what a sound and sensible mind should do.

I believed the lie that I had to achieve it all and therefore worked full-time, managed the house, and took care of the family. We had a nanny who came to our home to take care of our baby. She cleaned the house and cooked dinner so it was ready and waiting for us. I would come home, feed my daughter, play with her, and then put her to bed. It was the ideal situation if you are going to work. Yet, deep in my spirit there was a constant emotional tug. I did not want to go to work. I wanted to stay home and raise my child. However, I would not quit working since I was driven to achieve. I couldn't trust that I wouldn't be abandoned.

It was not until after I left my job that I realized how my drive to achieve kept me from really knowing God, much less bringing Him glory.

C. Battle of Accumulation

The battle of accumulation is thinking possessions such as more money or things will make life complete. Enough is never enough. However, God says in 1 John 2:15, "Do not love the world nor the things in the world. If anyone loves the world, the love of the Father is not in him." When we value what God values, then we are content with what we have—exactly what a sound and sensible mind should do.

I grew up very poor, so most of my life we did not have money to spend on anything beyond the basics. When I worked full-time, though I didn't spend extravagantly, I could buy whatever I needed and some things I wanted. The thought of quitting my job and going back to not having enough money was terrifying. It didn't matter that my husband had started making more money or that my work expenses would be eliminated. I feared it would not be enough. My desire for money kept me from what I truly wanted, which was to be a stay-at-home mom.

God used painful circumstances to bring me home full-time, changing the mental ruts that had formed in my thinking. I am not saying everyone needs to quit his or her job, but that my motives were based on my own thinking and not God's Word. This event started the renewing of my mind, and I began to win a few of the mental battles, but the war is constant.

Whether we struggle with one of the three A's—the battles of achievement, accumulation, or appearance—or some other challenge such as addiction or approval, the answer is to "set your mind on the things above, not on the things that are on earth" (Colossians 3:2). Then we will have the right perspective to contend with any of Satan's attempts to deceive us.

V. Protecting the Thought Life

A. Combat inner thoughts.
At times, it seems easier to control the outside influences than it is to calm the storm within our own heads. We have cluttered minds and runaway thoughts.

1. Cluttered minds: overextended and overwhelmed
The pressing issue of the moment, with all that needs to be done, can cause our minds to race. Short-term memory can only hold on to five to seven thoughts, so as a new thought comes in, an old thought goes out and we forget. Our thoughts are all over the place, making it hard to keep focused on any one idea. The constant mental juggling of trying to remember is very stressful for the brain and can even keep us awake at night. We need a way to take "every thought captive to the obedience of Christ" (2 Corinthians 10:5). To bring order to our brain, we can write down our thoughts. There are several ways to do this:

a. **Controlling thoughts**
  1. Create a mega to-do list by just jotting down thoughts as they come to mind. It can be on paper, computer, or a mobile device.
  2. Organize lists by types of activity, such as calls, e-mails, or immediate and long-term projects.

b. **Working it out.** Most of us have some method of managing our to-do list and calendar, from sticky notes to a phone app. It may be very helpful to presort categories of tasks when working through the list. For example, group all similar tasks together such as phone calls or errands. When similar tasks are completed during the same block of time, it helps our minds stay focused. It is so easy to lose track of time with a quick call or check of e-mail. Before you know it twenty minutes have gone by. Smart scheduling leaves bigger chunks of time for other things.

Whatever method of managing your to-do list works best for you, keep it handy so new thoughts can be immediately written down as they come to mind. It is a great way to alleviate mental stress and forgetfulness while ordering your mind.

2. Runaway thoughts: anxiety and fear

Anxiety and fear are at the root of many runaway thoughts. One momentary thought can multiply until it has gripped our minds. "But God hath not given us the spirit of fear; but of power, and of love, and of a sound mind" (2 Timothy 1:7, KJV). Just as our minds need to be transformed against the lies of the world, God's Word can transform fearful thoughts. He tells us, "Do not fear, for I am with you" (Isaiah 43:5).

When I was eleven years old, I was nearly abducted by a suspected pedophile. When I was sixteen years old, I had to fight off an attacker, as my mother was being dragged away by a stranger who had grabbed her at our front door. When I was twenty-one, a man sexually harassed me at a grocery store and then proceeded to follow me around town in his car. By the grace of God, I was not hurt, but you can understand the fear I had when I was out after that, especially at night. God worked mightily in my life to remove the spirit of fear. I thought I had victory in that area until my teenage daughters wanted to go out with friends or even take a job working at night. The spirit of fear was back. It is so easy for my mind to fixate on all of the terrible things that could happen that I was tempted to stifle their independence. But I had to trust God. So I personalize Isaiah 43:5: "Do not fear, for I am with your girls."

B. Pursue peace.

We are surrounded by stimulation all day long. Our brains need rest. When we take time to "Be still, and know that [He is] God" (Psalm 46:10, NIV), we develop a peace that surpasses understanding and that will guard our minds (see Philippians 4:7).

In addition to the peace of God, we also need sleep. According to the National Institute of Health, too little sleep leaves us with an inability to concentrate, impaired memory, and mood swings. In other words, sleep is necessary for the mind to be sensible.

VI. Conclusion

Have you allowed the Enemy to hijack your thought life? Are you struggling with a lack of order in your mind? There is hope, for God is the voice of truth. Those who respond to His voice will develop a sound mind, controlled by God's Spirit, and will live in His strength and power, bringing Him glory. Now that's an amazing woman!

Now What?

What were the most important points for you personally in this message, "Battle for the Mind: Be Sensible: Sound Mind"?

Homework Day 2

What?

"Set your mind on the things above, not on the things that are on earth" (Colossians 3:2).

So What?

Satan is called the god of this world and "a liar and the father of lies" (John 8:44). The "world" is defined as the system of living, devised by man, that leaves God out. Let's look at some of the common lies bombarding our minds and how God's truth challenges us.

1. Achievements or accomplishments are my goal.

a. Why were you made (see Isaiah 43:7)?

b. How does this challenge your thinking about what you want to achieve, and why?

2. Accumulations prove my worth.

a. The Enemy uses common motivators to cause dissatisfaction within us. Which of the following are most effective in causing you to desire more? (Circle the ones that apply.)

- Pride—if you have more, you are on top.
- Fear—if you don't have more, you won't be on top.
- Inadequacy—if you don't have more, then you are not good enough.
- Coveting—if they have more, you must have more too.
- Greed—you need more, you need more, you need more.

b. What does God warn (see 1 John 2:15)?

c. How does this challenge your motivation to accumulate more?

3. Appearance defines me.

a. What is your biggest struggle with your appearance?

b. What do you learn about God and yourself in Scripture (see Psalm 139:14-15)?

c. How does this change your thinking about your appearance?

1. What is God's solution as to how to renew our mind (see Romans 12:1)?

2. What are we to do and not do to arm ourselves to win the battle for our minds (see Romans 12:2)?

3. Renewing our minds gives the sensible, sound, self-controlled mind commanded by God. Based on what you've learned in this lesson, what has God revealed about your mind-set? What changes do you need to start making today?

Homework Day 3

What?

"But God hath not given us the spirit of fear; but of power, and of love, and of a sound mind" (2 Timothy 1:7, KJV).

So What?

The storm within our own heads can be caused by fear or being overwhelmed with life. Runaway thoughts, lack of focus, and forgetfulness are symptoms of a mind that is out of control. Let's look at the importance of a self-controlled mind and how we can achieve it.

1. Regardless of the cause of your inner storm, what two things must you do to experience the Lord's perfect peace (see Isaiah 26:3)?

2. What hinders you from keeping your mind steadfast, or fixed on the Lord?

3. What was Peter's mind problem and ours (see Mark 8:33)?

4. What are we commanded to do?

    Colossians 3:2

    2 Corinthians 10:5

1. It will be helpful to take every thought captive. Make a list of any fears or frustrations that are presently troubling your mind.

2. Using what we learned in "Session 2: It's the Truth! Student of the Word," do a word search to find Scripture to combat the fears, doubts, unforgiveness, anger, or anxiety resulting from those things you listed in the previous question. List your findings here.

3. Responsibilities can overwhelm us. Make a list of your responsibilities, tasks, and any other thoughts on your mind right now.

4. Arrange the tasks you listed for the previous question by type, such as phone calls, e-mails, errands, and so on. Try to focus on one type of task at a time and notice the amount of time saved. Write down new tasks as soon as you are aware of them.

Keep the Main Thing the Main Thing!

Priorities

Michele Helms

"That the word of God will not be dishonored."

Titus 2:5

DVD Outline

I. **The Gift of Womanhood**
    A. The Truth: Womanhood is a gift from God.
    B. The Lie: We can and should have it all.

II. **Biblical Priorities: What They Should Be**
    A. Your Relationship with Jesus
    B. Husband and Marriage
    C. Children
    D. Home
    E. Other Activities

III. **The Burdens We Pick Up**
    A. We sign our young children up for all activities.
    B. We say yes to everything.
    C. We compare ourselves to others.
    D. We find much of our self-worth by the positions we hold, our career, or even extracurricular activities.
    E. We feel inadequate as a wife and mother.
    F. We do not have strong boundaries when it comes to our parents or other family members.

IV. **When We're Overwhelmed**
    A. Unexpected Events
    B. Mixed-Up Priorities
    C. Depending on Our Own Strength

V. **How to Set Priorities**
    A. Ask questions.
        1. Does this please the Lord? God *never* works contrary to His Word.
        2. How does this affect my husband?
        3. How does this affect my children?
        4. How does this affect other commitments?
    B. Pray before making commitments.
    C. A Few More Suggestions

VI. **Conclusion**

PART ONE: Be Amazing in Character

Discussion Questions

1. What is the most difficult aspect of setting and keeping priorities?
2. How much does guilt play a role in your decision-making process?

Homework Day 1

What?

"There is an appointed time for everything. And there is a time for every event under heaven" (Ecclesiastes 3:1).

So What?

Read the following notes from the DVD message "Keep the Main Thing the Main Thing! Priorities" and answer the "Now What" question at the end.

I. The Gift of Womanhood

A. The Truth: Womanhood is a gift from God.

Have you ever thought about womanhood being a gift from God? It is! God created you uniquely for His purpose. The Bible says that He formed you in your mother's womb (see Psalm 139:13). He even has a plan for you: "'For I know the plans I have for you,' declares the Lord, 'plans to prosper you and not to harm you, plans to give you hope and a future'" (Jeremiah 29:11, NIV). It is exciting to know that God always has a plan for you and me! However, women have often taken the gift of womanhood and filled it with burdens and even lies.

B. The Lie: We can and should have it all.

One lie perpetuated by Hollywood and our culture is that we can have it all: a career, the best kept house and yard, the perfect marriage and children, time to volunteer for committees and bake sales and hit the gym every day, all while being an aggressive beast in the bedroom! It is maddening! The good news is that we can have biblical priorities so that we are not weighed down with burdens and lies.

II. Biblical Priorities: What They Should Be

A. Your Relationship with Jesus

As Christians we always say that God is our top priority, but is He? Of course we should be having a regular quiet/study time and an intentional time of prayer, but everything about the Christian life should reflect that Jesus is a priority. He should permeate all of our relationships, efforts, and decisions. He isn't first because we give Him time in the morning; He is first because He is what motivates everything we do! Matthew 22:37 says, "And He said

PART ONE: Be Amazing in Character

to him, 'You shall love the Lord your God with all your heart, and with all your soul, and with all your mind.'"

B. Husband and Marriage

It has been said that the nearest place to heaven on earth is a godly marriage and home. A good marriage takes work. Your husband must be a priority in your life. Ephesians 5:33 says, "Nevertheless, each individual among you also is to love his own wife even as himself, and the wife must see to it that she respects her husband."

C. Children

Notice that children *do not* come before our husband! Children do not raise themselves. The years spent raising children is a relatively short period of time in our life. There will be time for all sorts of things after they are gone. Deuteronomy 6:5, 7 says, "You shall love the Lord your God with all your heart and with all your soul and with all your might. . . . You shall teach [these words] diligently to your sons [children]."

D. Home

Titus 2:3-5 says we are to be keepers of the home. It is difficult to be the CEO of our home when we are so busy with other things. Remember that the home was the first institution established by the Lord in the Garden of Eden. It is important to Him!

E. Other Activities

After these top four come the other priorities such as volunteering (in church, school, community), our job, social activities, sports such as tennis, golf, exercise class, and so on. Fun, work, and ministry are important, but make sure you do not view your relationship with the Lord and serving in church as the same thing.

In the church I grew up in there was a woman who appeared to be a "super Christian." She was involved in many areas and activities at church. There was hardly ever a time that I would drop by when she wasn't there. Her small children were there as well, *all* the time! Morning, evening, anytime anything was going on, she was there with her children running around somewhere. Her children are all grown now, and none of them go to church. Her marriage appears shallow. She was so busy doing good things that she neglected the best things.

III. The Burdens We Pick Up

Instead of following these biblical priorities, we have bought the lie that we can and should have it all. As a result, we end up picking up many undue burdens.

A. We sign our young children up for all activities.

We want our children to be involved in as many activities and sports as possible because we want them to be "well-rounded."

B. We say yes to everything.

We say yes to everyone who asks us to commit to something without thinking of the impact it will have on our family and our other commitments. We are unable to say no except to our family.

C. We compare ourselves to others.

Social media has perpetuated this. It is sometimes called "Facebook envy"!

D. We find much of our self-worth by the positions we hold, our career, or even extracurricular activities.

E. We feel inadequate as a wife and mother.

Because of the inadequacies we feel, marriage and parenting are not what we thought they would be.

F. We do not have strong boundaries when it comes to our parents or other family members.

We're not talking about respecting parents or caring for aging or ill parents. In these cases, we should be joyfully serving them. We're talking about adults whose parents are still calling all the shots. The adult child either keeps running back or allows overbearing parents to interfere. Maybe we have a sibling or even a friend who is constantly taking advantage of our time or resources. We need boundaries!

● ● ●

Often these things we pick up are rooted in guilt and keep us from using our time wisely. Facebook, shopping, and Pinterest, though helpful, can be time stealers. Setting a timer could guard the time. Almost without realizing it, we become so weighed down, and this beautiful gift of womanhood becomes a huge burden that we drag around. We are drowning in discontentment and we don't know how to get out.

This is *not* God's plan! God wants us to have an abundant life. The Bible says in John 10:10, "The thief comes only to steal and kill and destroy; I came that they may have life, and have it abundantly." The word *abundant* in the Greek means "more than necessary, superior, extraordinary, more remarkable."

IV. When We're Overwhelmed

A. Unexpected Events

Sometimes we are overwhelmed because of life events that may be unexpected or difficult, such as sickness. I recently had this experience when I unexpectedly found myself in the ICU for a condition that came out of the blue. It couldn't have been a worse time, just before Thanksgiving. I remember lying in my hospital bed and thinking about how I didn't really have time for this illness and the long recovery that I knew was coming. It was hard, but it was also a sweet time in my life as I watched friends and family take care of things. At times like this, we must remember that God is sovereign.

B. Mixed-Up Priorities

Other times we are overwhelmed because of mixed-up priorities. When I get into that overwhelmed state I ask myself, What are my priorities? Do the things that I am spending my time and effort on reflect those priorities? When our priorities are out of whack, then everything in our world is out of control.

I personally found myself completely overwhelmed and miserable about two years after my husband went into full-time ministry. I came to realize that when unfulfilled expectations meet reality, what you get is frustration. You see, I had many expectations about ministry. My husband and I eagerly stepped out in faith to full-time ministry. We were so excited about the opportunities that Eric would have to speak in churches and schools. Our very well-known pastor sent out a phenomenal recommendation to hundreds of pastors. I expected that many would call, Eric would preach, and there would be offerings to pay the bills. I waited by the phone! But the reality was very different. Eric was very busy speaking in schools (where the kids don't pay honorariums), but we didn't receive even one single call from a church! We were quickly going through all our savings. I was not only homeschooling all five of our kids and keeping up with the house, but I also took on jobs that the ministry could not pay for. I was bookkeeper, secretary, lawyer — anything we needed to keep the ministry afloat. On the side, I was selling anything I could to keep the bills paid — collectibles, wedding china, you name it. It was stressful to say the least!

I really talked myself into believing that I was doing all of it for the sake of the gospel, but the truth of the matter was that I was miserable! Many people were coming to Christ, but I was having a hard time rejoicing. I was so stretched that I couldn't enjoy my kids, and I pretty much thought that Eric was the enemy. I found myself facedown in my bedroom, sobbing, crying out to Jesus and informing Him that I couldn't bear it anymore!

And then in that still, small voice that He uses, He said, "You picked up stuff I *never* intended for you to carry!" I had been so busy *doing* that I hadn't stopped to ask the Lord if I was supposed to pick those things up. They were all good things, but they were not intended for me! For me it was an issue of pride. It was ugly, and it was far from godly!

C. Depending on Our Own Strength

God never promised that we would not have work. The things that God calls us to are oftentimes difficult, but look at what Matthew 11:28-30 says: "Come to me, all you who are weary and burdened, and I will give you rest. Take my yoke upon you and learn from me, for I am gentle and humble in heart, and you will find rest for your souls. For my yoke is easy and my burden is light" (NIV).

Notice that these verses do not say that we will not work. However, as we walk in the work that the Lord has for us, even in the midst of hard times, our burden can be light. When you get to a place that you are so weighed down, one of two things is true:

1. We have picked up things we were never meant to carry (even good things!).
2. We are trying to carry them in our own strength.

V. How to Set Priorities

A. Ask questions.

As you are going through your decision-making process, you can ask, How does this affect my priorities? Here are a few questions to help you make wise decisions and keep your priorities in order:

1. Does this please the Lord? God *never* works contrary to His Word.
2. How does this affect my husband?
3. How does this affect my children?

    If we are not careful, we will "do" all kinds of things for our kids but never actually spend time with them.

4. How does this affect other commitments?

    Have you heard the saying "jack of all trades, master of none"? Sometimes we spread ourselves so thin that we are not doing any job well.

B. Pray before making commitments.

Prayer becomes the filter. Pray over your priorities, and this will become the filter through which every decision flows.

Several years ago I was finishing up teaching math at our homeschool co-op and I needed to tell the administration which classes I wanted to teach the following year. I had every reason to go back: it was a Christ-honoring program, my husband was happy with it, and my children loved it. And yet I could not find peace. Every time I prayed through it I felt unsettled in my spirit. I could not explain it. It didn't make sense, but I could not move forward with a commitment that I didn't have peace about. I pulled myself and my kids out for the next school year and spent the summer preparing to homeschool without the help of the co-op.

Although I didn't have a glimpse of the reason, I did have peace that the right decision had been made. In October of that year my mom was diagnosed with colon cancer and went through a terrible surgery and a long, hard recovery. I was freely able to care for her and my dad during that time. I was so glad I had obeyed even when it didn't make sense!

C. A Few More Suggestions

Before making any commitments or saying yes to anything, get into the habit of saying things such as:

- "Let me check my calendar and I will get back with you."
- "Give me a few days to pray about that or discuss it with my husband and I will let you know."

Do not be afraid to say no immediately: "I am so sorry. I would love to help you, but there is no way I can fit that into my schedule."

Remember, sometimes when we volunteer for a job that wasn't meant for us, we may be robbing someone else the joy of doing that job.

VI. Conclusion

When we do not have our priorities in order we become stressed, irritable, quarrelsome, depressed, or just downright ill! You see, the Enemy would love for us to fall into immorality, drunkenness, or drug abuse. However, he will gladly start with making you overwhelmed and ineffective!

The Bible says that living with an irritable woman is like a constant dripping. Ladies, do you know what water torture is? Seriously! The Bible also says in Proverbs 14:1, "The wise woman builds her house, but the foolish tears it down with her own hands." We have great influence, and we set the tone for our homes. In order to have a godly, peaceful, joyful home, we must set and live by biblical priorities. And that makes us amazing women!

Now What?

What were the most important points for you personally in this message, "Keep the Main Thing the Main Thing! Priorities"?

Homework Day 2

What?

"Older women likewise are to be reverent in their behavior, not malicious gossips nor enslaved to much wine, teaching what is good, so that they may encourage the young women to love their husbands, to love their children, *to be sensible*, pure, workers at home, kind, being subject to their own husbands, so that the word of God will not be dishonored" (Titus 2:3-5).

So What?

Self-control is a fruit of the Spirit and enables us to master our own desires. However, there is a battle in and for our minds, so it is encouraging to know that God has a plan. However, God's Word says there are two plans, as "the thief" has a plan for us as well.

1. What is "the thief's" plan (John 10:10)?

2. Now look at the rest of the verse. What is the Lord's plan for you?

Notice the word *only*. This is Satan's only goal for you. He will play on your insecurities, fears, and failures in order to steal, kill, and destroy your faith and render you ineffective or useless. A big part of overcoming him is understanding the tactics of your adversary Satan, the Devil.

3. What are Satan's (the Devil's) tactics, as described in the following verses?

Mark 1:13

Mark 4:15

PART ONE: Be Amazing in Character

John 8:44

2 Corinthians 11:14

Revelation 12:9

Now think about Jesus' words. His plan is abundant life. *Strong's Concordance* says the word *abundant* means "more than necessary, superior, extraordinary, more remarkable." So, not only do we as Christians have eternal life, but Jesus wants us to have a superior life here on earth. A life rich with joy, meaning, and power!

Both the Lord Jesus and the Enemy have plans for you. Can you see the connection between the lies of the Enemy and the lack of living an abundant life? You can be free to be the amazing woman the Lord created you to be; however, inappropriate priorities can keep you from the abundant life God has for you.

4. What does Ecclesiastes say about time (see 3:1-8, 11)?

Now What?

Wrong priorities are a way Satan steals our time, kills our joy, and keeps us from God's will. In preparation for tomorrow's homework, make a time journal for the next week. You can use the space on the next page. How do you use your time? Include your commitments, volunteer positions, work, lunch dates, shopping trips, carpooling, church, computer and phone time, television time, meal time, activities, and so on.

My Time Journal

Homework Day 3

What?

"Come to me, all you who are weary and burdened, and I will give you rest. Take my yoke upon you and learn from me, for I am gentle and humble in heart, and you will find rest for your souls. For my yoke is easy and my burden is light" (Matthew 11:28-30, NIV).

So What?

When our priorities are out of order and we are feeling overwhelmed, we may be trying to carry everything in our own strength, or we may be carrying things God never intended us to carry.

We learned yesterday that Jesus wants us to have an abundant life. As a Christian, my first priority is my relationship with Jesus. As a wife and mother, my next priorities are my husband and then my children in that order. Then I have to prioritize everything else in my life.

Unfortunately, we tend to give great time and effort to things that should be way down on the list, while the things that should be most important suffer. We say yes to things without considering the effect on our top priorities.

If you are single, your priorities are Jesus, family, and then other things. Even if you are without a husband or children or if they are grown, you still have a challenge to keep Jesus your first priority. Remember, going to church or doing a Bible study is not necessarily making Him a priority. Do your life and priorities bring glory to God?

1. How did Jesus make decisions, and what does this say to you (see John 5:30)?

2. What are we to do with our time, and why (see Ephesians 5:15-16)?

Now What?

1. At the end of the week, look at your time journal from yesterday's homework. This is only helpful if you are completely honest! What are you spending your time and effort on?

2. Does this accurately reflect your priorities? You may need to let go of some activities or projects.

Write out God's priorities for you on an index card. Put the card in a prominent place so you will be reminded daily. Make a commitment *not* to say yes to anything until you have considered the impact on these priorities.

Keep in mind that there are many seasons in life, each one with its unique blessings and challenges. You might need to give something up in this season and pick it back up in another. Don't get so busy doing good things that you miss the best things!

What Are You Thinking?

Purity

"That the word of God will not be dishonored."

TITUS 2:5

DVD Outline

I. **What is purity?**

II. **Purity of Mind (Thoughts)**
   A. Magazines
   B. Novels
   C. Television and Movies
   D. Pornography

III. **Purity of Speech**
   A. God's Thoughts on Words
   B. What is unwholesome talk?
      1. Gossip
      2. Slander
      3. Cursing
      4. Coarse jokes
      5. Sarcasm
      6. Lying and deceit
      7. Criticism
      8. Sharing intimate details

IV. **Purity in Behavior**
   A. Integrity matters!
   B. Gatekeepers of the Home

Discussion Questions

1. How can we best train our children in a sex-soaked culture to be pure as God commands?
2. How can we set ourselves apart while living in today's society?
3. According to God's Word, why is it important to *believe* what God says so we *behave* as God says when it comes to purity of thoughts, speech, and behavior?

Homework Day 1

What?

"Older women likewise are to be reverent in their behavior, not malicious gossips nor enslaved to much wine, teaching what is good, so that they may encourage the young women to love their husbands, to love their children, to be sensible, pure, workers at home, kind, being subject to their own husbands, so that the Word of God will not be dishonored" (Titus 2:3-5).

So What?

Read the following notes from the DVD message "What Are You Thinking? Purity" and answer the "Now What" question at the end.

I. What is purity?

When I worked on staff at a local church, several coworkers and I were innocently searching online for a Christian musician when up popped a very provocative picture! We desperately tried to get rid of it, even covering the computer screen with our bodies in case a pastor walked by. How did that happen? I was in church! The problem with pornographic pictures is that the image is now lasered on my brain.

Before we discuss purity, we need to understand Old Testament holiness, where holiness meant "set apart." In the New Testament, there is still an emphasis on separation, but as Christians we don't live in a separate nation but are scattered in every human society. How can we be morally pure while living in a culture that is not? Peter expressed God's call to us, saying, "As obedient children, do not conform to the evil desires you had when you lived in ignorance. But just as he who called you is holy, so be holy in all you do" (1 Peter 1:14-15, NIV). I know why Peter was so adamant. We need to look different.

God would not say "be holy" if it were not possible, even in a culture where you can turn on a computer at church and have an impure picture etched on your mind. James MacDonald, Bible teacher and pastor of Harvest Bible Chapel in Chicago, Illinois, defines sin as "any failure to conform to God's standard from His Word—in action, in failure to act, or in attitude."[3] Sin left unchecked has devastating results. God works to reveal our sin to us so we can turn away from it and turn back to Him.

When we think of purity, we usually think in terms of sexual purity. But purity, as defined by *The American Heritage Dictionary of the English Language*, means "cleanness, or freedom from physical or moral pollution." Since there is a principle in Scripture that says as we believe, so we behave (see Proverbs 23:7), let's start with our thoughts. It is important to match our thoughts, words, and actions with God's Word in order to be pure.

II. Purity of Mind (Thoughts)

In this study we have talked about having a sound or sensible mind and the importance of guarding it. Jesus warned, "for from within, out of men's hearts, come evil thoughts. . . . All these evils come from inside and make a man 'unclean'" (Mark 7:21, 23, NIV). Therefore, let's look at some things pulling on women's minds in today's culture.

A. Magazines

Some magazine articles offer tips on sex, including explicit sexual encounters. The grocery aisle is full of them, and some stores even place a cover over them so children won't see. If they are too impure for children's eyes, why do we think they are appropriate for ours? Psalm 119:37 says, "Turn my eyes away from worthless things; preserve my life according to your word" (NIV).

B. Novels

Some fiction takes us to unrealistic places. Reading it can make us unhappy in our relationships by sowing seeds of discontent and providing distortions about relationships. If it promotes dissatisfaction in your real relationships, put the book down and pick up reality. Proverbs 23:17 says, "Do not let your heart envy sinners, but live in the fear of the LORD." I heard of a Christian woman reading clean romance novels that caused her such dissatisfaction that she chose to stop reading them.

C. Television and Movies

Movies in the 1950s didn't even show a man and woman in the same bed. Today, they are not only in the same bed, but we see them engaging in sexual activity. Movies and sitcoms are full of sexual innuendo. The more we watch, the more desensitized we become. We have forgotten how to blush and how to feel shame. Beware what your eyes see! Our daughter has Psalm 101:3 on her television. It says, "I will set no worthless thing before my eyes."

D. Pornography

We can't focus on thought life without talking about the most dangerous subject with the largest potential for evil in our thoughts and those of our husbands and children. Pornography! The Internet is a wealth of information, but it is also a haven of evil for those who are not guarded. Many have personally experienced the devastation pornography causes.

Let's look at a few of the effects on marriage that Internet porn has presented:

- Increased marital infidelity
- Diminished trust in marriages

- Decreased marital intimacy and sexual satisfaction
- Increased appetite for more graphic types of porn
- Sexual activity associated with abusive, illegal, or unsafe practices
- Lack of attraction to family and child-raising

Here are some shocking pornography statistics:
- 12% of websites on the Internet are pornographic. That's 24,644,172.
- Every second, 28,258 Internet users are viewing porn.
- 40 million Americans are regular visitors to porn sites.
- 1 in 3 porn viewers are women.
- 25% of all search engine requests are pornography related. That's 68 million a day.
- There are 116,000 searches for child pornography every day.
- The average age at which a child first sees porn online is 11. Even more disturbing is the fact that porn producers strategically market children by researching textbooks to learn what children will be looking for when they do school projects and then posting porn there. They target 11- to 17-year-olds because they are the largest user base and will be customers for life if they become addicted as teens.[4]

These figures are from 2010! What are they today? These numbers ought to jolt us out of any complacency and get us in the battle. We are the gatekeepers of our homes! It is our job to protect our families by keeping evil out.

What can we do to be in the battle?
- Be educated.
- Our first defensive weapon against the Enemy is prayer. Pray over your children and grandchildren that their lives would be pure. Train them to guard their eyes. My three-year-old grandson covers his eyes when commercials come on during sporting events. He has been trained.
- Train your boys that women are to be respected. We must train them from a very young age in this area. Help them to appreciate their masculinity, to become strong leaders, to be loyal and faithful men, and to be on guard.
- Train your girls that they have great value. They should wait to be pursued rather than pursuing. Teach them to dress for respect. And teach them that flirting is a promise not delivered.
- Wisdom tells us not to trust our children in the area of sexual purity. We should expect integrity, but inspect behavior.
- To keep the thought life of our family pure, we must guard technology in our homes and be aware of what our children are up to elsewhere. Therefore, keep all computers in public areas of the home (not in a child's room where it can be used behind closed doors). Put a filter on the computer, but beware because none of them are 100 percent effective (a good one is Bsecure.com).

We have an Enemy who seeks to steal, kill, and destroy our loved ones! We may be aware there is a battle going on, but do we live like it? The battle is for the hearts of our children, as well as captivity for our husbands and even ourselves. Purity in the heart produces power in the life (see Matthew 5:8).

III. Purity of Speech

A. God's Thoughts on Words

"Do not let any unwholesome talk come out of your mouths, but only what is help-ful . . . that it may benefit those who listen" (Ephesians 4:29, NIV).

B. What is unwholesome talk?

It is talk that is injurious to physical, mental, or moral health or that is offensive or loathsome.

Guess Who I Am?

I have no respect for justice and no mercy for defenseless humanity. I ruin without killing. I tear down homes. I break hearts and wreck lives. You will find me in the pews of the pious as well as in the haunts of the unholy. I gather strength with age. I have made my way where greed, distrust, and dishonor are unknown; yet my victims are as numerous as the sands of the sea, and often as innocent. My name is Gossip.[5]

1. **Gossip** falls under unwholesome talk. It is idle talk or rumors about others. It betrays a confidence. According to Proverbs, "A gossip betrays a confidence, but a trustworthy man keeps a secret" (11:13, NIV).

2. **Slander** is defined by *The American Heritage Dictionary of the English Language* as "the utterance of defamatory statements injurious to the reputation or well-being of a person." Proverbs tells us, "He who spreads slander is a fool" (10:18). I have experienced slander when someone said things that were not true. The problem is that there is a residual effect with words: you can't take them back.

3. **Cursing** is defined by *The American Heritage Dictionary of the English Language* as "to swear at; profane abusively." Even saying, "oh god" is cursing. God instructs us, "You shall not take the name of the LORD your God in vain, for the LORD will not leave him unpunished who takes His name in vain" (Exodus 20:7). We have lost reverence for God's name by trivializing it. Teach your children not to use any expression that misuses God's name, even though it may be commonly used in society.

4. **Coarse jokes** are sometimes told or shared through conversation or e-mail. But the Bible tells us, "Put away perversity from your mouth; keep corrupt talk far from your lips" (Proverbs 4:24, NIV).

5. **Sarcasm** is defined by *Merriam-Webster* as "a sharp and often satirical or ironic utterance designed to cut or give pain." The word comes from a Greek word that meant "to tear flesh." Just because people laugh doesn't mean it is funny.

6. **Lying and deceit** can make us look better; they can cover up what should be brought into the open. But, "there are six things which the LORD hates, yes, seven which are an abomination to Him: . . . a lying tongue . . . and one [a woman] who spreads strife among brothers [sisters]" (Proverbs 6:16-17, 19).

7. **Criticism** is self-exalting. The critical woman looks at a situation from a human point of view—her own. James MacDonald defines it as "dwelling on the perceived faults of another with no aim for their good."[6] The root of it is a sinful heart. When criticism is present, there is usually a deeper issue such as unforgiveness, bitterness, anger, disappointment, impatience, unmet expectations, or pride. Paul tells us in Philippians, "Do nothing from selfishness or empty conceit, but with humility of mind regard one another as more important than yourselves" (2:3).

8. **Sharing intimate details** about our sex life or listening to others share theirs is inappropriate and unwise. I have a young friend in college who tells me sex is the constant topic of the college students around her. We need to watch what we share with women. Let's practice purity in our speech.

IV. Purity in Behavior

A. Integrity matters!

"How can a young man [or woman] keep his [or her] way pure?" The answer? "By living according to your word" (Psalm 119:9, NIV). There are no degrees of integrity. We either have it or we don't. *The American Heritage Dictionary of the English Language* defines integrity as "completeness or wholeness." My husband and I have agreed that we will not have lunch with someone of the opposite sex because it can give the "appearance of evil" (1 Thessalonians 5:22, KJV). This choice protects our marriage. We need to ask ourselves the following questions:

1. How do we behave in the company of men other than our husbands? Are we flirtatious? Do we dress for attention?
2. Do we teach our daughters it is not wise to ride in a car with a man, including not accepting a ride home from babysitting?
3. Do we go to lunch with or ride in the car with men who are not our husbands? Millard Fuller, the leader of Habitat for Humanity, lived and had his office about two and a half hours from the airport. When he needed to fly, his assistant would inquire at the office as to who was driving to the airport that day so he could share a ride. One day he accepted a ride with a female employee who then accused him

of inappropriate behavior. He denied the accusations, and an internal investigation found "insufficient proof of inappropriate conduct," though not before he lost his job and reputation. While it seems outdated and inconvenient, we should go overboard to protect our reputations, marriage, family, and work.

4. Do we Facebook with men from our past? My friend became reacquainted with a high school friend on Facebook and left her husband six months later.

5. Do we sext? This may not be an issue for us, but it can be for our children. Remember, if a child lives in our house, we can look at his or her computer or phone.

Thoughts become actions, and sin ensnares. So beware!

B. Gatekeepers of the Home

The purpose of this study is to experience the life change that comes from hearing and obeying God's Word. It may be necessary to cry out in repentance for our families in the area of purity. God tells us that when sin is acknowledged, He is faithful to forgive. James MacDonald says, "Repentance is a recognition of sin for what it is, followed by a heartfelt sorrow, culminating in a change of behavior."[7]

We are the gatekeepers, so we must stand guard against all sin that threatens our families. It starts with *us*. As gatekeepers, we have several jobs:

1. We are to train our children in the importance of living within God's boundaries throughout life. We need to model it. God's laws are meant to protect us!

2. We are not to be afraid to give our teenagers clear boundaries when interacting with the opposite sex. In high school, there should be no times for girls and boys to be together at home alone. Teach your kids the importance of staying pure sexually until marriage and how easy it is to be tempted. This was a rule in our home. One day I came home to find my daughter and a male friend sitting on the driveway. She had obeyed the rule.

3. We should think of the possible drawbacks (both physically and morally) for taking young daughters to the doctor for birth control pills even as a solution for cramps.

4. We have the control when it comes to buying our children clothes that are modest. It is called the credit card.

Gatekeepers protect themselves, their families, and their home from the onslaught of evil. Good gatekeepers are truly amazing women!

What were the most important points for you personally in this message, "What Are You Thinking? Purity"?

You Tell on Yourself

You tell on yourself by the friends you seek,
By the very manner in which you speak,
By the way you employ your leisure time,
By the use you make of dollar and dime.

You tell what you are by the things you wear,
By the spirit in which your burdens bear,
By the kind of things at which you laugh,
By the records you play on the phonograph (CD player, Ipod, etc).

You tell what you are by the way you walk,
By the things of which you delight to talk,
By the manner in which you bear defeat,
By so simple a thing as how you eat.

By the books you choose from the well-filled shelf;
In these ways and more, you tell on yourself.[3]

Homework Day 2

"Just as he who called you is holy, so be holy in all you do" (1 Peter 1:15, NIV).

So What?

God is holy. We are to be holy and live purely, set apart from evil, while we live among people who remain uncommitted to the divine standards. Purity is defined by *The American Heritage Dictionary of the English Language* as "freedom from sin or guilt; innocence; chastity." Divine purity includes our thoughts, words, and actions. Impurity left unchecked has devastating results.

1. Since purity of thoughts is essential for pure actions, we must train our minds to have pure thoughts. Do the things you fill your mind with lead you toward God? Do they support what God teaches in His Word? Or are you filling your mind with movies and television that portray immorality, fiction that takes you places you shouldn't go and portrays relationships you shouldn't have, and magazines with sexually explicit articles and advertisements?

2. Where are we to fix our thoughts (see Philippians 4:8)?

3. How can we control our minds and desires so that we can be more like Christ (see 1 Peter 1:13-15)?

4. Remember, "What's in your well comes up in your bucket." Our speech reflects what is in our hearts. What do we want the words of our mouth to be (see Psalm 19:14)?

5. The tongue weighs little, but few can hold it. James 1:26 says that the tongue can corrupt the whole person. Our words are mighty weapons. Do we use them to build up or tear down? To what did James compare the tongue (see James 3:5-9)?

Now What?

1. To be pure, is there anything you need to repent of so God can forgive and restore you?

2. In light of all we've learned, what can you do to protect your words and behavior so they are pure and Christlike?

Homework Day 3

What?

"How can a young man keep his way pure? By keeping it according to Your word" (Psalm 119:9).

So What?

The psalmist pondered how he could live a pure life and concluded the key was to obey God's teaching. *As we believe, so we behave!* Behavior follows what we think or believe. Therefore, our heart or mind is always the key to our conduct.

1. What must we do to present ourselves to God as one approved (see 2 Timothy 2:15)?

2. To have a pure heart, what must we do (see 2 Timothy 2:22)?

3. List what the will of God is for you (see 1 Thessalonians 4:3-5).

4. As gatekeepers of our homes, we are given rules for holy living. Record what Paul said we are to put to death (see Colossians 3:5-10).

As we master our passions, we will learn to recognize the things or people that have the potential to compromise our purity.

Now What?

An amazing woman desires an amazing home. If we want to be pure, choose what is pure. If we want our children to be pure, model purity and teach them! "Even a child is known by his actions, by whether his conduct is pure and right" (Proverbs 20:11, NIV).

1. As gatekeepers of our homes, purity must start with us. In light of whose you are and what you've learned about purity and holiness, is there anything you need to stop doing, watching, or speaking?

2. As you think of your past as a gatekeeper, in what areas have you been lax in guarding yourself and your family, especially your children?

3. As you consider the future, what are some actions you need to take to protect your family?

God's perfect plan is for His people to be holy. Holiness or purity protects us and provides the freedom we all desire. Let's be amazingly pure pictures to a world that longs to be free.

Session 6
· · · · · · · · · ·

You're Going Out in That?

Modesty

Pat Harley

"That the word of God will not be dishonored."
TITUS 2:5

DVD Outline

I. Illustration and Introduction
    A. We all wear a sign.

    B. The world screams, "Look at me!"

II. Is dress neutral?
    A. Genesis 38:14-15: Tamar

    B. Genesis 41:42: Joseph

    C. Exodus 28:2-42: The Priests

    D. 2 Samuel 14:2: A Woman in "Mourning"

    E. Esther 5:1: Esther

    F. Esther 6:11: Mordecai

III. What is modesty?
    A. Modesty gives the impression of moral purity.

    B. Modesty is an element of Christian character.

IV. Did God design clothes?
    A. Adam and Eve in the garden were naked and unashamed.

    B. God designed the clothing of the priests.

    C. The saints in heaven are clothed in "fine linen, bright and clean."

V. Does the Designer have a dress code?
    A. Dress discreetly.

    B. Dress attractively.

VI. How does dress affect men?
    A. Dress can be a great stumbling block.

    B. Dress can diminish respect.

VII. Will you stand against the culture?
    A. Know Who you represent.

    B. Know your Enemy.

    C. Take courage and stand firm.

    D. Understand what modesty, decency, and femininity look like.

    E. Know the clothes that are best for your body.

    F. The two words "purely alluring" should be the message on your sign.

VIII. What are the blessings of modesty?
    A. Peace

    B. Power

PART ONE: Be Amazing in Character

C. Purity
D. Protection
E. Privilege
F. Praise

Discussion Questions

1. What is your greatest challenge when it comes to dress?
2. How have women's fashions changed, and what effect do you think it has made on society?
3. Tell of someone who dresses in a way you admire.

Homework Day 1

What?

God commands, "Likewise, I want women to adorn themselves with proper clothing, modestly and discreetly" (1 Timothy 2:9).

So What?

Read the following notes from the DVD message "You're Going Out in That? Modesty" and answer the "Now What" question at the end.

I. Illustration and Introduction

Some years ago I was sitting at a table at a wedding reception. At the table behind me were three or four men. I overheard them laughing and began to listen to their conversation. The object of their jokes was a young woman who had just entered the room. She was absolutely gorgeous—tall, long, blond hair, and very well endowed. She was wearing a floor-length dress made from a material that revealed her every curve. The back of the dress was cut down below the waist, and the front was cut so low it revealed almost her entire breasts.

But it was the men's response that was most disturbing. Sexual innuendos abounded, referring to her in the most disrespectful, inappropriate way. As I observed this young woman, I also saw elderly men blushing and giggling as they approached her to dance. No woman spoke to her. During the time when she was not being hit on by lechers, she was alone.

I was intrigued and so introduced myself to her and began a conversation. She was intelligent, witty, charming, and kind. She had graduated from a Christian school, attended a church, and was now a student at a prestigious college. Yet she was wearing a sign that did not accurately represent who she was. And I saw a great deception. She had bought into one of Satan's crafty and oft repeated lies without even knowing it!

A. We all wear a sign.
What we are wearing is the first thing people will notice about us. It is that which will make the first impression. It is what we wear that is the first "sign," and it will speak volumes about who we are, Whose we are, and what we represent.

B. The world screams, "Look at me!"
Magazines scream from the pages, "Look at me! Look at me!" More often than not the message is sensuous: "Hot new styles!" "Sexy clothes for the summer!" "Sleek and sexy

weekend wear." Movie stars parade in the most outrageously revealing clothes. Everything from cars to perfume is sold by flashing nakedness before our eyes. "Hot and sexy" seem to be the key words for fashion and design.

Even children have become victims of this deceit. There has been a changing scene in young children's clothes. No longer do we find little girls' dresses with lovely innocence, pastel colors, and ruffles. This has been replaced by black fishnet stockings, miniskirts, and tight tank tops. As for teens, it is now almost impossible for mothers to find clothes that are not designed to be sexual in appearance, and forget finding modest bathing suits. Though they do exist, mothers too quickly cave in to the demands of the daughters or become weary from trying to find an appropriate one in the local department stores.

There is another voice calling for attention through wild makeup, spiked clothes, chains, various colored hair, excessive tattoos, and anything else with shock value. Adults trying to "fit in" or "relate to youth" have abandoned dignified dress and joined the ranks of the indecent.

And then there is the voice of sheer sloppy attire, which is disguised as being relaxed and comfortable clothing. In the name of modesty some Christian women have turned to homely, dowdy, and unattractive clothing. Even in churches some have come to believe a lie that dress is neutral and makes no difference at all.

Let's take a look at what the Bible has to say and then determine the decisions we may need to make to live in obedience to our Savior and dress in a way that brings honor to Him and respect and dignity to us.

II. Is dress neutral?

The Bible gives many examples of the way dress makes a statement. It is a sign and gives many messages to those looking on. Here are some examples:

A. Genesis 38:14-15: Tamar
Tamar intentionally dressed like a harlot in order to deceive her father-in-law. Her dress sent a message that she was sexually available, and Judah responded to it in kind.

B. Genesis 41:42: Joseph
Pharaoh clothed Joseph in garments of fine linen as a sign of authority and position.

C. Exodus 28:2-42: The Priests
The priests wore different robes and clothing to distinguish them from the common man. It identified them as holy unto the Lord.

D. 2 Samuel 14:2: A Woman in "Mourning"

Joab had a woman dress in mourning garments. She was able to deceive David by what she was wearing.

E. Esther 5:1: Esther

Before she went before the king, Esther put on her royal robes, showing her authority and position.

F. Esther 6:11: Mordecai

Mordecai was given the king's clothes to wear as he went through the streets. The clothes identified him with the king and gave him great status.

So as we can see, dress is a sign that can communicate to others something about us. Tamar's dress said she was a harlot, while Esther's dress said she was a queen. Our clothing is the first impression someone will have about us, and people will make a judgment call on what they see.

III. What is modesty?

A. Modesty gives the impression of moral purity.

Modesty is a state of mind or disposition that expresses a humble estimation of oneself before God. Modesty, like humility, is the opposite of boldness or arrogance. It doesn't seek to draw attention to itself or show off in an unseemly way. In *Christian Modesty and the Public Undressing of America,* Jeff Pollard said, "Webster apparently links chastity with modesty because chastity means moral purity in thought and conduct."[9] Modesty has the general meaning of being respectable and honorable, especially in dress.

B. Modesty is an element of Christian character.

Our dress should make the same profession that we do. God calls us to be holy as He is holy, and our dress should reflect that.

IV. Did God design clothes?

A. Adam and Eve in the garden were naked and unashamed.
   1. No sin (lust, greed, pride) had entered the world (see Genesis 3).
   2. As soon as sin entered, they made coverings for their groin area.
   3. God covered their bodies with tunics (coats or robes) of skin. "While Adam covered his privates, God covered his body."[10]

PART ONE: Be Amazing in Character

B. God designed the clothing of the priests (see Exodus 28).

C. The saints in heaven are clothed in "fine linen, bright and clean" (Revelation 19:7-8, 14).

V. Does the Designer have a dress code?

A. Dress discreetly.
1. Deuteronomy 22:5 says, "A woman shall not wear man's clothing, nor shall a man put on a woman's clothing; for whoever does these things is an abomination to the LORD your God." This is a command to dress in a feminine manner that is different from the way men dress. It sets us apart as women.
2. First Timothy 2:9 says, "Likewise, I want women to adorn themselves with proper clothing, modestly and discreetly" (having good judgment, pleasantly noticeable, not showy or obtrusive).
3. First Peter 3:3-4 says, "Your adornment must not be merely external — braiding the hair, and wearing gold jewelry, or putting on dresses; but let it be the hidden person of the heart, with the imperishable quality of a gentle and quiet spirit, which is precious in the sight of the God."

B. Dress attractively.
1. Proverbs 31:22 says, "She makes coverings for herself; her clothing is fine linen and purple."
2. In summary, God's dress code for women is feminine, modest, discreet, and attractive.

VI. How does dress affect men?

"It is inevitable that stumbling blocks should come; but woe to that man [or woman] through whom the stumbling block comes!" (Matthew 18:7).

A. Dress can be a great stumbling block.
Drew was concerned for her son who was fourteen. He had joined the senior high youth group and they were going on a beach retreat. Drew approached the youth pastor, concerned about the girls in their bikinis. She felt modest bathing suits should be required. The pastor considered her a prude and informed her that the boys didn't pay any attention because they were used to it. But the truth is that boys, young men, and even old men *do* pay attention. A man in his seventies told me it was difficult to go to church because the young women in his congregation dressed so immodestly that it was hard for him to concentrate on worship.

A website called "The Rebelution" (www.therebelution.com), designed by Alex and Brett Harris, asked young men to respond to the way women dress today. Here are two of the letters they received.

"Sisters in Christ, you really have no concept of the struggles guys face on a daily basis. Please take a higher ground in the ways you dress. True, we are responsible for our thoughts and actions . . . but it is so good to enjoy the companionship of women when we don't have to constantly be on guard against ungodly thoughts brought about by the way they dress." (age 24)

"In high school the place of greatest temptation toward lust was my church. Girls wore things to church that they thought were fashionable and dressy, but they never would have passed the dress code at my public school." (age 26)

B. Dress can diminish respect.
A survey of one thousand men done by "The Rebelution" revealed the following:
- 92 percent agreed that modest women make a difference.
- 76 percent had less respect for immodest women.
- 98 percent said women can dress attractively and still be modest.
- 96 percent said that modesty was important for his future wife.

VII. Will you stand against the culture?

"You are the light of the world. . . . Let your light shine before men in such as way that they may see your good works, and glorify your Father who is in heaven" (Matthew 5:14, 16).

I ran into the local grocery market many years ago. I had been scrubbing the floors that morning and was in a hurry, so I had not bothered to change clothes. I had on old sweatpants with filthy knees and an old jacket over an even older, raggedy sweatshirt. I was wearing no makeup and had barely combed my hair. "No one will see me," I reasoned, because it was so early in the morning. I had bought into the lie of sloppiness. I ran through the door of the market and right into Eleanor and Bob Lewis! They both were neat and clean. El had on a black coat and a white scarf. She was wearing a little makeup, her hair was combed, and she looked altogether lovely.

I was ashamed. I had a black coat at home that I could have easily put on to hide the work clothes. It would have taken no more than three minutes to give some thought to my appearance before leaving the house, and it would have been worth it. I am the light of the world, and I represent Christ. It was a good lesson.

A. Know Who you represent.

Your body is the temple of the living God. Therefore, you are a daughter of the King. You represent Him and His kingdom. The sign you wear should reflect Whose you are. "Do you not know that you are a temple of God and that the Spirit of God dwells in you?" (1 Corinthians 3:16).

B. Know your Enemy.

Satan came to steal, kill, and destroy. He is our Enemy, and he will lie about everything, including the sign you wear. He will attack every one of God's commands. So be prepared to fight Satan by knowing Scripture.

C. Take courage and stand firm.

"Therefore, take up the full armor of God, so that you will be able to resist in the evil day, and having done everything, to stand firm" (Ephesians 6:13). Who would think that how we dress would be part of a battle!

D. Understand what modesty, decency, and femininity look like.

We have given you guidelines in the homework that will help you in making good decisions. Modesty does not detract from beauty; it simply adds to it.

E. Know the clothes that are best for your body.

This includes knowing the styles that are best for your body type, the colors that are best for your skin tones, and the labels that fit you the best. We have provided some fashion tips that will help you select clothing that is best for your body type on page 97.

F. The two words "purely alluring" should be the message on your sign.

We are to be feminine, modest, discreet, and beautiful—never a stumbling block but representing Christ as the light of the world.

VIII. What are the blessings of modesty? *by Nancy Leigh DeMoss*

A. Peace

There is peace in knowing you are obedient to God.

B. Power

Power comes in being free from the enslavement of fashion, fads, and the opinions of others.

C. Purity

You will attract the right kind of attention.

D. Protection

You will be guarded from the wrong kind of attention from men.

E. Privilege

You will experience greater freedom in marriage.

F. Praise

You will be valued for spiritual and heart qualities more than physical appearance.

Shara McKee, a pastor's wife and worship leader in Texas, said it well:

Modesty is a wall to the uninvited,
A guardian to what is protected,
An invitation to the respectful,
A statement of values to the unbeliever,
A sense of dignity to the culture that wages war on our worth,
And a gift of honor to the One we represent.[11]

Now What?

What were the most important points for you personally in this message, "You're Going Out in That? Modesty"?

Homework Day 2

What?

"Because the daughters of Zion *are proud and walk with heads held high and seductive eyes,* and go along with mincing steps and tinkle the bangles on their feet, therefore the Lord will afflict the scalp of the daughters of Zion with scabs, and the LORD will make their foreheads bare. In that day the Lord will take away the beauty of their anklets, headbands, crescent ornaments, dangling earrings, bracelets, veils, headdresses, ankle chains, sashes, perfume boxes, amulets, finger rings, nose rings, festal robes, outer tunics, cloaks, money purses, hand mirrors, undergarments, turbans and veils. . . . Your men will fall by the sword" (Isaiah 3:16-18, 25).

So What?

Today we are constantly told that the way to gain attention is to be sexy, trendy, or even sloppy. We are told that dress does not matter. It is neutral. None of these are true. When women dress sensuously to attract the attention of men, or choose to be comfortable at the expense of decency and femininity, we have moved beyond the biblical dress code set down by our Creator. We have embraced that which is a stumbling block, unattractive, or masculine. The sign women wear reveals who or what they represent.

1. Read Isaiah 3:16-26. (We have included only a portion of those verses above.) What attitude did the women have? How was that attitude reflected in their dress?

2. What was the result of this practice? List all of the consequences.

3. Review the Designer's dress code on page 89. Write what you learn in the following verses.

Deuteronomy 22:5

1 Timothy 2:9

1 Peter 3:3-4

4. What can we learn about clothing from the Proverbs 31 woman that we can apply to ourselves and our family (see Proverbs 31:21-22, 25, 30)?

5. What should be our motive for dressing modestly, according to the following verses?

Matthew 5:14-16

1 Corinthians 3:16

2 Corinthians 6:16-18

Now What?

From what you learned in the verses we just studied, write out a personal dress code.

PART ONE: Be Amazing in Character

Homework Day 3

What?

"Your adornment must not be merely external — braiding the hair, and wearing gold jewelry, or putting on dresses; but let it be the hidden person of the heart, with the imperishable quality of a gentle and quiet spirit, which is precious in the sight of God" (1 Peter 3:3-4).

So What?

God does have a dress code for women: feminine, modest, discreet, and attractive. Yesterday you wrote out a personal dress code. Now it is time to make a personal assessment of your own attitude toward the clothes you choose to wear.

1. Do I dress to attract the attention of men?

2. Do I dress to give the impression of financial extravagance?

3. Do I dress in a sloppy and unattractive manner with the excuse that it is comfortable?

4. Do I dress in clothes that are masculine?

5. Are the clothes I wear appropriate for my body type?

6. Do I take the time to honestly look at the sign I am wearing?

Now What?

Now it is time to get to work. With your dress code in hand, go through the clothes in your closet and look at each piece of clothing. Does it fit your personal dress code? If not, give it away, throw it away, or alter it to comply with your personal, biblical dress code. You may be able to make it fit your guidelines, such as by adding a scarf for a neckline that is too low or wearing a camisole under a transparent blouse. Also, if you do not have a full-length mirror, purchase one and hang it in a place that is easily accessible.

The following are questions that may help you:[12]

- Does the neckline expose the breast or cleavage? (Consider when you bend over or when viewed from above or from the side.)
- Does your top show the midriff?
- Is the fabric transparent or clinging?
- Are there writings or pictures that draw attention to private areas?
- Are the clothes tight or do they reveal private areas?
- Is the clothing inappropriate for public wear, such as undergarments and pajamas? Pajamas are for home comfort and should never be worn in public.

The sign you wear every day should reflect who you are, Who you belong to, and Whose kingdom you represent. And remember, you are the light of the world, the daughter of the King . . . an amazing woman!

How to Dress the Amazing Woman

by Sheila Frye, fashion consultant

Dressing for your unique body type is the key to balancing your silhouette and emphasizing your best features. Once you know your body type, you can choose clothing styles that flatter your assets and downplay any problem areas. Women's body types come in approximately five different shapes:

- Hourglass — the top and bottom are evenly proportioned through the shoulders and hips with a defined waist. Accentuate existing proportions by wearing fabrics that drape well around your body and softly hug your curves. Avoid clinging, tight-fitting garments, which can overaccentuate the bust, hips, or bottom.
- Triangle — the hips and thighs are broader than the upper body. The goal for the triangle is to add fullness to the upper body and minimize the hips. Draw attention to the top part of the body by wearing brighter, bolder patterns on the top. Downplay your lower half by choosing pants or skirts in dark or neutral colors. Avoid tight-fitting skirts and pants, which overemphasize the bottom area.
- Wedge — the bust and back are larger than the waist and hips. Downplay large shoulders by adding fullness to the hips. Wear darker colors above the waist and brighter colors, prints, and detailing below the waist. Avoid tops with large lapels, gathered sleeves, or a tight fit.
- Rectangle — the waist, bust, and hips show little difference proportionately. The goal for the straight figure is to slightly define the body with shaping. Look for clothing that helps define the waist. Use pattern and texture to give the illusion of more curves. Avoid patterns or detailing around the middle area.
- Oval — the waist is wider than the hips or shoulders. Look for tops with structure and bottoms with a little bit of volume to help balance out the midsection. Avoid skinny pants and skirts, which will make the top half look even larger by comparison.

Knowing your body type can take the guesswork out of dressing and help you choose an appropriate and flattering wardrobe.

Session 7

• • • • • • • • • •

Kindness in a Mean Girl World

Kindness

Linda Sweeney

"That the word of God will not be dishonored."

TITUS 2:5

99

DVD Outline

I. **God commands women to be kind.**
   A. Kindness Defined
   B. Kindness is a fruit of the Spirit.

II. **A Deeper Look at Kindness**
   A. Are you deceived?
   B. Are you applying truth?

III. **Exercise kindness.**
   A. Kindness is Christlike.
   B. Kindness comes from the heart.

Discussion Questions

1. Share an act of kindness that made a difference in your life—either one you received or one you gave.
2. What is one truth you heard today that you could apply to your life? What difference might it make?

Homework Day 1

What?

"Older women likewise are to be reverent in their behavior, not malicious gossips nor enslaved to much wine, teaching what is good, so that they may encourage the young women to love their husbands, to love their children, to be sensible, pure, workers at home, *kind*, being subject to their own husbands, so that the word of God will not be dishonored" (Titus 2:3-5).

So What?

Read the following notes from the DVD message "Kindness in a Mean Girl World: Kindness" and answer the "Now What" question at the end.

I. God commands women to be kind.

Have you ever had someone do something so kind you will never forget it? Following a long period of unemployment, my husband got a job and God miraculously made it possible for us to purchase a home. Since we had been renting for about six years, this was a very exciting time in our lives. However, we had almost no money to change the inside of the house so it would go with my furniture, colors, and decorating style.

I had a fabulous group of girlfriends who volunteered to be my decorating team. They didn't ask but told me they had signed up to scrape wallpaper, patch walls, and paint my entire house! It took all of us working together for about two weeks, but we laughed, sang, and worked until my home was beautiful. That was way beyond kindness in my book, and it was a special time of poured-out love I will never, ever forget!

A. Kindness Defined

Titus 2:5 includes being kind on the list of character qualities older women are to train and encourage the younger women to have. Therefore, all women are to be kind.

As God's daughters we're to be good-natured, gracious, benevolent, caring, gentle, considerate, tender, compassionate, and pleasant. Now, this makes a "pretty picture." Two beautiful women were Mother Teresa and Corrie ten Boom. They were beautiful because of what was on the inside and what motivated them—putting others first! They were kind and therefore beautiful, but not in the way that our culture defines beauty. The media glamorize meanness, and the world stresses outer beauty, but there's nothing lovelier than a kind woman. A Christian woman known for kindness is the one who spreads the sweet aroma of

Christ and who draws others to want what she has. She cares, she empathizes, she helps, she gives, she loves, and she shines far above the rest! People are drawn to her and want to be like her. Tabitha—also known as Dorcas—is a biblical example. In Acts 9:36-42 we're told that "this woman was abounding with deeds of kindness and charity which she continually did." In other words, she didn't just do random acts of kindness, but kindness was part of her character. When she died, all the widows wept and showed the garments she made for them.

B. Kindness is a fruit of the Spirit.

God says, "Be kind," and this is one of His attributes or character traits. God *is* kindness. Kindness is found on the list of the fruits of the Spirit. "Fruit" in Galatians 5:22 means "that which originates or comes from something; an effect or result such as work, act, or deed."[13] In other words, if we belong to Christ, we will possess the fruit of His Spirit. Exhibiting His "fruit" is evidence that we belong to Him. His Spirit in us gives us His power to be an example to others. We will have a good influence in our marriages, communities, and churches. Our goal should be to become like Jesus in character so we can influence the culture.

We are given God's requirements for His people in Micah 6:8, which states, "He has told you . . . what is good; and what does the LORD require of you but to do justice, to love kindness, and to walk humbly with your God?" First Corinthians 13:4 defines it this way: "Love is kind." Being kind is a command! Do you remember the great photo op I told you about when we started? We talked about the fact that our pictures are being taken all the time and that surely we all want to make a good one! Being kind will make us "photo-ready" at all times!

II. A Deeper Look at Kindness

A. Are you deceived?

On the surface, this seems to be one of the easier teachings to grasp and obey because we like to see ourselves as kind. This is a lot like looking in our mirror and seeing only what we want to see. After all, everyone knows that kindness is an admirable quality, and we want to think of ourselves this way. This is a command we can easily dismiss as "done" and go about our business feeling pretty confident we have hit the mark.

Sometimes I am too hasty in thinking I am kind. I was recently confronted with this very issue and upon closer examination realized I had failed this test miserably. I thought I was okay in the "kind department" but soon realized I was basing this on my dealings with people I like and who like me, those who agree with my thinking and don't cause me grief.

Here's an example: My husband and I were watching a Bible study series and throughout the sessions we were introduced to several "colorful characters" who all had opinions very different from mine. One young man was shabbily clothed, almost totally tattooed, and angry, so most of the time his opinions just made me mad. Subconsciously I had developed a "Who cares what you think" attitude. I thought this until the end of the series when he

PART ONE: Be Amazing in Character

was interviewed on a more personal level and he talked about his background. What he shared made me so ashamed of my lack of compassion and kindness that I cried. Truthfully, it affected me for days.

He talked about one woman he'd met who he felt was the only person to legitimately deserve the title "Christian," and he said it was because she was kind to him when no one else had ever been! Did you hear that? The only one! I was so convicted! I hung my head in shame because I knew that had I crossed paths with him, he would not have seen me as a Christian but as a mean girl. My attitude reeked of a "I don't have time for you; you don't look like me or talk like anyone I hang around with" hypocrite! This attitude does not reflect Jesus, and it is sin. It's not the same as robbing a bank or murdering someone, but it is still sin. Second Timothy 2:24 says, "Be kind to all."

B. Are you applying truth?

As we've already learned, sometimes we women do not think sensibly (with a sound mind) because we are overly concerned with the things of this earth and not the things above. We can be consumed with an attitude of "me, myself, and I." Maybe you've met women like this; you may even hang out with them or are one yourself!

For Christians, being Christlike should be a priority. Unfortunately, 2 Timothy 3:1-4 tells us what will happen: "But realize this, that in the last days difficult times will come. For men will be lovers of self, lovers of money, boastful, arrogant, revilers, disobedient to parents, ungrateful, unholy, unloving, irreconcilable, malicious gossips, without self-control, brutal, haters of good, treacherous, reckless, conceited, lovers of pleasure rather than lovers of God." It continues in verses 6-7 to say, "Among them are those who [are] . . . always learning and never able to come to the knowledge of the truth." Do you see it? They are stuffing knowledge in their heads but not their hearts. They are not applying what they are learning; therefore, they remain the same.

1. Sometimes we are kind only to those who are kind to us or who can help us. This is the wrong motive for demonstrating kindness. God warns that we are not to do nice things just for those who are nice but that we are to love or be kind to even those who don't deserve it.

Luke 6:32-33, 35-36 states, "If you love those who love you, what credit is that to you? Even 'sinners' love those who love them. And if you do good to those who are good to you, what credit is that to you? Even 'sinners' do that. . . . But love your enemies, do good to them, and lend to them without expecting to get anything back. Then your reward will be great, and you will be sons of the Most High, because he is kind to the ungrateful and wicked. Be merciful, just as your Father is merciful" (NIV).

2. We sometimes say things that are very hurtful, things that embarrass others, discourage others, or elevate us at someone else's expense. Someone has said, "Speaking ill of another is

a dishonest way of complimenting oneself."

For example, why do women sometimes feel compelled to tell other women that they look "tired, sick, or troubled"? These can be hurtful words disguised as concern. If you aren't any of those things, you probably soon will be, and if you are, you will feel even worse! Over and over God says we are to be uplifting and encouraging to others. First Thessalonians 5:11 says, "Therefore encourage one another and build up one another." Hebrews 3:13 tells us, "But encourage one another day after day." Hebrews 10:25 states that we're to assemble together for the purpose of "encouraging one another."

There was a lady I once knew who insisted on asking me, "Are you okay?" When I would say, "Yes, why?" she would continue with, "You look so pale [or tired or sad]." It ruined my day every time, and I spent far too much time looking in the mirror and quizzing my husband about my appearance. And it always happened on the days I thought I looked fairly good! To me this isn't kind. When someone who is usually very talkative is very quiet or is noticeably upset, of course express concern! Otherwise, encourage!

3. At times, we make assumptions about people and then spread our thoughts around; this is called gossip! If we are not careful, we Christians can veil gossip as a "prayer request." We can listen to others gossip, and even if we don't speak, we are compromising ourselves. Romans 1:32 ends a long list of grievous sins with a startling statement: "Although they know the ordinance of God, that those who practice such things are worthy of death, they not only do the same, but also give hearty approval to those who practice them." In other words, even if we are silent, we are expressing approval, and by listening, we are participating. We are guilty too!

4. We may fail to express gratitude. Saying "thank you" has become almost obsolete. Remember when Jesus cleansed those ten lepers and only one thanked Him (see Luke 17:11-19)? He made note of that, didn't He? He said, "Were there not ten cleansed? But the nine—where are they?" (verse 17). Often sin begins with an ungrateful heart!

5. Keeping your word is kind. Do what you say even if it is difficult or inconvenient. Matthew 5:37 states, "Simply let your 'Yes' be 'Yes,' and your 'No,' 'No'; anything beyond this comes from the evil one" (NIV).

6. We may criticize others. Some people seem to think criticism is a spiritual gift! It's not. We can tear down our husbands, children, and others with our words and body language. What are you saying with your words, tone of voice, or "you know what I mean" looks that might be received as criticism?

My husband, Ed, has told me it's not what I say but *how* I say it that he doesn't like. I must admit I didn't like hearing that correction because, frankly, I didn't believe it. Considering what a joy I've always felt myself to be, this was hard to hear. One day God gave me a hard lesson on this! I called home to speak to Ed about a matter of importance at an agreed upon time, and he did not answer the phone. I was not happy that he didn't pick up because we had an understanding about when I was to call. So I left him a message. When I got home, I saw the indicator light blinking on the answering machine but had forgotten all about the entire incident. I wondered who I might have missed while I was out. Much to my surprise, it was me leaving a not so kind message for Ed! It wasn't what I said so much as how I said it that was startling to me. It reminded me of how I didn't believe I had a southern accent until I first heard myself recorded. Now, that was a shock! We can't hear ourselves as we really sound; therefore, we need to make an effort to be kind not only in what we say but in how we say it!

7. Children are not taught to be kind, which is one reason bullying is in the news. The opposite of kindness is a mean spirit.

III. Exercise kindness.

A. Kindness is Christlike.

Let's review the characteristics of kindness: benevolence, generosity, helpfulness, grace, understanding, forgiveness, and empathy. We are often times kinder to those outside our homes than we are to those inside. If a visitor's child spills his milk we say, "No problem." If ours does the same, we yell and ridicule. Unkindness can be the result of a day gone wrong. So those closest to us seem to receive the brunt of our frustration or wrath. I would venture to guess that those who irritate us the most are our husbands and children (in that order), but often our unkindness spills over to others. More than that, our attitude is contagious! Think about who's seeing the pictures we're making. Women have incredible influence, and we set the "temperature" for the home. It makes sense that God would want us to demonstrate His characteristic of kindness, especially since we live in a culture of unkindness.

B. Kindness comes from the heart.

We live in a hurting world in need of kindness. Every person you meet is fighting a battle. If we remembered that, we might be more prone toward kindness. Kindness comes from a heart of love. Eleanor says, "What's in our well comes up in our bucket." When we get right down to it, it is definitely a heart issue. God loved David's heart because he had a heart like God's. Surely we want to have a heart like God's as well!

I heard about a woman who befriended a homeless man who had taken up residence on the front lawn of her church. The pastor had been challenging his congregation to show the world that Christians care and that they are kind by "putting feet" to his messages. She engaged the homeless man in conversation for several days and gave him food to eat. He seemed to be warming up to her, and she felt he was responding to her kindness. Then, to her great surprise, the man began to take off his old clothes, which were a disguise, and she recognized him to be her pastor. This was a test, and she had passed! God tests our hearts. Proverbs 17:3 says, "The refining pot is for silver and the furnace for gold, but the LORD tests hearts."

Will you and I pass His test? Don't ask for kindness to be thrust upon you, because it usually doesn't happen that way. Instead, expect to be given an opportunity to practice kindness, and don't be surprised if it is to a person you would probably not have chosen. There is power in even small expressions of kindness. Matthew 10:42 says, "And if anyone gives even a cup of cold water to one of these little ones because he is my disciple, I tell you the truth, he will certainly not lose his reward" (NIV). Such a small kindness, but it affects eternity. Now, that makes an amazing woman!

Now What?

What were the most important points for you personally in this message, "Kindness in a Mean Girl World: Kindness"?

Homework Day 2

What?

"The fruit of the Spirit is love, joy, peace, patience, *kindness*, goodness, faithfulness, gentleness, self-control" (Galatians 5:22-23).

So What?

God desires for us to have a character of kindness, which means we should be good, generous, pleasant, caring, loving, benevolent, and forgiving. We live in a hurting world in need of kindness. God is not asking for random acts of kindness but for us to be kind always. It should not just be what we do but should be who we are. Kind acts flow from a kind heart. The Holy Spirit is the source of kindness.

1. Read Ephesians 4:29-32. What do verses 31-32 say about kindness?

2. How do you think forgiveness and kindness go together?

3. What are our words supposed to do for others (see Ephesians 4:29)?

4. What is the result of speaking unwholesome words (see Ephesians 4:30)?

Now What?

We have all been touched by words. Some words have built up and some have torn down.

1. Kindness is good, generous, pleasant, caring, loving, benevolent, and forgiving. Which of these characteristics of kindness are most challenging for you?

2. How might things be better in your home if you were to choose to be kind regardless of how others act or react?

Recognizing the power of words, place a note this week with a specific, sincere compliment on the pillow of your husband and each child (or send an e-mail or note to a friend). Remember, there is power in words to devastate or to elevate!

Homework Day 3

What?

"Do not let kindness and truth leave you; bind them around your neck, write them on the tablet of your heart. So you will find favor and good repute in the sight of God and man" (Proverbs 3:3-4).

So What?

God is calling women to a higher standard than the world and culture around them because we are to have a heart like His. Proverbs 31:26 tells us that an amazing woman "opens her mouth in wisdom, and the teaching of kindness is on her tongue." One of the kindest things we can do is to teach children to be kind and continually model kindness for them.

1. List some things we are to do to have a heart of kindness (see Colossians 3:12-17).

2. Circle those things in the list above that are lacking in your life.

Now What?

God gives clear instruction about teaching our children (see Deuteronomy 6:1-9). Children must be taught that it is wrong to be unkind. To hurt another person by word or deed is not acceptable. My granddaughter and grandson have both been victims of bullying, and they attend a Christian school! It is hurtful and can be damaging in many ways. I still remember the harsh words of mean kids who teased me about my height, braces, clothes, and my skinny frame (yes, I was once skinny!).

Recently, in an effort to reverse this situation, a principal read her students excerpts from a book called *Have You Filled a Bucket Today?* It is not a Christian book, but it is excellent. The concept is that we all have an invisible bucket that we carry with us wherever we go. The bucket's sole purpose is to hold good thoughts and feelings about ourselves. When our bucket is full, we feel happy, but when it is empty, we feel sad, lonely, and left out. Although

God's Word is the ultimate bucket filler, other people's kindness can help fill our bucket, and our kindness can help fill theirs. Some people are bucket fillers, and some are bucket dippers, which means they take away the good things in someone else's bucket in hopes of putting it into their own; however, we can't fill our own bucket by dipping into someone else's.

1. With children and adults in your sphere of influence, stimulate a conversation about being a bucket filler. Record the results.

Almost everyone responds well to kindness, and there are many ways of expressing it. We can speak only kind words, do something nice for someone, teach a child a lesson on kindness, write a long overdue note expressing gratitude, keep silent when a harsh word is spoken and instead reply in love, and be ready to keep our word even when it is inconvenient.

2. As the gatekeeper of your home, you have the power and responsibility to keep unkindness out. What are some changes needed in your heart or your home?

It's Not All About Me?

Others-Centered

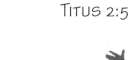

"That the word of God will not be dishonored."

TITUS 2:5

DVD Outline

I.   Introduction

II. **People for a Reason**
     A. Those Going Through Difficult Circumstances
     B. Serve through your giftedness.

III. **People for a Season**
     A. Seasons of Change or Crises
     B. Bearing Others' Burdens
        1. Unemployment
        2. Special-needs kids
        3. Widowed or divorced
        4. The elderly

IV. **People for a Lifetime**
     A. Learn their love language.
     B. Special Moments or Surprises
     C. Letters

V.   **Conclusion: Make God visible to others.**

Discussion Questions

1. What are some ways you have been cared for by others?
2. Why is it important to be focused on the needs of others?
3. Can you think of a time you were in another person's life for a specific reason or season?
4. What challenges you about focusing on the needs of others?

Homework Day 1

What?

"Do not merely look out for your own personal interests, but also for the interests of others" (Philippians 2:4).

So What?

Read the following notes from the DVD message "It's Not About Me? Others-Centered" and answer the "Now What" question at the end.

I. Introduction

In 2006, I was diagnosed with cancer. How could I have colon cancer? I was healthy, fit, young, and I was serving God. Besides, I was too busy to be sick. However, what I thought did not matter, because I spent the rest of the year in treatment, including multiple surgeries, chemotherapy, and radiation. But God blessed me with people—angels—who came alongside my family to help so we were strengthened physically, emotionally, and spiritually.

My friends were living out Philippians 2:4-5, which says, "Do not merely look out for your own personal interests, but also for the interests of others. Have this attitude in yourselves which was also in Christ Jesus." By caring, they made Christ visible in difficult circumstances.

As believers, we have opportunities to look beyond ourselves and to minister to others. However, selfishness is part of our nature. Anyone who has children knows this. One of their first words is often "mine"! As women, we may not say "mine," but we may ask questions such as these:

- "Why me?" when something bad happens
- "Why not me?" when good fortune comes to someone else
- "What about me?" when our needs or desires are not being met

Our older daughter, away at school, rarely gets home and is most likely going to attend grad school in another state next year. Our younger daughter works evenings and attends a local college. Therefore, this past Christmas, my husband and I wanted to savor our family time and planned some fun events. It was not the family outings that I looked forward to as much as the impromptu discussions, laughter at dinner, or staying up way too late watching really old reruns. However, our girls scheduled lots of activities with friends and were often gone. I felt sad and deserted. It is good to spend family time together, so shouldn't they feel the same way I do? I was not considering their needs and desires but was being selfish. I wanted it my way.

"Do nothing from selfishness or empty conceit, but with humility of mind regard one another as more important than yourselves" (Philippians 2:3). What Paul was saying is that we are to consider the needs of other people, but it takes humility. It is changing our mantra from "What about me?" to "It's not about me." God gives us plenty of opportunities to look beyond ourselves by putting others in our lives for a specific reason, season, or for a lifetime.

II. People for a Reason

A. Those Going Through Difficult Circumstances

When someone we care for is facing a challenging situation, whether illness, an accident, the death of a loved one, or the loss of a job, they need us to care about their interests. Jesus tells us when we are caring for others we are caring for Him (see Matthew 25:35-40).

A few months before my diagnosis, a dear friend lost her long-fought battle with cancer. Imagine how scared I was, receiving the news that I had the same disease. This came at a demanding time for our family. It took every bit of energy I had to focus on my medical care as I was anxious to meet my daughters' needs and keep my home running. I am so grateful for the army of angels God sent to provide for me during this trying time. Every meal that was prepared for us was more than physical nourishment; it was emotionally calming. We didn't feel like we were alone. We felt loved and cared for by our friends and God.

There are so many ways to ease the burden of someone going through a crisis. Here are some things to consider:

- Before making a meal, call to make sure there are no food allergies and ask for the best time to deliver it. Remember to do the following:
  - ★ Keep it simple for them to heat and eat.
  - ★ Pack the meal in disposable containers.
  - ★ Consider bringing some staples for breakfast and lunch at the same time.
- Give the person in need a break by taking him or her for an outing away from the circumstances, if possible.
- Lend a helping hand—offer services such as yard work, housecleaning, laundry, grocery shopping, babysitting, taxi services, and so on.
- Be loyal and remain a friend. The Bible says that "a friend loves at all times" (Proverbs 17:17). Too often, when someone enters a difficult time, people don't know how to respond and drop out of his or her life.

When a person is going through difficult circumstances, family or close friends may not always be available to assist. They are often affected by the difficulty as well, and most people are not comfortable asking for help. My best friends just jumped in and were there in every

PART ONE: Be Amazing in Character

way, especially keeping my spirits up. Other people who I thought would be very supportive actually disappeared; they didn't know how to respond to my sickness. Still others, some just acquaintances or even strangers, provided consistent help throughout the illness. God put them in my life for a reason.

It took a full year to go through cancer treatments, a full year to recover, and almost four years before I settled into a "new normal." It became a new season in my life.

B. Serve through your giftedness.

If you have a special talent or hobby, consider blessing your friend out of your giftedness. Here are some ideas:

- If you enjoy photography, offer family portraits. This is especially thoughtful before chemotherapy starts for cancer patients.
- If you enjoy gardening, bring fresh flowers or produce to your friend.
- If you enjoy reading, sit with her and read her favorite book.

III. People for a Season

A. Seasons of Change or Crises

A new season of life is when the normal flow changes into a new routine, usually started by an event such as a marriage, a new baby, an empty nest, or retirement. Seasons of life are normal and even anticipated; however, challenging seasons are often triggered by a crisis or tragic circumstances that cause life to be taxing and overwhelming. "Therefore encourage one another and build up one another" (1 Thessalonians 5:11). When we walk alongside a friend who is in a weary season, we help her shoulder the burden (see Galatians 6:2).

A pressure cooker is a cooking pot that has a locking lid, so pressure from the trapped steam builds. The trapped steam cooks the food significantly faster than a conventional pot. There are pressure relief valves that allow small amounts of steam to escape, keeping the pot from exploding. When we share even a small act of kindness with a friend going through a trying season, we act like a relief valve in her life as we release some of her stress.

B. Bearing Others' Burdens

The following are some common seasons that people may find themselves in and a few suggestions for acts of kindness that could be especially encouraging for them.

1. Unemployment. A job loss is upsetting enough, but when a new job doesn't come for a long period of time, it is discouraging. This is especially hard financially, so the following could be done (even anonymously).

- Deliver groceries to their door.
- Pay their utility bills.

- Bring clothes and shoes to them with gift receipts.
- Give them gift cards for gas, groceries, or a discount department store.
- Hire them to help you around your house to earn some money.

If you don't have money, you can still help by doing the following:
- Invite them for a meal and at the same time share fellowship and compassion.
- Shop from your house and share things you already have.

2. Special-needs kids. Having a special-needs child is a blessing but also requires lots of specialized attention, which can drain the parents. You can help by doing the following:
- Babysit for them.
- Educate yourself about the special need so you understand what your friend is dealing with and how you can better help.

3. Widowed or divorced. These women with children deal with life without daily support. They are doing a job that God designed for two people: a husband and a wife.

My parents divorced when I was four years old. My father was disengaged from our lives and my mother worked long hours but could barely make ends meet. The dynamics in our home were difficult. My life was so centered on what I did not have that I often found myself asking, "Why me?" or "Why not me?" But there was a family with a daughter my age who invested time in my life, including rescuing me one rainy night when my car died. They challenged me to be my best and loved me enough to tell me not to sing in public! So I encourage you to do the following:
- Continue to invite the widowed or divorced to couple events.
- Consider mentoring their children.
- Babysit for them.
- Help them with their honey-do list.

4. The elderly. If you have elderly parents or even grandparents you are caring for, you know that they require varying degrees of help. But mostly they need to feel valued.
- Spend as much time as possible with them.
- Take them to run errands.
- Ask them about their past.
- Play games with them.

If you have friends or family taking care of elderly parents, offer them a respite by sitting with the ones in their care. Sometimes offering rest can be the best help.

Following my cancer treatments, I entered a season of healing. Friends celebrated with me when treatments were finished by throwing a party. But my journey was far from over. In

PART ONE: Be Amazing in Character

many ways recuperating was more difficult than going through chemo and radiation because I no longer had the medicines that kept me from feeling terrible and I no longer had meals coming or help driving my kids. More importantly, I didn't have the daily prayer support I had. Even though we scaled back our life to the essentials, it took everything I had just to keep up. I had already received so much help that I didn't want to burden anyone by asking for more. Regardless of what season a friend is in, we should try to remain loyal and continue to love her (see Proverbs 17:17) and "not grow weary of doing good" (2 Thessalonians 3:13).

IV. People for a Lifetime

Focusing on others is not limited to someone in a crisis; for our family it should happen every day. We are to make each family member feel loved and special. Think about what would please your family. Here are some possible ideas.

A. Learn their love language.

A love language is how each person feels love. If we know our family members' love language, it is then possible to express love in a way they can receive it. My husband's love language is touch; therefore, I hug him often and hold his hand. My older daughter's is words of affirmation; she needs to hear how much we value her.

B. Special Moments or Surprises

Regularly plan a favorite outing or new adventure, such as "spontaneous doughnut." This is when we jump in the car and drive to the doughnut shop to see if the Hot Doughnuts sign is lit.

C. Letters

Words on a page can be read over and over. At least twice a year I write two letters to my daughters. The first one is to challenge them in an area I feel they need to grow. The second one is to encourage and bless them for who they are.

We can all agree that staying connected with extended family takes work. Friends may come and go, but family lasts forever. Some ways we can build relationships include the following:

- Planning meals with our family who live locally
- Planning vacations or reunions with family who live farther away
- Staying connected to keep up on their lives. Facebook has really helped me keep track of my nieces and nephews.

V. Conclusion: Make God visible to others.

When we grasp the depth of love Jesus has for us, then our love should overflow to others. Jesus said the second greatest command is to "love your neighbor as yourself" (Mark 12:31). This is not limited to your friends but extends to the people on your street and community. Even if you don't know them, even if they are unlikable, even if they have wronged you, you are to love them. Acts of love may be simple gestures, but they will help uplift and encourage someone in need. It's teaching them about Jesus.

Once we become a believer in Jesus Christ, our lives are no longer to be about us, but about Him. As we shift our thinking from "me, myself, and I" to Jesus, the natural response is selflessness. It changes how we view and treat the people who are in our life for a reason, a season, or a lifetime.

In Philip Yancey's book *Finding God in Unexpected Places*, he tells the story of Joanna Thomas, who worked diligently in the most violent South African prison. By preaching the gospel, teaching Bible studies, and forming small groups, she successfully reduced the violent acts within the prison from close to three hundred cases a year to just two. When asked how she brought God into the prison, her response was, "God was already there. I just made Him visible." Most of us are not called to prison ministry, but when we have the opportunity to minister to others, we make God visible.

Serving others should define our lifestyle because "we are ambassadors for Christ, as though God were making an appeal through us" (2 Corinthians 5:20). When we love and serve others, our life says, "It's not about me!" That is an amazing woman!

Now What?

What were the most important points for you personally in this message, "It's Not All About Me? Others-Centered"?

Homework Day 2

What?

"Let your light shine before men in such a way that they may see your good works, and glorify your Father who is in heaven" (Matthew 5:16).

So What?

Making God visible is at the core of what it means to focus on others. Our words and actions can influence others for Christ's kingdom in every relationship we have. When we realize that with God there are no chance encounters, we will see each person, either a total stranger or a trusted friend, as an opportunity to reflect kindness and therefore shine the spotlight on Him.

1. What was John the Baptist's role (see John 5:33-35)?

2. Who lights our lamp (see Psalm 18:28)?

3. A lamp is a vessel that casts light, though it is not the source of light itself. Who is the Light (see John 8:12)?

4. When we have accepted Jesus as our Savior, we have His light within us. What are we supposed to do as His lamp (see Luke 8:16)?

5. What is the purpose of the light within us (see Matthew 5:16)?

Now What?

1. What is being asked (see Psalm 4:6)?

2. How are we to love others (see 1 John 3:18)?

3. What changes do you need to make in order to shine the light of Christ for others?

PART ONE: Be Amazing in Character

Homework Day 3

What?

"But through love serve one another" (Galatians 5:13).

So What?

A poem titled "Reason, Season, or Lifetime" by an unknown author states that people come into your life for a specific reason, a short season, or a lifetime. Perhaps you have experienced a "chance" encounter with a stranger who gave you the insight you needed at the time. She was there for a reason. Or perhaps a fellow mom you considered a close friend drifted away after the kids grew up. She was there for a season. Most of us can claim family as our lifetime relationships. Regardless of the length of time, God is asking us to serve others.

1. What did Jesus come here to do (see Mark 10:45)?

2. What was Peter's mother-in-law's response to being touched by Jesus (see Matthew 8:14-15)?

3. What is our reward if we serve others (see Mark 10:43)?

4. What are we supposed to do with our gifts, and why (see 1 Peter 4:10)?

Now What?

How can you serve those in your life? The graph that follows has three sections: reason, season, and lifetime. In the "Person" column, list people God might want you to have an impact on. In the "Touch Point" column, list a possible way you could touch their lives by helping, praying, or encouraging.

REASON

Person	Touch Point

SEASON

Person	Touch Point

LIFETIME

Person	Touch Point

Serving others is being kind and is evidence of an amazing woman!

Be Amazing

in Relationships

How to Accept Yourself, Understand Others, and Love Them Anyway!

Temperaments

Eleanor Lewis

"That the word of God will not be dishonored."

Titus 2:5

DVD Outline

Getting Started: Discovering Your Temperament

I. **Why study the temperaments?**
   A. They affect everything you do.
   B. They do not keep you from doing anything.

II. **Possible Origin of the Temperaments**
   A. Man was created perfect: body, spirit, and soul.
   B. Sin affected all.

III. **Temperaments and Relationships**
   A. Jesus must be the center.
   B. To love others we must accept ourselves.
   C. To love others we must understand them.

IV. **Temperaments and Sin**
   A. Understand how we tend to sin.
   B. Weaknesses are not sin.
      1. Weaknesses are not sin unless acted on.
      2. Weaknesses are not an excuse to sin.

V. **We need the Spirit of God.**
   A. Uncontrolled temperaments God calls "flesh."
   B. The Holy Spirit produces fruit.
   C. God cleanses and prunes us to be more fruitful.

Discussion Questions

1. What is your temperament, and what do you like and appreciate about it?
2. Share an insight about your temperament that helps you understand the advantages or difficulties you have in relationships.

Homework Day 1

What?

"Love the Lord your God with all your heart, and with all your soul, and with all your mind.... You shall love your neighbor [another] as yourself" (Matthew 22:37, 39).

Getting Started: Discovering Your Temperament

About the Temperaments

Hippocrates, Ole Hallesby, Tim LaHaye, and Florence Littaur have all written about the temperaments. There is an old theory of behavior that says we were born to respond to things in a certain way. The University of Minnesota, Pennsylvania State University, and Harvard have all conducted studies comparing identical twins raised in the same environment with those raised in separate environments. They concluded we are more a product of our genetics than our environment.

If you have a brother or sister or more than one child you already knew that. How could the same two parents, raising children in the same environment, have children so different? One is sweet, like you, one is like your husband, and one is unlike anyone you've ever met in your life! This is explained by the temperaments or personality types. Let's find yours.

Discovering Your Temperament Worksheet

The worksheet that follows is a brief test you cannot fail! Go down all four columns looking at each word. Check those that describe you 95 percent of the time. For example, the first word is *animated*. If you came out of the womb shouting, "Yahooo!" check it. If you just admire animated people, leave it blank. You have less than ten minutes to complete the test, so there is not time for you to analyze each word. Go with your first instinct. We are trying to discover what you are naturally, not what you can be. After you have completed the worksheet, add all your checks in each column so you have a total at the bottom of each one. Find the letter (A–D) of your two higher numbers and then find the corresponding personalities on page 129.

How to Accept Yourself, Understand Others, and Love Them Anyway!

Discovering Your Temperament Worksheet

A	B	C	D
☐ Animated	☐ Independent	☐ Adaptable	☐ Analytical
☐ Easily Hurt	☐ Strong-willed	☐ Peace-loving	☐ Sensitive
☐ Fun-loving	☐ Outspoken	☐ Quiet but fun	☐ Loves detail
☐ Inspiring	☐ Goal-oriented	☐ Easygoing	☐ Thinker
☐ Friendly	☐ Decisive	☐ Patient	☐ Indecisive
☐ Emotional	☐ Leader	☐ Listener	☐ Planner
☐ Talkative	☐ Outgoing	☐ Dependable	☐ Faithful/loyal
☐ Outgoing	☐ Determined	☐ Cool & calm	☐ Precise/exact
☐ Restless	☐ Active	☐ Teases	☐ Fearful/worrier
☐ Forgetful	☐ Not sensitive	☐ Not aggressive	☐ Gifted/talented
☐ Interrupts	☐ Bossy/opinionated	☐ Sometimes lazy	☐ Perfectionist
☐ Scatterbrained	☐ Impatient	☐ Unenthusiastic	☐ Hard to please
☐ Easily bored	☐ Not affectionate	☐ Fearful/worrier	☐ Easily hurt
☐ Disorganized	☐ Argues/debates	☐ Stubborn	☐ Quiet
☐ Messy	☐ Gets even	☐ Slow/unhurried	☐ Moody
☐ Quick-tempered	☐ Time conscious	☐ Procrastinates	☐ Pessimistic
Total A	**Total B**	**Total C**	**Total D**
_____	_____	_____	_____

PERSONALITY A

Sanguine: Talker
Motto: Let's Have Fun!
Fears: Losing Approval

STRENGTHS	WEAKNESSES
Overview	
Warm, Outgoing	Unpredictable
Talkative	Restless
Carefree	Spontaneous anger
Emotional	Undisciplined
Optimistic	Weak-willed
In Personal Relationships	
Friendly	Undependable
Sensitive	Poor listener
Popular	Impulsive
Inspiring	Brash
Encourager	Loud
In Work Activities	
Enthusiastic	Disorganized
Natural salesman	Talks, Should work
Good starter	Poor finisher
Creative, good ideas	Easily distracted

PERSONALITY B

Choleric: Doer
Motto: I Can Do It Myself!
Fears: Losing Control

STRENGTHS	WEAKNESSES
Overview	
Confident	Anger, Revenge
Strong-willed	Opinionated
Optimistic	Insensitive
Self-sufficient	Unemotional
Not easily discouraged	Impatient
In Personal Relationships	
Born leader	Unsympathetic
Controls	Sarcastic, Cruel
Exhorter	Domineering
Decisive	Inconsiderate
Stimulates activity	Unforgiving
In Work Activities	
Organizer	Manipulative
Practical	Bored with details
Goal-oriented	Demanding
Delegates work	Intolerant of errors

PERSONALITY C

Phlegmatic: Watcher
Motto: Why Overexert Myself?!
Fears: Losing Peace

STRENGTHS	WEAKNESSES
Overview	
Calm, Relaxed	Unenthusiastic
Easygoing	Worrier, Fearful
Patient, Kind	Pessimistic
Peace-loving	Compromising
In Personal Relationships	
Likable	Stingy
Dry, witty humor	Selfish
Good listener	Stubborn
Faithful friend	Indifferent
In Work Activities	
Good under pressure	Procrastinates
Adaptable	Unmotivated
Practical, Finds easy way	Indecisive
Steady, Reliable	Reluctant leader
Efficient planner	Spectator

PERSONALITY D

Melancholy: Thinker
Motto: If It Is Worth Doing, Do It Right!
Fears: Making a Mistake

STRENGTHS	WEAKNESSES
Overview	
Gifted, Genius-prone	Moody, Depressive
Analytical	Pessimistic, Negative
Sensitive	Too introspective
Deep and thoughtful	Hypochondria
In Personal Relationships	
Self-disciplined	Critical, Picky
Dependable, Loyal	Unsociable
Self-sacrificing	Remembers past
Faithful friend	Sulks
In Work Activities	
Perfectionist, Intellectual	Theoretical
Conscientious	Tires easily
Likes detail work	Hard to please
Finds creative solution	Indecisive
Likes charts, graphs	Plans too much

Description of the Four Temperament Types

Each of the four boxes (personality A, B, C, and D) is a description of someone who matches that personality type completely. However, most people are a blend of two. Because you are probably a blend, you will not likely have all the characteristics of one.

Sanguine

If one of your two higher numbers is in column A, you may be a sanguine.

The sanguine is a born talker. His motto is, "Let's have fun!" She is an extrovert and a people person.

Strengths: Sanguines are outgoing, emotional, and friendly. Something has always happened to them, and they have to tell you about it. Tim LaHaye says that if you were with them when the real event took place, you almost don't recognize their version. They aren't concerned with facts but with entertaining you. They are huggers, touchers, kissers. They will hold on to your arm while they tell their story so you won't get away until they are finished.

Weaknesses: They are good starters but poor finishers. They have drawers full of unfinished projects. They have creative ideas but forget them. If they write them down, they will lose the piece of paper. They don't like to plan, but rather are spontaneous, weak-willed, and undisciplined. They may be on a diet but if they see a bag of chips, they will eat the whole thing!

Choleric

If one of your two higher numbers is in column B, you may be a choleric.

The choleric is a born doer. His motto is, "I can do it myself!" She is an extrovert and a project person.

Strengths: Cholerics are confident, strong-willed, self-sufficient, and decisive. They make decisions for parents, teachers, bosses, and mates. They always have goals and projects and accomplish much. They are opinionated; they have an opinion on all subjects and also a compulsion to tell you what it is.

Weaknesses: They are not sensitive, emotional, or sympathetic. That is, they don't cry and don't know what to do if you do. They don't say, "I love you," but will do something for you instead. They have a need to be in control so are not sympathetic with sickness because they can't control it. They are impatient and will drive fast even when they are not going anyplace!

PART TWO: Be Amazing in Relationships

Phlegmatic

If one of your two higher numbers is in column C, you may be a phlegmatic.

The phlegmatic is a born watcher. His motto is, "Why overexert myself?" She is an introvert and a people person.

Strengths: Phlegmatics are calm, relaxed, patient, and kind. They are born nice! They are peace loving, but this becomes a weakness when they compromise their opinions to keep the peace. If their opinion is different from yours, they will hide in the bathroom for a week rather than discuss it!

Weaknesses: They are procrastinators. They hate pressure, but when the pressure is on they do what they have put off and are good at it! They appear calm externally but internally worry about the things not done. They are stingy, selfish, and stubborn, but they are sweet about it! They are quietly stingy with their energy, selfish with their comfort, and quietly but sweetly stubborn!

Melancholy

If one of your two higher numbers is in column D, you may be a melancholy.

The melancholy is a born thinker. His motto is, "If it is worth doing, do it right!" She is an introvert and a project person.

Strengths: Aristotle said every genius is of the melancholy temperament; however, because they are perfectionists they are never satisfied. They are very hard on themselves. They are extremely dependable and loyal. If you want something done, and done right, ask a melancholy. They are conscientious and love order, lists, charts, graphs, and schedules.

Weaknesses: They are easily depressed because they are negative thinkers. They see what is wrong and tend toward hypochondria. They analyze life and have a perfect plan in mind; however, people and life don't cooperate. This depresses them, so they put on their robe and go to bed. They can be very sociable but have to go home and nap afterward because it is tiring.

So What?

Read the following notes from the DVD message "How to Accept Yourself, Understand Others, and Love Them Anyway! Temperaments" and answer the "Now What" question at the end.

I. Why study the temperaments?

A. They affect everything you do.

They explain why we view and do things differently.

- The **sanguine** would say, "Let's have a picnic. That would be fun!"
- The **choleric** would say, "Okay, Saturday, 11:00 a.m. at the lake. You bring the potato salad and you bring the baked beans. Now it is organized."
- The **phlegmatic** would think, *I'll take my lounge chair and some take-out chicken and lemonade. We'll have a good time.*
- The **melancholy** would think, *It's supposed to rain Saturday. The bugs are bad this time of year!* The melancholy wants to come but will analyze everything that could go wrong and come prepared. She will bring paper towels, garbage bags, a first-aid kit, sanitary wipes, an umbrella, bug spray, and a change of clothes, just to name a few.

B. They do not keep you from doing anything.

There have been U.S. presidents of all four types.

- **Sanguine:** Reagan and Clinton were *inspirational leaders.*
  - ★ Reagan told wonderful stories and had jelly beans at cabinet meetings.
  - ★ Clinton was charming with sanguine weaknesses. He lacked self-control.
- **Choleric:** Nixon (choleric/melancholy) and G. W. Bush (choleric/sanguine) were *independent leaders.*
  - ★ Neither led by polls. They are a good example of the difference in temperament blends.
  - ★ Nixon, a choleric/melancholy, was a cool personality. He had few friends and was a project person.
  - ★ George W., a choleric/sanguine, was more warm. He was a project and people person.
- **Phlegmatic:** Ford was an *intermediating leader.*
  - ★ Ford became president by default when Nixon was put out of office, but he was the perfect person for the time. He was a peacemaker and a conciliatory mediator.
- **Melancholy:** Carter was an *intellectual leader.*
  - ★ Carter was a deep thinker and detailed. He would edit and correct memos received and return them to the sender. Because he was a detailed person, his library was twice the size of Reagan's, though he was in office half the length of time.

II. Possible Origin of the Temperaments

A. Man was created perfect: body, spirit, and soul.

Man was created in God's image, so he was perfect (see Genesis 1:26-27, 31). He had a body, soul, and spirit. However, man sinned, resulting in death (see Romans 5:12). We're all like sheep who have gone astray because we want our own way (see Isaiah 53:6).

S**I**N ("I" is at the center of sin) is going *my way* instead of *God's way.*

B. Sin affected all.

When man sinned his entire being was affected.

- Body started to die. "It is appointed for men to die once" (Hebrews 9:27).
- Spirit immediately died (see Ephesians 2:1). We are dead to God, for God is Spirit (see John 3:1-6; 4:24).
- Soul (mind, emotions, and will) became imbalanced, resulting in the temperaments.
  - ★ Emotional = Sanguine
  - ★ Strong-willed = Choleric
  - ★ Quietly strong-willed = Phlegmatic
  - ★ Mental = Melancholy

III. Temperaments and Relationships

A. Jesus must be the center.

God says, "Two are better than one" and "a cord of three strands is not quickly broken" (Ecclesiastes 4:9, 12, NIV). A cord of three strands would be you, Jesus, and another person. Since a cord of three strands is not quickly broken, Jesus must be at the center of every relationship to make it strong and lasting.

B. To love others we must accept ourselves.

"You shall love the Lord your God with all your heart, and with all your soul, and with all your mind. . . .You shall love your neighbor [another] as yourself" (Matthew 22:37, 39).

One meaning of "love your neighbor" is "to be contented with." To love others as ourselves, we must first be content with ourselves! To do that we must get right with God. "I will give thanks to [God], for I am fearfully and wonderfully made" (Psalm 139:14).

However, when we look at others, we see their strengths, but when we look at ourselves, we see our weaknesses. Therefore, others always seem better than us! If we don't accept ourselves, we are saying God made a mistake. Have you complained about something in regard to yourself? "Will the clay say to the potter, 'What are you doing?'" (Isaiah 45:9; see also Romans 9:20). Thank God for the way you are made! We must realize that though others are different, they are "fearfully and wonderfully made" as well. Therefore, the next step to better relationships is to realize that others are different and that's okay, so change your expectations!

C. To love others we must understand them.

God said we are all like sheep who go astray because we want our own way. If you know anything about sheep you know they aren't too bright. So the real problem comes when one dumb sheep marries another dumb sheep and produce little dumb sheep. Do you think people who are alike get married? No! Opposites attract! If you are one of the two temperaments above the line on the graph on page 129, you will usually be attracted to someone who falls below the line, and vice-versa. However, what attracted us when we were dating begins to annoy us once we've been married awhile. We forget why we married our spouse and try to change him to be perfect like us! Our view changes.

	When Dating	Once Married
Sanguine	delightfully spontaneous	annoyingly spontaneous
Choleric	decisive	dictatorial (bossy)
Phlegmatic	laid-back	lazy
Melancholy	particular (detailed)	picky, picky, picky

Instead of trying to change the other person, we need to change our expectations. Don't expect your spouse to be like you, because he isn't! I'm a choleric/sanguine blend who married a phlegmatic. At first we had conflicts. I expected we would "go and do," and he wanted to stay home, relax, and "recharge his batteries." A choleric/sanguine is born with charged batteries! I learned we can't change another. In fact, we need each other. He needs me to light his fire, I need him to put mine out!

IV. Temperaments and Sin

A. Understand how we tend to sin.

Weaknesses acted upon can become sinful. We all want, but don't always get, our own way, but the way each temperament sins may look different.

1. **Sanguine** wants "the fun way."

These people lack self-control and discipline. Because they live in the moment and lack self-control, they may repeat the same sin. "No one who is born of God practices sin" (1 John 3:9). It is hard for them to see sin because they avoid thinking about it (it's not fun).

2. **Choleric** wants "my way."

These people lack love and are controlling. Because they are bossy and blunt, what they do and say can be sin. "Be angry, and yet do not sin" (Ephesians 4:26). They need Jesus at a young age to become loving. It is hard for them to see their own sin because their way is "right," so instead they blame others!

3. **Phlegmatic** wants "the easy way."

These people lack motivation. Their sin may be not only in what they do but also in what they don't do. "Therefore, to one who knows the right thing to do and does not do it, to him it is sin" (James 4:17). It is hard for them to see their own sin because they are so nice.

4. **Melancholy** wants "the right way" (as they define right).

These people lack faith and are fearful. Their sin shows itself in what they don't believe. "Whatever is not from faith is sin" (Romans 14:23). Faith overcomes fear and doubt. These people see their sin but lack the faith to believe God will forgive it.

B. Weaknesses are not sin.
1. Weaknesses are not sin unless acted on.

They are red flags warning where we will tend to sin. Therefore it is important to be honest about seeing your weaknesses.

2. Weaknesses are not an excuse to sin.
   They are not an excuse for a:
   - **Sanguine** to be undisciplined, disorganized, or untruthful
   - **Choleric** to be bossy, blunt, or sarcastic
   - **Phlegmatic** to be lazy, stubborn, or a procrastinator
   - **Melancholy** to be negative, moody, or hard to please

V. We need the Spirit of God.

A. Uncontrolled temperaments God calls "flesh."
God calls our natural, uncontrolled temperaments our "flesh." Flesh is our human nature devoid of the Spirit of God and dominated by sin. It is living in our weaknesses. God says, "Those who are in the flesh cannot please God. However, you are not in the flesh but in the Spirit, if indeed the Spirit of God dwells in you" (Romans 8:8-9). Therefore, to overcome our flesh, or weaknesses, we must have God's Holy Spirit. Does the Holy Spirit dwell in you? When we receive Jesus as our Savior, we are sealed with the Holy Spirit. If we don't have the Spirit of God in us there is no hope for fixing our weaknesses. We not only can't change others, but we can't even change ourselves! Only God can change people.

B. The Holy Spirit produces fruit.

The Holy Spirit produces fruit to overcome every weakness of our flesh. "The fruit of the Spirit is love, joy, peace, patience, kindness, goodness, faithfulness, gentleness, self-control" (Galatians 5:22-23).

- **Sanguine** needs the fruit of self-control.
- **Choleric** needs the fruit of love and patience.
- **Phlegmatic** needs the fruit of God's true inner peace.
- **Melancholy** needs the fruit of joy.

C. God cleanses and prunes us to be more fruitful.

God accepts us the way we are, but He doesn't want us to stay that way! To produce spiritual fruit God will cleanse and prune us. "I am the true vine, and My Father is the vinedresser. Every branch in Me that does not bear fruit, He takes away [takes up or lifts up to cleanse]; and every branch that bears fruit, He prunes it so that it may bear more fruit" (John 15:1-2).

God uses people and circumstances to prune each temperament in order to bear fruit.

- **Sanguine:** God uses *temptations* to produce *self-control*.
- **Choleric:** God uses *slow people or delays* to produce *patience*.
- **Phlegmatic:** God uses *conflict or unhappy people* to produce true inner *peace*.
- **Melancholy:** God uses *imperfect people and situations* to produce God's *joy*.

"It is good for me that I was afflicted, that I may learn Your statutes" (Psalm 119:71).

There is a story of Michelangelo receiving an exquisite piece of marble. He walked around it and suddenly began flailing at it wildly with his chisel. Chips flew in all directions. An apprentice yelled, "What are you doing? You will ruin that beautiful marble!" Michelangelo replied, "I see David in there and I've got to let him out." God looks at us and says, "I see Jesus in there and I've got to let Him out."

That is the value of understanding our temperament and trusting that God will use trials to prune us so we may be more like Him and can be amazing women with amazing relationships!

Now What?

What were the most important points for you personally in this message, "How to Accept Yourself, Understand Others, and Love Them Anyway! Temperaments"?

Homework Day 2

What?

"You wove me in my mother's womb. I will give thanks to You, for I am fearfully and wonderfully made" (Psalm 139:13-14).

So What?

The temperaments study shows we are created differently, but all four personality types are important and necessary. We will look at biblical women of each temperament type to see what we can learn about God and ourselves. We'll first look at Rebekah, a sanguine.

Abraham, a man of great wealth and position, sent his servant to another country to find a wife for his son, Isaac. The servant met a beautiful young woman named Rebekah at a well.

1. Review the characteristics of the sanguine and record the ones you see in Rebekah (see Genesis 24:15-28, 55-58). You may need to look beyond the different culture and treatment of women at that time.

Sanguines talk easily with strangers, desire to please, and love a spontaneous party! Rebekah not only talked with a stranger but gave him and his camels a drink and invited him home for the night. Only a sanguine who talks and acts without forethought would agree to leave home, go to a foreign land, and marry a complete stranger—immediately!

2. Rebekah married Abraham's son, Isaac, and had twin sons, Jacob and Esau. Esau was adventurous, dramatic, and spontaneous like his mother, while Jacob was quiet, laid-back (perhaps he was a phlegmatic), and very much her opposite. Which son did Rebekah prefer, the one like or unlike herself (see Genesis 25:27-28)?

Often we have trouble with people who are too much like us because we see our weaknesses in them. We may be attracted to those unlike us because we admire their strengths, which we do not have. As a talker, Rebekah probably enjoyed Jacob, the listener. She also may have felt he needed her to motivate and inspire him.

How to Accept Yourself, Understand Others, and Love Them Anyway!

3. Sanguines, controlled by present circumstances, often fail to think of future consequences. What did Esau's sanguine, live-for-the-moment nature cost him (see Genesis 25:29-34)?

4. Sanguines are born persuaders who can sell their ideas; however, they may exaggerate or even lie to make the sale. What was the real reason Rebekah wanted her favorite son, Jacob, to go away (see Genesis 27:41-45)? What reason did she give her husband (see Genesis 27:46)?

Instead of communicating truth, sanguines (and the rest of us) may stretch the truth or manipulate to get what we want. The sad result for Rebekah was that the few days Jacob was to stay away became twenty years, and it appears she never saw her dear son again.

Now What?

It is important to see ourselves from God's point of view . . . as "fearfully and wonderfully made." Look at the strengths of your temperament and write down three things you like about yourself. Perhaps you are a good communicator, leader, thinker, or diplomat. You may be good with computers, people, numbers, machines, ideas, music, color, or your hands. You might be practical, creative, loyal, or fun. Resist negative thoughts and stop comparing yourself to others, because they have weaknesses too. Thank God for the way you are made.

1.

2.

3.

Homework Day 3

What?

"All of us like sheep have gone astray, each of us has turned to his own way" (Isaiah 53:6).

So What?

God says "all have sinned" (Romans 3:23), which means every temperament has a problem with sin, though the sin for each may look different. Sometimes it is what we do or what we don't do. It may be what we believe or don't believe. However, God is in the life-changing business. We will continue our study by looking at a biblical example of a choleric. (We will look at the other temperaments next week.)

Jesus owned no property and had "nowhere to lay His head" (Luke 9:58). Therefore, He spent time in the home of his good friends Martha; her sister, Mary; and their brother, Lazarus.

1. Review the choleric characteristics and list the good and bad ones you see in Martha (see Luke 10:38-42).

Cholerics are doers, and Martha was never one to sit around. However, Martha's project of preparing a meal for friends became more important than the friends themselves! She became angry when others didn't work as hard as she did. We all might have had the same thoughts as Martha—"Lord, do You not care . . . ?"—but only a strong-willed choleric would be bold enough to verbalize it.

2. Lazarus died while Jesus was away. When He returned, how did Martha, in true choleric fashion, verbally challenge Jesus (see John 11:21, 39)?

Cholerics always try to get in the last word, even with God and even when they are wrong! However, as Martha learned to trust Jesus, she was changed.

3. After she witnessed God's power raising her brother from the dead, what did Martha do? Did she continue to complain (see John 12:1-3)?

4. This family is now a picture of what God desires for us: Martha *served* Jesus without complaint. Lazarus sat with Him in *fellowship*. Mary anointed His feet in *worship*. How are you doing in these three areas?

Now What?

1. Can you identify your husband's temperament?

2. What are his strengths that you appreciate?

3. How do your temperament differences cause conflict?

4. What new insights have you gained from this study that you can apply to your marriage?

How to Accept Yourself, Understand Others, and Love Them Anyway!

Temperaments, Part 2

Eleanor Lewis

"That the word of God will not be dishonored."

TITUS 2:5

DVD Outline

I. **Temperaments Review**
   A. Sanguine
   B. Choleric
   C. Phlegmatic
   D. Melancholy

II. **Temperaments and Communication**
   A. Communicating with Others
      1. Communicating requirements
      2. Communicating problems
   B. Communicating with God
      1. Knowing and going God's way
      2. Temperaments and a quiet time

III. **Temperaments and Parenting**

IV. **Temperament Needs and Fears**
   A. Sanguine
      1. Needs approval
      2. Fears losing social acceptance and being embarrassed
   B. Choleric
      1. Needs control and a project
      2. Fears losing control or being taken advantage of
   C. Phlegmatic
      1. Needs appreciation and others' expectations
      2. Fears not living up to others' expectations
   D. Melancholy
      1. Needs encouragement and information
      2. Fears making a mistake or being criticized

V. **Temperaments Changed by God's Spirit: Biblical Examples**
   A. Sanguine Peter
      1. Before: a people pleaser
      2. After: a God pleaser
   B. Choleric Paul
      1. Before: controlling
      2. After: loving

C. Phlegmatic Abraham
　　1. Before: timid
　　2. After: bold
D. Melancholy Moses
　　1. Before: fearful
　　2. After: joyful

VI. Conclusion

Discussion Questions

1. What difficulties do you have in your prayer life and Bible study? What insights have you received that will help you understand how to improve in those areas?
2. What is one weakness you see in yourself that you need the Holy Spirit to change?

Homework Day 1

What?

"Therefore if anyone is in Christ, he is a new creature; the old things passed away; behold, new things have come" (2 Corinthians 5:17).

So What?

Read the following notes from the DVD message "How to Accept Yourself, Understand Others, and Love Them Anyway! Temperaments, Part 2" and answer the "Now What" question at the end.

I. Temperaments Review

Titus 2 says amazing women are to have good relationships. To love others it helps to understand our temperaments and to do the following:

- Thank God for the way you are made.
- Realize others are different and that's okay, so *change your expectations*!

We are all fearfully and wonderfully made but different! Let's review the characteristics of each of the temperaments.

A. Sanguine
The sanguine is a born talker with a compulsion to have fun. She is a people person.

I was standing in the grocery and a little sanguine in the cart beside me said, "Hi, my name is Molly" and then proceeded to introduce me to her entire family. We were new best friends in the meat department.

B. Choleric
The choleric is a born doer with a compulsion to take charge. She is a decisive project person.

My neighbor who has two dogs babysat a three-year-old choleric who decided she didn't like the names of the dogs, so she renamed them. Within a few hours the dogs were responding to their new names!

C. Phlegmatic
The phlegmatic is a born watcher, so she is easygoing and has few compulsions. She is a people person.

My friend's phlegmatic child brought home a note from kindergarten that said he didn't know his address, his phone number, or how to tie his shoe. He had known all these for quite a while. When she asked him about it he said, "When I ask my teacher to tie my shoe, she does, so why should I do it? And I don't want to tell her my address or phone number because she might come over or call me!" The philosophy of the phlegmatic is, "Why over-exert myself?"

D. Melancholy

The melancholy is a born thinker with a compulsion to be orderly and perfect. She is a project person.

I am a choleric/sanguine. What that means is I am choleric enough to put everything in file folders, but sanguine enough not to label any of them! A six-year-old melancholy was visiting and saw me trying to find something in a file eight inches thick. She quietly said, "You need to put that in alphabetical order." I said, "You are right, but it would take too long." She said, "Just do a little bit each day!"

Often we take our differences personally, thinking others are being difficult. Actually we need each other. Sanguines make the world more fun. Cholerics make sure we get things done. Phlegmatics keep the world from fights. Melancholies make sure we do things right!

II. Temperaments and Communication

A. Communicating with Others

1. Communicating requirements

To communicate we need talking, listening, and coming to an understanding. In our temperament types (flesh) we have two good talkers and two good listeners but often no real communication or "meeting of the minds."

- **Sanguines** talk to inspire, entertain, and encourage. They may talk over you while you are talking or think about what they will say when you are quiet. They have difficulty listening.
- **Cholerics** talk to motivate to action. They may talk at you in commands, such as, "You don't think that!" They don't discuss but debate. Because they have strong opinions, they don't listen well.
- **Phlegmatics** are good listeners and excellent counselors who give good advice. However, they may talk like you because of their fear of offending. The danger is they may just agree or remain silent rather than share their wisdom.
- **Melancholies** are good listeners but will analyze not just what you say but what you mean. If I told a melancholy, "You look nice in that shade of blue," she would think, *What does she mean that shade? Didn't she like the blue I had on last week?* You can hurt their feelings by paying them a compliment.

2. Communicating problems
- **Sanguines** and **cholerics** finish your sentences. They ask questions but don't wait for answers.
- **Cholerics** are bottom-liners, so they want others to get straight to the point.
- **Phlegmatics** avoid conflict and therefore may not say what is on their mind. If interrupted by a talker, they will smile sweetly and become silent. They have a need to give their counsel.
- **Melancholies** have thought through everything but don't feel a need to share their thoughts. Instead they may have an attitude of approval or disapproval. My melancholy mother listened to her sanguine brother talk about a property he was going to buy. She didn't say a word. When he left I said, "Mom, I don't think you approve. Why didn't you tell him?" Her reply? "By my silence he should know I don't approve."

B. Communicating with God

As we strive to understand the temperaments, we need to do the following:
- Understand how we will sin by going our own way.
- Seek to go God's way!

1. Knowing and going God's way

Sin is going "my way," so we must learn to go God's way. Isaiah tells us, "'My thoughts are not your thoughts, nor are your ways My ways,' declares the LORD. 'For as the heavens are higher than the earth, so are My ways higher than your ways and My thoughts than your thoughts'" (55:8-9).

Going God's way requires communicating with God: talking, listening, and coming to an understanding of His mind. We have the same problems communicating with God that we have communicating with each other.

2. Temperaments and a quiet time
- **Sanguines** struggle with Bible study and prayer because they require discipline and focus. My sanguine friend had a rich quiet time because she had a chair for Jesus, played music, and imagined Him there singing and talking with her personally.
- **Cholerics** are disciplined, so they will set a time. However, they will pray "bless my plan" prayers, telling God what to do, rather than listening to what God wants done. They often apply God's Word to others instead of to themselves.
- **Phlegmatics** are good when in a routine but will struggle with getting started. They do best with structure: the same chair at the same time each day with a plan to follow that isn't overwhelming. They need a directed Bible reading and prayer time. Once in a routine they will be consistent.

- **Melancholies** are best at prayer and Bible study becuase they desire to learn. Their problem is getting bogged down in details instead of hearing God speak. Their biggest struggle can be legalism or negativity. They may feel condemned instead of convicted. They need to practice praise.

III. Temperaments and Parenting

The temperaments affect everything you do, including the way you parent. "Train up a child in the way he should go" (or in the way he is "bent") (Proverbs 22:6).

Have you heard a parent say, "I raised all my kids the same; I don't know what happened!" Do you see that you can't raise them the same because they are not the same? We are each born with a different "bent." I met a sanguine mother who worried about her melancholy son because in her opinion he didn't have enough fun. Thinking like a sanguine, she signed him up for activities, playgroups, and so forth. What he really enjoyed was being alone building with Legos. The more she tried to make him have fun, the more depressed he became. If we try to "bend" a melancholy to be a sanguine, we may break him!

The following characteristics of each temperament apply not only to parenting but to all relationships—with children, husbands, friends, and coworkers.

- **Sanguines** are fun parents who will play with and enjoy their children and be appreciated by their friends. However, their desire to be a friend can overshadow their impact as a parent. Their own lack of personal discipline makes it difficult to consistently discipline another. Spontaneous anger may lead to sharp, hurtful words. "Life and death are in the power of the tongue" (Proverbs 18:21).
- **Cholerics** are great disciplinarians who will not enable bad behavior. However, being uncomfortable with emotion (which they perceive as weakness), they have a hard time showing or expressing love. Cholerics also struggle with angry or blunt words. They make commands instead of requests, tell people what they are doing wrong, and rarely praise what they are doing right. "Fathers, provoke not your children to anger, lest they be discouraged" (Colossians 3:21, KJV; *Strong's Concordance* says *discouraged* means "broken in spirit").
- **Phlegmatics** are so nice and even-tempered that they create a peaceful home environment. However, I heard psychologist Dr. Henry Brandt, called "The Father of Modern Day Biblical Counseling," say, "When a child asks for a fight, give it to 'em!" Since phlegmatics hate conflict and love comfort, they often overlook or adapt to bad behavior that needs to be disciplined. They can be enablers. They especially need God's strength to deal with a choleric who does not respect weakness. "Discipline your son while there is hope" (Proverbs 19:18).
- **Melancholies** are often strongly gifted in some area, and they will help their children develop interests in writing, technology, art, music, math, and so on. They

are sensitive to their children's abilities and needs. However, being analytical and negative, they can discourage others, saying things such as, "How could you miss this question on the test? Everyone knows that." More than words they often give a look that sends the message, "I am not pleased. How could you be so stupid?" "But as for a broken spirit who can bear it?" (Proverbs 18:14).

IV. Temperament Needs and Fears

A. Sanguine

1. Needs approval

Sanguines need praise, attention, and lots of approval. When they do something, they make an announcement, such as, "I mowed the lawn!" And you are supposed to say, "And you did it better than anyone ever has!" But a phlegmatic will say, "So?" A choleric will say, "It's about time!" and a melancholy will say, "Yes, but you didn't trim." Criticism deflates a sanguine! They aren't as confident as they appear and therefore need praise. They often don't achieve because they don't finish. They quit when something is no longer fun. Therefore, have a rule for sanguine children that they must finish the school year or the sports season. Train them to finish!

2. Fears losing social acceptance and being embarrassed

Because they fear losing social acceptance, don't correct a sanguine adult or discipline a sanguine child in front of others. I watched five-year-old Gracie not listen to her mother's instruction. Her mother wisely took her into another room rather than embarrass her by disciplining her in front of others. In true sanguine fashion I heard the child try to charm her way out of discipline, saying, "But, Mommy, I love you, I love you!"

B. Choleric

1. Needs control and a project

Cholerics will naturally take charge. Even choleric children need to control something, just not their parents! Give them an area of control such as their bedroom. As students and in careers they do better with practical subjects because they don't relate with abstracts, analogies, or emotion (unless they are a choleric/melancholy blend).

A choleric is not prone to depression; however, my choleric father became depressed when he retired and felt he had lost control of his life and had no goals or projects.

2. Fears losing control or being taken advantage of

Since conquering everything is their comfort zone, having someone take advantage of them is in their mind a sign of weakness. In an attempt to control every situation, a choleric tries to get the last word in. A child will end any attempt at discipline with, "That didn't hurt," or "I didn't want to go anyway." Adult cholerics will get the last word in as well!

C. Phlegmatic

1. Needs appreciation and others' expectations

A phlegmatic is motivated by others appreciating them. However, their quiet efforts are often overlooked. Their lack of drive can keep them from living up to their full potential. They need someone to have an expectation for them because they often don't have goals for themselves. However, don't make your expectation so high it overwhelms them. My phlegmatic husband, Bob, went to college on a football scholarship, and it was hard. He had to practice, play, and study, and every day he wanted to quit. He had a phlegmatic mother who would have said, "Whatever makes you happy!" However, he had a sanguine father who bragged about his son, the college football player. That is what kept Bob in school. His father had an expectation, and Bob wanted to please him.

2. Fears not living up to others' expectations

However, another person's expectation can be not only the greatest need of phlegmatics but also their greatest fear. "Will I please everyone and keep them happy? How can I keep them from being upset?" Therefore, their greatest fear of not living up to others' expectations can be their greatest motivator.

D. Melancholy

1. Needs encouragement and information

Melancholies need much encouragement. However, they are easily discouraged and difficult to encourage because they are hard on themselves. My melancholy neighbor was a dean's list student in college. Her alarm didn't go off and she missed an exam. She couldn't be consoled as she said, "Now I'll never get into grad school!" They also need information, clear instructions, and a quiet environment. They don't do well with confusion or disorder and need time to analyze. If you ask them a question, don't expect an immediate response because they need time to process information.

2. Fears making a mistake or being criticized

If they don't do something perfectly the first time, they will want to quit, saying, "I'll never get it right!" Mistakes mean failure. They may fear competition because it can be "failure with witnesses." Being criticized is one of their greatest fears. They are sensitive not only to people's words but also to their tone of voice, facial expressions, and even actions. Redoing their efforts can be perceived as criticism.

V. Temperaments Changed by God's Spirit: Biblical Examples

As we study the temperaments, we see that our greatest need is for the Holy Spirit. God's Spirit produces a fruit to overcome every weakness. For God to produce spiritual fruit we must be sealed with the Spirit (see Ephesians 1:13), walking in the Spirit (see Galatians 5:16-17), and filled with the Spirit (see Ephesians 5:18). The fruit the Spirit will produce is "love, joy, peace, patience, kindness, goodness, faithfulness, gentleness, self-control" (Galatians 5:22-23).

Turn from your own way by being filled with God's Spirit. The Spirit will change your character and your conduct. We can learn from biblical characters how God sometimes used other people and hard circumstances to prune people and produce spiritual fruit in order to change their temperament weaknesses.

A. Sanguine Peter
1. Before the Holy Spirit

A servant girl and bystanders said, "'You also were with Jesus.'. . . He began to curse and swear, 'I do not know this man you are talking about!' Immediately a rooster crowed" (Mark 14:67, 71-72).

 a. Peter talked on the Mount of Transfiguration, and God told him to listen.
 b. He relied on emotions, feeling he would never deny Jesus. He had good intentions, but sanguines live in the moment and are controlled by their circumstances.
 c. A sanguine people pleaser, he wanted others' approval and behaved like those he was with. Peter didn't deny Jesus before authorities but instead before a servant girl and bystanders.
 d. He needed the fruit of *self-control*.

2. After the Holy Spirit

Filled with the Holy Spirit, Peter told the rulers about Jesus. He was imprisoned and commanded "not to continue teaching in this name [Jesus]," but Peter replied, "We must obey God rather than men" (Acts 5:28-29).

 a. Filled with the Spirit, Peter was a God pleaser rather than a people pleaser.
 b. He boldly spoke before thousands and was willing to be ostracized.
 c. He was flogged but went out "rejoicing that they had been considered worthy to suffer shame for His [Jesus'] name" (Acts 5:41). He was willing to suffer floggings, prison, and the loss of social approval.

B. Choleric Paul
1. Before the Holy Spirit

"Paul began ravaging the church . . . dragging off men and women, he would put them in prison" (Acts 8:3). His goal was to destroy the church.

 a. A choleric will naturally take control.
 b. Paul was passionately doing something even though it was wrong!

    c. Paul was probably a choleric/melancholy, which is the coolest temperament. He
       was better with projects than people.

    d. He needed the fruit of *love*.

2. After the Holy Spirit

"Suddenly a light from heaven flashed around him; and he fell to the ground. . . . Saul
got up from the ground, and though his eyes were open, he could see nothing; and leading
him by the hand, they brought him into Damascus. . . . Ananias . . . said, 'Brother Saul, the
Lord Jesus, who appeared to you . . . has sent me so that you may regain your sight and be
filled with the Holy Spirit'" (Acts 9:3-4, 8, 17).

    a. Paul had to lose control and be made blind in order to "see."

    b. God pruned him hard: he was shipwrecked, beaten, and imprisoned, but, still
       strong-willed, he told his captors what to do. He told them to throw food
       overboard.

    c. Paul went from destroying the church to loving the church. In love, he was will-
       ing to be separated from God if it would bring his fellow Jews to Jesus. Paul
       wrote, "If I . . . do not have love, I am nothing" (1 Corinthians 13:2).

C. Phlegmatic Abraham

1. Before knowing God intimately

God told Abraham to leave his family and go where God told him to go. Abraham
took his family and went partway. Partial obedience is disobedience.

    a. God said, "Sarah your wife will bear you a son" (Genesis 17:19). To avoid conflict,
       Abraham obeyed his wife and slept with her handmaid, Hagar.

    b. He was timid and because of fear twice said his wife was his sister.

    c. He needed the fruit of God's *peace* (not based on his circumstances).

2. After knowing God intimately

God asked Abraham to offer his only son, Isaac. Immediately he obeyed, believing "God
will provide for Himself the lamb for the burnt offering." He also believed "God is able to
raise people [Isaac] even from the dead" (Genesis 22:8; Hebrews 11:19).

    a. He had immediate, total obedience rather than procrastination and partial
       obedience.

    b. He had great faith to believe God was able to provide a lamb or resurrect his son.

    c. He knew God had an expectation for him, and he wanted to please God.

D. Melancholy Moses

1. Before knowing God intimately

From a burning bush God asked Moses to deliver Israel. Moses said, "Who am I?" God said it didn't matter who Moses was because "I will be with you" (Exodus 3:11-12). Moses had more doubts and fears, wondering who God was and thinking no one would believe God sent him. He told God, "I have never been eloquent" (Exodus 4:10).

Moses prayed, "Why have I not found favor in Your sight, that You have laid the burden of all this people on me? . . . Where am I to get meat to give to all this people? . . . I alone am not able to carry all this people, because it is too burdensome for me. . . . Please kill me at once, if I have found favor in Your sight" (Numbers 11:11, 13-15).

    a. He was fearful, seeing everything that could go wrong.

    b. He tried to figure things out. He wouldn't commit until he understood what, how, and who.

    c. He struggled with faith, which comes from hearing God, believing Him, and obeying Him, without seeing the end result.

    d. He needed the fruit of God's *joy.*

2. After knowing God intimately

Just as Moses feared, Israel didn't heed his words and Pharaoh's heart was hardened. However, as Israel stood before the Red Sea with the Egyptian army in hot pursuit, "Moses said to the people, 'Do not fear! Stand by and see the salvation of the LORD" (Exodus 14:13). And he sang a song of praise!

    a. God graciously worked to remove Moses' doubts by showing His presence and power through the burning bush, rod, and plagues.

    b. Moses' doubt and insecurity were replaced by faith and joy.

    c. Praise replaced Moses' fear.

VI. Conclusion

Apart from God's Spirit we will always wrestle with our relationships; however, God will produce His character in us. If you were born a sanguine, choleric, phlegmatic, or melancholy, you will die the same. However, God wants us to be the very best we can be—amazing women who have amazing relationships with God and each other.

Now What?

What were the most important points for you personally in this message, "How to Accept Yourself, Understand Others, and Love Them Anyway! Temperaments, Part 2"?

Homework Day 2

What?

"'For My thoughts are not your thoughts, nor are your ways My ways,' declares the LORD. 'For as the heavens are higher than the earth, so are My ways higher than your ways and My thoughts than your thoughts'" (Isaiah 55:8-9).

So What?

Since sin is going our own way instead of God's way, it is important we learn to go God's way, which requires communicating with God. We will learn from a woman who did just that. Hannah was married to a man named Elkanah and lived at a time of great ungodliness. There was trouble in her home, her "church," and her community. It was a time when "every man did what was right in his own eyes" (Judges 17:6). Hebrew women greatly desired children, for they knew God had promised to send a special Son who would bring the Holy God and unholy men together. Review the phlegmatic characteristics as we learn from Hannah.

1. What was Hannah's problem (see 1 Samuel 1:6-8)?

A sanguine with the problems Hannah had would have been emotional, a choleric would have been angry, and both would have been verbal. They may have said, "It's my husband's fault" or, "It's God's fault!" They would have blamed others or at least been noisy about it.

2. What did phlegmatic Hannah do instead (see 1 Samuel 1:9-13)?

Hannah poured out her concern to God. She prayed a very specific prayer. True faith is *hearing* God's Word (see Romans 10:17), *believing* God's Word (see Romans 4:20-21), and *obeying* God's Word (see Hebrews 11:8) *without seeing* the outcome (see Hebrews 11:1, 8).

3. Did Hannah have faith? How do you know? Did she hear, believe, and obey God without seeing a result (see 1 Samuel 1:15-18)?

What a lesson for us! Though not yet pregnant, Hannah believed God's Word, evidenced by her eating and having joy even before the answer came.

4. How did God reward Hannah's quiet faith (see 1 Samuel 1:19-20; 1 Samuel 2:21)?

Now What?

1. Can you identify the temperaments of each of your children? If so, what are they?

2. What are their strengths that you need to encourage?

3. What are their weaknesses that you can help them overcome?

4. What new insights have you gained from this study that you can apply to your parenting?

Homework Day 3

What?

"You did not choose Me but I chose you, and appointed you that you would go and bear fruit, and that your fruit would remain" (John 15:16). "But the fruit of the Spirit is love, joy, peace, patience, kindness, goodness, faithfulness, gentleness, self-control" (Galatians 5:22-23).

So What?

We need to turn from going our way by being filled with God's Spirit so He can produce His fruit. We see from melancholy Ruth how a personal relationship with the living God can change the way we live. It can also change the direction of our lives and the choices we make.

There was a famine in Israel, and Naomi, a follower of Almighty God, went with her husband and two sons to a foreign land for food instead of trusting God to provide. While there, her sons married pagan women, Orpha and Ruth. Soon her husband and both sons died. The grief-stricken Naomi decided to go back to her homeland.

1. Although both of Naomi's daughters-in-law had the same experience, go back over the melancholy characteristics and record the ones you see in Ruth (see Ruth 1:8-18).

The two young women had the same circumstances but made very different choices. We see in Ruth the melancholy characteristics of loyalty, dependability, faithfulness, and sensitivity.

2. What were these two women choosing besides where to live (see Ruth 1:16-17; 2:11-12)?

They were choosing the god they would worship and trust: their pagan gods or the one true and living God. Being a melancholy thinker, Ruth made the right choice.

3. In relationships, melancholies are self-sacrificing. In performing tasks, they are conscientious, precise, and detailed. How did Ruth respond to Naomi's instructions that reveals her conscientiousness (see Ruth 3:5)?

4. How was Ruth blessed for her right choices (see Ruth 4:13-17; Matthew 1:1, 5)?

Ruth's son, Obed, was the father of Jesse, who was the father of King David, of the line of Jesus!

Now What?

1. Look at your temperament weaknesses (remember, these are not sins but red flags warning where you will have a tendency to sin). Write down the top two that need to be dealt with.

   a.

   b.

2. Why are you not getting victory in these areas?

3. What have you learned through this study that will help you improve your relationships with God and others?

You Don't Know My Husband!

Love Him?

Linda Sweeney

"That the word of God will not be dishonored."

TITUS 2:5

DVD Outline

I. **Introduction**

   A. God commands wives, "Love your husband!"

   B. Love is a choice.

   C. Change yourself, not him.

II. **Understand "loving your husband."**

   A. Definition of Love

   B. Truths to Learn and Apply

   C. Hindrances to Loving Our Husbands

      1. Familiarity

      2. Fatigue

      3. Family

      4. Forgiveness withheld

   D. Practical Ways to Show Love to Your Husband

      1. Pray for him.

      2. Get rid of unrealistic expectations.

      3. Choose your battles.

      4. Honor and respect him.

      5. Encourage him.

      6. Make your home a refuge.

      7. Learn about his temperament.

      8. Present yourself well.

      9. Pray a "hedge of thorns" around him.

III. **Conclusion**

Discussion Questions

1. What are some things you could do differently that might make loving your husband easier? If you're not married, how could this advice help you?

2. How could learning your husband's temperament(s) make a difference as you learn to love him more biblically?

Homework Day 1

What?

"Older women likewise are to be reverent in their behavior, not malicious gossips nor enslaved to much wine, teaching what is good, so that they may encourage the young women to love their husbands, to love their children, to be sensible, pure, workers at home, kind, being subject to their own husbands, so that the word of God will not be dishonored" (Titus 2:3-5).

So What?

Read the following notes from the DVD message "You Don't Know My Husband! Love Him?" and answer the "Now What" question at the end.

I. Introduction

A. God commands wives, "Love your husband!"

In Titus 2:4 God says older women are to teach and encourage younger women to "love their husbands." However, before God's command barely passes through your ear canal you are probably saying, "BUT YOU DON'T KNOW MY HUSBAND!" You are right. . . . I don't. And you don't know mine either except for the things I reveal. We are using God's Word as our guide rather than the world's view because God teaches a completely different concept of marriage than what society teaches.

B. Love is a choice.

I heard a great definition of marriage: "Marriage is an irrevocable covenant of unconditional love with an imperfect person." With marriage come commitment and promises between a man and a woman to love one another. The number one reason I hear for "quitting marriage" is this: "I no longer love him/her and God would want me to be happy." However, *love is an act of the will*. It is a choice, not a feeling!

Disclaimer from me: I am not perfect. I do not have all the answers, do not have a perfect marriage, and have failed multiple times in what I'm teaching. I grieve over not knowing these truths sooner in my marriage. These truths work when I choose to apply them! I would so love to help you avoid my mistakes.

C. Change yourself, not him.

Right now, wherever you are, I pray you will have an open heart and the courage to examine yourself in light of God's truth. Ask Him to show you what you need to know about yourself and your marriage and to help you be humble enough to receive it.

Maybe your husband is a pill, but we're not addressing him. Changing him is God's work. We're talking about us! Remember Romans 12:18: "If possible, *so far as it depends on you,* be at peace with all men" (emphasis added). Well, we're to love in the same way—so far as it depends on us. This isn't about changing him; it's about changing us!

I can't resist smiling as I include a quote that says, "Being a woman is a terribly difficult trade since it consists principally of dealing with men." The best part is that it was a man who said it!

II. Understand "loving your husband."

A. Definition of Love

When the book of Titus was written to those on the Island of Crete, which was a very pagan place, this teaching was quite challenging. The Christian lifestyle was new and so was the idea of "the Christian home." Warren Wiersbe tells us, "Young women saved out of paganism would have to get accustomed to a whole new set of priorities and privileges. Those who had unsaved husbands would need special encouragement!"[14] This is the same situation that prompted the words in 1 Peter 3:1-4, where Peter encouraged the behavior of wives to be so pure and respectful and their character so gentle that their unbelieving husbands would be won without a word!

There are several different meanings for the word *love,* but the one we're studying is from the Greek word *philandros,* which means "friendship, respect, value." When women are instructed to "love their husbands" in this passage and in others that are similar in content, "respect" is the meaning. It is not based upon a wife's assessment of her husband's worthiness, and it is not a feeling. You will find the same word in Ephesians 5:33, which says, "The wife must see to it that she respects her husband."

B. Truths to Learn and Apply

A few years ago my husband and I were invited to attend a marriage conference. I felt he would not go as most often he says no to such invitations, so I spoke for us and declined. I was urged, however, to "just ask him." Because it was hard to explain not doing so, I asked him and quickly added, "and there will be good food for those who attend." He rarely turns down an opportunity to eat. Our running joke is, "Feed him and he will go!" We went.

During the time leading up to the conference I kept thinking, *This is good. Ed will hear things I want him to know but can't tell him, like how to love, value, cherish, and appreciate me much more!* I was getting excited. Once we arrived, I was shocked to learn pretty quickly that

God wanted me there regardless of whether or not Ed participated. I soon forgot my plan to watch him take notes on how to be a better husband because I was too busy taking my own notes relating to my role as his wife! Up to that point I would have told you that I was a really good wife—a rare gem and a total joy, no doubt! However, I heard things explained in ways I'd never heard before, and looking back I realize the teaching was so powerful because it was truth straight from Scripture. The teacher wasn't particularly charismatic or good-looking. He was short and bald, he wasn't funny, he used no stories, and I learned later he wasn't even married! Here are a few things I learned and am trying to practice:

1. Marriage requires work.
2. God has only one job opening: servant! (I'll admit I chewed on this for a while, but I've noticed that when I serve Ed, he tends to do the same. However, my motive cannot be to get something from him but rather to obey Jesus. Look at the picture on page 168.
3. You can have a happy marriage that is neither righteous nor holy. But holy marriages have a better chance of being happy!
4. God gives commands, not advice, on marriage.
5. There are two problems with focusing on having a good marriage:
   a. God never commands us to have a good marriage. He directs us to reform ourselves, not our marriages. Scripture gives instruction on being a good wife or husband, but God's Word never defines a good marriage.
   b. God's objective is to sanctify us, not pacify us. (That may be a surprise to some!) In other words, marriage requires joint effort—the cooperation of two people. Thus, individual obedience is the only way to approach your marriage. It requires work! When I work on becoming a better person, it will not guarantee a better marriage, but it will please God.
6. I am expected to "clock in" and fulfill my obligation to God and my marriage because God will not judge us as a couple. The idea of standing alone before God without Ed was a new and sobering thought for me.
7. Lack of romance will not be important on judgment day!

Here are some interesting thoughts:
- Persistent love is a choice, not an emotion. It is "I do" or "I will" and never "I feel."
- The most reliable test of your love for God is your love for others (see 1 John 4:7).
- We need an attitude of giving, not trading (this includes sex!).
- The question that should be asked of all engaged couples is, "Who do you want to serve and forgive for the rest of your life?" That might make a difference in how many marriages stand the test of time.
- Don't compare workloads. There is no comparison and was never meant to be because our roles are different.

You Don't Know My Husband!

C. Hindrances to Loving Our Husbands

1. Familiarity. Knowing and being known can produce ingratitude, or even a judgmental spirit. It can also lead to bitterness: "I liked you before I got to know you so well." This is dangerous territory. The longer you live with someone, the more intentional your love needs to be. Philippians 1:9 applies here: "And this I pray, that your love may abound still more and more in real knowledge and all discernment."

2. Fatigue. It distorts our thinking and causes us to cut corners. Watch for this one; it is subtle.

3. Family. It is easy for family to take priority over our husbands. Children's needs seem more immediate because they are young, and feedback from them is usually more rewarding. This means we're tempted to redirect energy toward our kids or grandkids, not our spouse.

A wife should be her husband's press agent! The greatest gift you can give your children is to demonstrate your love for your husband.

4. Forgiveness withheld (mutual). It's absurd to resent your spouse for being a sinner! That's like resenting snow in Michigan. We think we don't sin as much as our husbands. Matthew 6:14-15 says, "For if you forgive others for their transgressions, your heavenly Father will also forgive you. But if you do not forgive others, then your Father will *not* forgive your transgressions" (emphasis added). If I don't forgive, I won't be forgiven.

Forgiveness is the only path to reconciliation. We justify withholding forgiveness by thinking, *But you don't know what he's done!* There is nothing unforgivable. Jesus' sacrifice paid for our forgiveness! His life in us gives us the power to forgive others.

Women have a hard time with forgiveness. We keep good, thorough records, and often the smallest offense causes the lid to blow off all we've had in storage. It's been said that women are not only hysterical at times but often historical as well!

D. Practical Ways to Show Love to Your Husband

1. Pray for him. Here's a good exercise and perhaps a tough challenge: find something to be thankful for about your husband for thirty days. Each day must be a new thing, even if it's just "he takes out the garbage"! After thirty days, you'll have a changed attitude and most likely a pretty good list of things you appreciate about him. You might even have a changed marriage!

2. Get rid of unrealistic expectations. Let me save you a lot of time and frustration. You will not change him!

3. Choose your battles carefully and ask, "Is this worth going to war over?" Usually it's not! Remember, it's the second word that starts the argument.

4. Honor and respect him. Do not talk about him or complain about him to your friends or family, not even to your mother or mother-in-law. Later you may forgive him, but they can't forget what you've told them and may not forgive. It is an issue of proper boundaries for your relationships.

Several years ago, my husband and I entered a season of unemployment, and it was a nightmare for me. Frankly, it was not just unsettling; it was frightening. There were times when I let fear of the "what ifs" paralyze me as I listened to the lies of the Enemy instead of trusting God's promises. During that time, I said things I came to regret—hurtful words that were disrespectful and discouraging. I thought Ed should be out job hunting every day until he found work, not sitting and waiting for the phone to ring. He went to several networking meetings where other unemployed men met to swap resumes and try to help each other find work, meet new contacts, and so on. He told me later that the number one hardest thing for the men to endure was wives who weren't supportive, who said hurtful things in an effort to motivate them, and who gave them unkind, disapproving looks. Men were created to work. When they aren't able to fulfill their role due to circumstances beyond their control, it's our job to be their supporter, cheerleader, helper, biggest fan, and encourager! If you are in this place today, I pray you choose your words carefully. We have no idea of the far-reaching damage that can come from our tongues. James says the tongue is a fire that can cause a forest fire (see 3:5-6). Even if we are disappointed, we should not show it.

5. Encourage him with kind and loving words of affirmation. One of Ed's love languages is words of affirmation. He takes great joy and pride in the upkeep of our home, especially in caring for our lawn. After he cuts the grass he wants me to come "see how good it looks!" Now, I've got to tell you that one cut yard looks pretty much like another to me, but it's important that I affirm him in this as I know it's important to him.

6. Make your home a refuge. You've learned what he likes and what he doesn't, so do those things that please him. If you want your husband to be excited about being at home, consider the following:

- If he hates clutter and disorganization, get busy and clean up the mess!
- If he loves a home-cooked meal, head for the kitchen (help is on the way for both the home and food preparation later in our study).
- If he wants peace and quiet after driving in the rush-hour traffic, don't hit him with all the day's problems within the first five minutes of his arrival.
- Greet him with a kiss and a "How was your day?" before you tell him about yours.
- Let everything you do say, "I'm glad you're home and I hope you are too!"

7. Learn about his temperament. This is one of the most important things I've learned about loving my husband. It has changed my marriage! Be sure to do this week's homework assignment on this subject.

8. Present yourself well. Men are visual. You looked nice when you were dating, so make it a daily goal to look nice for him now. Ed often comments on this, so I know he appreciates it.

9. Pray a "hedge of thorns" around him by asking God to somehow make him unattractive and unattainable to the women he encounters in the world. Women are often naïve

You Don't Know My Husband!

by not realizing there may be someone out there who has eyes for him and who would do most anything to snare him away.

When Paul Newman was asked how he managed to remain faithful to his wife, Joanne Woodward, he answered, "Why fool around with hamburger when you have steak at home?"[15] Now, you've got to admit, we'd all like to have this said about us!

It's understood that many women must work today, and it is hard working both inside and outside the home! I know; I've done it. However, taking to heart these suggestions benefits both the husband and the wife.

III. Conclusion

The greatest way we can love our husbands is to live according to God's Word. We're to do everything we do as unto the Lord. First Corinthians 10:31 says, "Whether, then, you eat or drink or whatever you do, do all to the glory of God." One Valentine's Day Ed and I attended a marriage retreat (timely, huh?), and it was at a Christian retreat center. When I complimented a staff member on how wonderful everything was, the reply was, "The owners always want to exceed your expectations." I wonder what would happen if we applied this to our marriages by always desiring to exceed our husbands' expectations. Wouldn't we be amazing women?

Now What?

What were the most important points for you personally in this message, "You Don't Know My Husband! Love Him?"?

PART TWO: Be Amazing in Relationships

Homework Day 2

What?

"Whatever you do, do all to the glory of God" (1 Corinthians 10:31).

So What?

There is a principle in the Bible that teaches, *When you go where you should not go, you most often bring back what you should not have!* This was the case with Abraham and Sarah in their attempts to have a baby (see Genesis 12:10-20; 16:1-3). In this case, they went to Egypt, where they should not have gone, and brought back Hagar, whom they should not have had. This principle applies to many circumstances and places, such as where we go with our feet, ears, eyes, mind, and so on. God has said this world is not our home; we are only passing through and are not to conform to its ways. He is calling us to a higher standard. God's plan is for our marriage to be a picture of our relationship with God. The home is to be a picture of heaven on earth. We must reflect our knowledge of and obedience to God's Holy Word because our attitudes and choices are examples to the next generations.

1. Record any thoughts you have regarding how you may be conforming to this world in your attitude toward men (see Romans 12:2).

2. What does God tell wives to do in the following verses?

   a. Titus 2:4

   b. Ephesians 5:33

Wives are to love and respect their husbands. This means God desires that we honor our husbands in the way we interact with them in front of others and in private. An undercurrent of disrespect can be demeaning and damaging and can send the wrong message to our children.

3. Meditate on God's words in Titus 2:4 and Ephesians 5:33. What are God's requirements, and how might you carry them out in your home?

Now What?

Read 1 Peter 3:1-9 and list what God is asking of you and how you are applying these truths at home. An application of this might be as simple as biting your tongue and being silent when you believe you are right. Are you willing to give this a try at your next opportunity? If you are not married, based on the verses you just read, how would you encourage someone who is married?

Homework Day 3

What?

"If I speak with the tongues of men and of angels, but do not have love, I have become a noisy gong or a clanging cymbal" (1 Corinthians 13:1).

So What?

Last week we saw that our differences often come up because we have different temperaments. Learning about the temperaments was one of those "aha moments" when a light came on in my brain. I could finally understand why there was so much butting heads going on in my marriage! Before this, instead of understanding Ed, I just fumed because we weren't on the same page. Can you relate?

1. Regardless of our temperament differences, Titus 2:5 says a woman is to love her husband. List what God says love is in 1 Corinthians 13:4-8.

Now What?

Your assignment for today is to look at the list of temperaments provided on page 129.

1. What is your temperament? What is your spouse's temperament?

2. Look at the list of the needs of each temperament on pages 148–149.

   a. What is the greatest need of someone with your temperament?

You Don't Know My Husband!

b. What is the greatest need of someone with your husband's temperament? Remember, he also *needs* respect from you.

3. Read the list of the fears of each temperament on pages 148–149.

a. What is the greatest fear of someone with your temperament?

b. What is the greatest fear of someone with your husband's temperament?

Think over your history and the times you did not think or act alike. This frustration now has a name: "We have different temperaments!" He isn't trying to annoy you; God made him different! You might spend some time discussing this with your husband.

4. After doing this exercise, spend some time asking God how you might use this information to find ways to be more understanding and to better love your husband by meeting his needs and understanding his fears. Record what action steps you will take to love your husband.

PART TWO: *Be Amazing in Relationships*

It's All About Sex!

*Making **Real** Love*

Pat Harley

"That the word of God will not be dishonored."

TITUS 2:5

DVD Outline

I. **What was God's plan for sex?**

II. **Man perverted God's design.**
    A. How was sex misused?
    B. Why are these stories in the Bible?
    C. Where are we today?

III. **God's Laws on Sex**
    A. Adultery
    B. Lust
    C. Incest
    D. Bestiality
    E. Homosexuality
    F. Fornication

IV. **What does the Bible say about sex inside of marriage?**
    A. Don't defile the marriage bed. It is a sin.
    B. Don't withhold sex from one another. It is a sin.

V. **What if I have committed sexual sins?**
    A. A repentant heart receives forgiveness from God.
    B. God promises total cleansing for all past sins.

Discussion Questions

1. What examples have you seen that show Christians are not clear on the sexual commands of God?
2. How do you think sexual immorality defiles the land? What do you think God meant by that statement?
3. What contributes to the sexual immorality that we see in our country today? What is the greatest culprit?
4. What steps can mothers take today to protect their children from sexual immorality?
5. What is the greatest contributor to sexual problems in marriage today?

Homework Day 1

What?

"Flee immorality" (1 Corinthians 6:18).

So What?

Read the following notes from the DVD message "It's All About Sex! Making *Real* Love" and answer the "Now What" question at the end.

I. What was God's plan for sex?

Just before my beloved and I were married, my sister had been given a very large bottle of expensive and extremely fragrant perfumed body oil. Knowing I was soon to be married, she poured a large amount of the bath oil in a mouthwash bottle for me to have for my new life as a married woman.

My husband and I had a two-day honeymoon and then spent the third day moving into our first home together. We were excited to get the work done and enjoy some intimate time together. That time finally came, so I bathed quickly, put on my cute little honeymoon attire, and climbed into bed, awaiting my beloved. He went into the bathroom to wash up, and at that moment I heard a loud and agonizing cry. He had poured a very large amount of thick bath oil into his mouth, thinking he was getting mouthwash. Needless to say, it put an immediate damper on the evening, and I began to realize that the sexual experience in marriage was far more complicated than I had imagined.

God's view of sex all begins in Genesis 1. God created man and woman, and it was a beautiful picture. The woman was brought to the man and he was thrilled. God told them to be fruitful, multiply, and fill and subdue the earth. He said the two shall become one. The man was to leave all others and cleave to his wife. Cleaving means sticking like glue that cannot come undone, joining together in an intimate, satisfying relationship. They were to be united for pleasure, fellowship, unity, protection, and procreation. Each was made to satisfy the needs of the other and to enjoy the sexual union that oneness provides. The anatomy of a man and woman alone points to the fitting together. From that sexual union could come children, so God made every aspect of this union good. Sex was a gift from God!

II. Man perverted God's design.

A. How was sex misused?

Within a short period of time after the Fall, man had corrupted the very thing God had created for good. By the end of Genesis we see great perversion and its consequences:

- **Lust:** Noah's nakedness was viewed inappropriately by his son, Ham, and Ham's family line was cursed (see Genesis 9).
- **Homosexuality:** Lot invited two men who were strangers into his home, and soon all the men of the city surrounded the home, wanting to rape the guests. Because of the sin of its inhabitants, God destroyed all of Sodom and Gomorrah (see Genesis 19).
- **Incest:** Lot's daughters got their father drunk and committed incest with him, producing the nations of the Moabites and Ammonites. Those two nations caused misery for God's people for centuries (see Genesis 19).
- **Rape:** Shechem raped Dinah, and her brothers took revenge and slaughtered every man in the town (see Genesis 34).
- **Prostitution:** Tamar dressed up like a prostitute and deceived her father-in-law into having sexual relations with her (see Genesis 38).
- **Seduction:** Potiphar's wife tried to seduce Joseph, and when he resisted he was imprisoned for years (see Genesis 39).
- **Polygamy:** Abraham and Jacob practiced polygamy and never had a happy home.

And that is only the first book of the Bible!

We know that even the gods of the nations surrounding Israel promoted sexual perversion, having both male and female temple prostitutes. Those gods and their ways were soon embraced by many of the Israelites, which led to the nation being disciplined and exiled. What was given for pleasure became a curse. What was given for unity brought division. What was given for satisfaction brought great sorrow. God has given sex to man and woman under the protection of marriage, and man has turned it into a perversion that has brought much misery to the earth. After giving the laws on sex, God clearly stated that sexual "abominations" led to the defilement of both the person and the land (see Leviticus 18:24-28). So it is not only the individual person who becomes dirty or polluted, but rather it is the whole society that suffers when man chooses to ignore God's laws on sexual behavior.

B. Why are these stories in the Bible?

First Corinthians tells us why: "Now these things happened as examples for us, so that we would not crave evil things as they also craved. . . . Nor let us act immorally, as some of them did. . . . Now these things happened to them as an example, and they were written for our instruction" (10:6, 8, 11).

The Bible clearly shows us the beautiful purpose of the gift of sex in marriage and the great evil that comes from breaking God's sexual laws.

The biblical stories of the history of Israel are true and clearly give us examples of the consequences of sexual immorality so that we can learn from them. They are there to teach us the way to not only guard ourselves from perversions that can enslave but also to freely enjoy the sexual experience in marriage.

C. Where are we today?

We live in a sex-obsessed society. Sex sells everything from beer to automobiles to perfume and purses. Clothing manufacturers tout sexy looks, and magazines include articles on sexual performance. Movies tell us that sex is for everyone at anytime and that a deep relationship with the person is of little importance. Sex is recreation. It is seen as a biological need, such as food and water, of which there should be no restrictions. After all, it is just a physical performance and nothing more.

Many Christians have bought into this lie and are often unwilling to stand with God on these issues. However, there has been a personal price to pay. Early sexual experience for women has been linked with dissatisfaction in their present marriages, unhappiness with their level of sexual intimacy, and the prevalence of low self-esteem.

Society is also reaping the consequences of these attitudes. Parents talk openly about their children's sexual immorality, children are born out of wedlock, there is irreverence for the marriage bed, living together is common, and there is scarcely a moment of shame. Christian mothers buy contraception for their daughters because "everyone is doing it." "It is what it is" is their answer. Yet God's laws have not changed; we have. The land has been defiled.

Here are some facts that prove this point:

- The majority of children in their teens have had premarital sex.
- More than 50 percent of married people will be unfaithful.
- Sex slavery has become big business, now second only to drug trafficking.
- It is estimated there are hundreds of thousands of child sex slaves in America.
- Porn websites gross billions.
- Date rape is common.
- Sexual abuse among children by a family member is skyrocketing.
- There are more than twenty-five sexually transmitted diseases, and some cannot be cured.

III. God's Laws on Sex

How do God's laws change society? A noted Jewish commentator made the following observations:

- God gave the laws on Mount Sinai to the people of Israel to curb the sexual lusts and commit them to the marriage bed. God demanded that sexual activity be channeled into marriage, and it changed the world.

- Sex was sanctified and placed in the home, in the bed of husband and wife.
- This sanctification of sex was one of the essential elements that allowed society to progress, as it elevated women, protected children, and channeled sexual passion into productive work. It was no longer someone doing something to someone weaker. It was now a shared pleasurable, intimate experience between a husband and a wife.

So what are God's laws?

A. Adultery

Man shall not commit adultery (see Exodus 20:14; Leviticus 20:10). Adultery breaks the marriage covenant and causes untold sorrow and misery. It breaks apart the family relationship and is an ultimate act of betrayal. The punishment in Bible times was death.

B. Lust

Jesus went on to say that a man shall not even look at another woman with lust because it is a sin. Jesus put it in the same category as adultery. The punishment was death (see Matthew 5:28; Leviticus 20:10). This would make pornography in today's culture not an innocent pastime but a capital crime.

C. Incest

Man should not commit incest. The law was clear and protected children from sexual abuse by a family member (see Leviticus 18:6-17; 20:11-12).

D. Bestiality

Man shall not have sexual relations with an animal. The punishment was death (see Leviticus 18:23; 20:15).

E. Homosexuality

Man shall not have sex with another man. It is an abomination and was punishable by death. Though culture would try to tell us otherwise, the Bible is absolutely clear on the issue of homosexuality. It is forbidden (see Leviticus 18:22; 20:13; Romans 1:27).

F. Fornication

Man shall not fornicate because it defiles the person and the land. Fornication means sexual relations between two persons not married to each other. Man shall not rape a woman, as it is fornication punishable by death.

Sex apart from marriage is not a hookup, friends with benefits, or recreation. It is sin. The New Testament is even clearer on this than the Old Testament.

IV. What does the Bible say about sex *inside* of marriage?

A. Don't defile the marriage bed. It is a sin.

"Marriage is to be held in honor among all, and the marriage bed is to be undefiled" (Hebrews 13:4). Undefiled means there should be nothing that makes sex in marriage dirty, polluted, contaminated, stained, or bitter. Defilement occurs when God's moral laws are ignored. So what can defile the marriage bed?

- Bitterness caused by unforgiveness
- Selfishness
- Sexual fantasy (bringing another mentally into the bed)
- Dwelling on past relationships
- Sexually explicit novels, television, movies, and pictures
- All pornography
- An unwillingness to accept the sexual freedom God has given in marriage

B. Don't withhold sex from one another. It is a sin.

"The husband must fulfill his duty to his wife, and likewise also the wife to her husband. The wife does not have authority over her own body, but the husband does; and likewise also the husband does not have authority over his own body, but the wife does. Stop depriving one another, except by agreement for a time, so that you may devote yourselves to prayer, and come together again so that Satan will not tempt you because of your lack of self-control" (1 Corinthians 7:3-5).

God calls for unrestricted and unconditional sex in marriage. Meeting our mate's sexual desires is not an option. We are not to deprive him of the sexual experience, but rather sex should be given freely and generously. We cannot allow our lack of desire to trump our moral obligation.

There is only one biblical reason for abstaining: by mutual agreement, for extended prayer, for a limited time! So the command is not about when to have sex but about when to abstain.

The purpose of sex is protection from immorality for both men and women. Before marriage there is self-control. After marriage there is sex. The question should be asked, "Is God pleased with my sex life?"

Warning: The bedroom is a demonic battleground. The greatest threat to immorality in the home comes from disobedience and disregard for this command. Satan will do everything he can to trap in this area.

God gives couples tremendous freedom to experience and enjoy pleasure in the sexual union. In the excellent study *Passion Pursuit: What Kind of Love Are You Making?* (Moody Press, 2013), Linda Dillow and Dr. Juli Slattery recommend three questions couples should ask when wondering what is permissible and what isn't. These are excellent guidelines:

1. Does God say no? See God's laws discussed earlier.
2. Is it good for us? Does it cause either one of us emotional or physical pain?
3. Is it only us? Hebrews 13:4 says the marriage bed should be honored by all and should be kept pure. This would eliminate pornography, fantasy, role-play, movies, and so on.

Many problems have come about because of unbiblical views or actions. At times both men and women will have different desires that need to be communicated and agreed upon. However, if sin such as pornography is involved and/or there is no mutual respect, consideration, and agreement, outside help will be necessary.

What are three reasons God gives for sex?

1. Sex in marriage is for procreation.

    God says, "Be fruitful and multiply." One of the core reasons for sex was to enlarge one's family through children. Children were not seen as a hindrance to life but as a gift from God (see Psalm 127:3).

2. Sex in marriage is for unity.

    It is something shared between two people that is not to be shared with anyone else. It produces oneness, refreshes the love between two people, and creates deeper intimacy. In Song of Solomon, the Shulamite rejoices in the unity of sex with her husband: "I am my beloved's and my beloved is mine" (6:3).

3. Sex in marriage is for pleasure.

Let your fountain be blessed,
And rejoice in the wife of your youth.
As a loving hind and a graceful doe,
Let her breasts satisfy you at all times;
Be exhilarated [intoxicated] always with her love. (Proverbs 5:18-19)

In order for a husband to be exhilarated, a wife should think about being exhilarating! She needs to find out what he likes and help him know what she enjoys. Couples should find sex exhilarating together.

V. What if I have committed sexual sins?

A. A repentant heart receives forgiveness from God.
God says,

> "Come now, and let us reason together. . . .
> Though your sins are as scarlet,
> They will be as white as snow;
> Though they are red like crimson,
> They will be like wool." (Isaiah 1:18)

B. God promises total cleansing for all past sins.
There is hope: "If we confess our sins, He is faithful and righteous to forgive us our sins and to cleanse us from *all* unrighteousness" (1 John 1:9, emphasis added). Repentance is our part; cleansing and renewal are God's.

We see a wonderful picture of the grace of God through Jesus in John 8:1-11. The Pharisees brought a woman caught in adultery to Jesus. Jesus offered grace along with a command for her to not only cease sinning but to not turn back to it. If God has forgiven you, then it is in the past and you are washed clean. Now go and sin no more.

God has given us sex as a unifying force in the marriage relationship. It is for procreation, unity, and pleasure, and it is to be limited within the confines of marriage. It is a gift from God, and it is good. How amazing!

Now What?

What were the most important points for you personally in this message, "It's All About Sex! Making *Real* Love"?

Homework Day 2

What?

"For from within, out of the heart of men, proceed the evil thoughts, fornications, thefts, murders, adulteries. . . . All these evil things proceed from within and defile the man" (Mark 7:21, 23; see also Matthew 15:19).

So What?

1. What was Jesus saying in these verses, and what does it mean to you personally? What is the source of sexual immorality (see Matthew 15:19-20; Mark 7:21-23)?

2. What do you think Paul meant when he said sexually immoral people will not inherit the kingdom of God (see 1 Corinthians 6:9)?

3. What are the reasons given for fleeing from sexual immorality (see 1 Corinthians 6:18-20)?

4. What do you think Paul meant when he said, "The deeds of the flesh are evident"? What does that mean to you (see Galatians 5:19-21)?

5. How does sexual immorality defraud our brothers (and sisters) in Christ (see 1 Thessalonians 4:3-8)?

Now What?

These verses show the gravity of sexual immorality. They should stand as clear commands to teach to your children and also to guide you through the crushing immoral influence of the culture.

Yet God's love and grace should also free you from any past immoral decisions you might have made. This may be a good time for reflection, for repentance, and for forgiveness . . . from God and from yourself.

1. What steps must you take to "possess [your] own vessel in sanctification and honor" (1 Thessalonians 4:4)?

Homework Day 3

What?

My beloved is dazzling and ruddy [having a fresh, healthy reddish color],
Outstanding among ten thousand. . . .
His mouth is full of sweetness.
And he is wholly desirable.
This is my beloved and this is my friend. (Song of Solomon 5:10, 16)

So What?

God's children have often had skewed pictures of the sexual relationship in marriage. Either they are not familiar with God's clear commands concerning sex in marriage or they have added unbiblical, legalistic laws for the sexual relationship. Yet God has given married couples great freedom for enjoyment in the sexual experience that enhances greater unity, deeper love, and exquisite pleasure for both the husband and wife.

Read about the wedding of Solomon and his bride (see Song of Solomon 3:6-11). Now read the description of the honeymoon (see Song of Solomon 4:1–5:1). It is believed that the words "Eat, friends; drink and imbibe deeply, O lovers" are said by God Himself.

1. What do these verses tell you about God's view of the marital sexual relationship?

2. What do these passages tell you about the way a husband and wife should view one another's bodies and the giving of themselves to each other?

3. Write out the principles God explicitly states for the sexual experience in marriage (see 1 Corinthians 7:3-5).

4. How can withholding sex from one's marriage partner bring about pain and suffering in the marriage? What message does that send?

5. Is there anything that is defiling your marriage bed? What steps will you take to make it pure and undefiled (see Hebrews 13:4; Titus 1:15)?

6. Read Philippians 2:3-4. How can these verses speak to the way a husband and wife should relate to each other sexually?

Now What?

1. Choose an appropriate time to talk openly with your husband about your sex life. Discuss the following questions:
   - Are there areas in which forgiveness needs to be granted?
   - Is there confusion about what is permissible?
   - Is there anything that is defiling the marriage bed?
   - If you have never done so, ask your husband what pleases him in the lovemaking experience and also be willing to freely tell him what pleases you.

2. Plan a special evening for you and your husband. Think of the things that would please him. It may be a special meal, fragrant candles, perfume, or other things that would make the sexual experience pleasing to him. Make the evening totally his.

Sex Outside of Marriage

Extra Study

"How can a young man keep his way pure? By keeping it according to Your word" (Psalm 119:9). Today sexual intimacy is as common as holding hands. "Friends with benefits" is the norm. We can be deceived by the world's standard of sexual behavior.

What is God's view on sex? The Scripture passages in the following chart give us insight on this. The word *immorality* in this chart means illicit sexual intercourse or sex between anyone other than a man and woman in marriage.

Scripture Passage	Topic Discussed
Genesis 2:23-24	The marriage covenant (Genesis 1:27-28: to "multiply" requires sex)
Romans 1:24-32	The sexual ramifications of turning from God
Romans 13:13-14	Proper behavior for those living in God's light
1 Corinthians 6:12-20	What immorality does and why
1 Corinthians 7:2-5	Sex in marriage keeps us from immorality
1 Corinthians 10:6-12	Immorality caused many to die
Ephesians 5:3, 5-6	Immorality keeps us from God's kingdom
Colossians 3:5-7	Immorality brings the wrath of God
1 Thessalonians 4:3-8	God's will is that we abstain from sexual immorality
Revelation 21:6-8	Immorality leads to the lake of fire, the second death
Revelation 22:15	Immorality places us outside the presence of God forever

Dictator or Darling?

Submission

Pat Harley

"That the word of God will not be dishonored."
Titus 2:5

185

DVD Outline

I. **Introduction: Two Conflicting Beliefs**
   A. The world says women should be coleaders of the family.
   B. The Bible says the husband is to lead and the wife should submit.

II. **What is submission?**
   A. Definition of Submission
   B. Submission is exemplified in the Godhead.
      1. Jesus submits to God.
      2. Jesus did the will of the Father.
      3. The Holy Spirit submits to Jesus.

III. **The problem originated in the Garden of Eden.**
   A. The Plan: Eve was created to be a helper.
   B. The Problem: Eve sinned and Adam followed.

IV. **The Role of Women in Marriage**
   A. Wives are to submit.
   B. How to Submit
      1. Trust God.
      2. Share your thoughts.
      3. Do not claim responsibility for your husband's actions or decisions.
      4. Speak the truth in love.
      5. Be trustworthy.
   C. The Benefits of Submission
      1. Freedom
      2. Intimacy
      3. Spiritual growth
      4. Safety

V. **Submission can be distorted.**
   A. Involuntary Submission
   B. Male Domination
   C. Negative Feminism
   D. Male Passivity
   E. Submission Dependent upon Agreement
   F. Submission to All Men

VI. When a Wife Should Not Submit
A. When There Is Physical Abuse
B. When It Involves Sinful Activity

VII. When the Helper Becomes the Leader
A. When There Is Serious Sin
B. When There Is Serious Illness

VIII. Conclusion

Discussion Questions

1. What is the greatest barrier facing women when it comes to the subject of submission?
2. How does the concept of trust fit into submission?
3. If you are married, is it difficult for you to submit to your husband? Is there anything from the lesson today that would make it easier for you?

Homework Day 1

What?

God commands, "Wives, submit to your husbands as to the Lord" (Ephesians 5:22, NIV).

So What?

Read the following notes from the DVD message "Dictator or Darling? Submission" and answer the "Now What" question at the end.

I. Introduction: Two Conflicting Beliefs

When I was in my early thirties, my marriage was disintegrating. It was at this time of deep misery that God brought me to Himself and began to reveal His Son as my Savior. My husband and I were invited to a Bible study on marriage. We were desperate for help, so we agreed. About the fourth lesson we opened the Bible to Ephesians 5:22, and I was introduced to the concept of submission. I was to be my husband's helper. He was to be the leader. Truthfully, I was appalled! I was steeped in feminism and this went against everything I had been taught. But throughout the next week I began to see that what the Bible had to say about my role as a woman, and especially my role as a wife, made sense and in the end could make for a peaceful home and a happy marriage. But above all, it gave me a clear path in which to live in obedience to my God.

I really began to see there are two conflicting beliefs:

A. The world says women should be coleaders of the family.

B. The Bible says the husband is to lead and the wife should submit.

II. What is submission?

A. Definition of Submission

1. Submission means to yield oneself to authority or control of another; to surrender. In the Greek, the word is *hypotasso,* implying that one subjects or subordinates himself to another. It implies *voluntary responsive obedience.* This word is used four times in the Gospels and forty-one times in the Epistles.

2. "Submission is not a confession of inferiority. It is a demonstration of the fact that

PART TWO: Be Amazing in Relationships

personal significance does not depend on one's role in society. The Christian is responsive to God, fulfilling his or her highest destiny in choosing to obey the Lord in the manner of submission."[16]

3. Submission must be the very structure in any society, or there will be chaos. We hear that seven times in Judges when the writer said, "Everyone did what was right in his own eyes" (21:25). There was chaos.

In a nation there must be a leader. In the workplace there must be a boss. In a school there must be a principal or director. In a town there must be a mayor. In a church there must be a pastor, deacons, elder board, or some other form of leadership. In all of these social institutions there must be one in authority.

In a family God has ordained that there must be *one* who has the final say, and that is the husband. The wife is to voluntarily submit or subject herself to his authority.

B. Submission is exemplified in the Godhead.
The Trinity is God the Father, Jesus Christ the Son, and the Holy Spirit. Three Persons in One. And within the Trinity there is submission, all working together in perfect harmony, each with different roles.

1. Jesus submits to God. God sent His Son: "I must preach the kingdom of God to the other cities also, for I was sent for this purpose" (Luke 4:43).

2. Jesus did the will of the Father even when it involved crucifixion. Jesus prayed in the Garden of Gethsemane, "Father, if You are willing, remove this cup from Me; yet not My will, but Yours be done" (Luke 22:42).

3. The Holy Spirit submits to Jesus. Jesus said, "When the Helper comes, whom I will send to you from the Father, that is the Spirit of truth who proceeds from the Father, He will testify about Me" (John 15:26).

All are equal with different roles.

III. The problem originated in the Garden of Eden.

A. The Plan: Eve was created to be a helper.
Adam and Eve were created as spiritually equal human beings and both bore the image of God. Neither was inferior in their design or relationship to God. We read in Genesis,

> Then God said, "Let Us make man in Our image, according to Our likeness; and let them rule over the fish of the sea and over the birds of the sky and over the cattle and over all the earth, and over every creeping thing that creeps on the earth." God created man in His own image, in the image of God He created him; male and female He created them. God blessed them; and God said to them, "Be fruitful and

multiply, and fill the earth, and subdue it; and rule over . . . every living thing that moves on the earth." (1:26-28)

Noted pastor Ray Ortlund Jr. said it well: "Man was created as royalty in God's world, male and female alike bearing the divine glory equally."

Genesis 2 continues the Creation story. God created man out of dust and formed woman. She was made to be a helper, and they were to become one flesh. There was no relationship between personal role and personal worth. Both had equal value and both were given the same goal, but they had different roles to play. Eve was created to be Adam's helper. Please note: this was a call on her life before the Fall.

Is the term "helper" seen as a debasing position? The very same term used for women as a helper is used of God Himself in Psalm 54:4: "Behold, God is my helper; the Lord is the sustainer of my soul." Therefore, to be a helper is not debasing but is a responsibility and a privilege.

B. The Problem: Eve sinned and Adam followed.

Genesis 3 is in many ways the beginning of every problem and every heartache on earth. Eve took charge and led the way into sin. Adam stood passively by, allowing and then participating in disobedience to the direct command of God. Both were to blame. Adam abandoned his role as protector, and Eve allowed the serpent to deceive her. Because they both disobeyed, they pulled the human race down into sin.

What were the consequences that followed?

- **For Women:** "Yet your desire will be for your husband, and he will rule over you (Genesis 3:16). This implies that our inclination will be to usurp our husband's authority.
- **For Men:** Through painful toil man would eat of the ground all the days of his life, fighting "thorns and thistles" (Genesis 3:17-19). Work for man would now be frustration.
- **The Conflict:** So now we have two people working against each other. No longer will they work together in harmony with a shared goal and shared communion. She will have a desire to rule, and he will be frustrated with work. They will be pulled in two separate directions, no longer working together for a common good.

IV. The Role of Women in Marriage

A. Wives are to submit.

Scripture is emphatic, clear, and concise. Wives are to submit to their husbands:

- "Wives, submit to your husbands as to the Lord" (Ephesians 5:22, NIV).
- "Now as the church submits to Christ, so also wives should submit to their

PART TWO: Be Amazing in Relationships

husbands in everything" (Ephesians 5:24, NIV).
- "Wives, submit to your husbands, as is fitting [proper, right, suitable] in the Lord" (Colossians 3:18, NIV).
- "For you have been called for this purpose, since Christ also suffered for you, leaving you an example for you to follow in His steps, . . . and while being reviled, He did not revile in return; while suffering, He uttered no threats, but kept entrusting Himself to Him who judges righteously. . . . In the same way, you wives, be submissive to your own husbands so that even if any of them are disobedient to the word, they may be won without a word by the behavior of their wives, as they observe your chaste and respectful behavior" (1 Peter 2:21, 23; 3:1-2).
- Older women are to teach the young women to be "subject to their own husbands, so that the word of God will not be dishonored" (Titus 2:5).

My first real challenge in submitting came when I wanted to get our daughter out of a public school and send her to a Christian school. My husband said it was too expensive, but I felt her eternal salvation was at stake, so I voiced my opinion very strongly. It was a very difficult time for me as I began to believe that my beloved did not care about our daughter's spiritual life. Feeling sure I was right, I went to Scripture and came across Ephesians 5:22, which says, "Wives, submit to your husbands as to the Lord" (NIV). I really began to meditate on the last part: "as to the Lord." And little by little I started to realize that God can change the hearts of kings (see Proverbs 21:1), so surely He could change my beloved's heart! I relaxed. I let go. I prayed, and I didn't bring it up again. I tried, and often succeeded, to trust Christ for our daughter. That year she went to public school. It turned out to be a most significant year for my daughter with opportunities that I would never have dreamed of. Instead of drawing her into the world, it drew her closer to Christ.

One important note: First Corinthians 7:13 says, "A woman who has an unbelieving husband, and he consents to live with her, she must not send her husband away." Even if the husband is not a believer, his wife is still to submit to him "as to the Lord."

B. How to Submit

1. Trust God. Scripture is clear that we are to submit to our husbands as if we are submitting to Christ Himself (see Ephesians 5:22; Colossians 3:18). It is the Lord we should trust, and we can trust Him with our lives, our family, and our husbands.

2. Share your thoughts. You are part of the oneness, and your role and opinions are important. Submission does not mean never having an opinion. God made us as helpers, which indicates that Adam needed help. Women have insights that men do not have, and vice-versa. We need each other!

3. Do not claim responsibility for your husband's actions or decisions. You are responsible to voice your opinion and then submit to his decision.

Dictator or Darling?

Years ago my husband and I strongly disagreed on a financial decision. I gave my opinion, and he made a decision contrary to what I had wanted to do. It was not a good decision and ended with a financial loss that greatly affected our future. Yet now, a few years down the road, we would both agree that during that time of great devastation for both of us, we began to see God work in ways that can only be called miraculous. He proved Himself to truly be our great provider, our great protector, and our healer. We would call it one of the best times of our lives—very hard, but so worth it. Guard against "I told you so" when your husband disregards your opinion that proves right. Neither of you are omniscient!

4. Speak the truth in love. A wife brings a great deal to the marriage. She is not a doormat, nor is she a wallflower. She is a vital part of the relationship. And yet, a gentle and quiet attitude allows a wife to disagree in a way that is winsome. Kindness and respect should be part of her conversation. Proverbs 31:26 says of the "excellent wife," "She opens her mouth in wisdom, and the teaching of kindness is on her tongue."

5. Be trustworthy. "An excellent wife, who can find? For her worth is far above jewels. The heart of her husband trusts in her, and he will have no lack of gain" (Proverbs 31:10-11). Are you trustworthy? Do you hide your spending or anything else from him?

In the end it is Christ you are to trust. We are to look to Him to be our protector and provider. "Trust in the LORD with all your heart and do not lean on your own understanding. In all your ways acknowledge Him, and He will make your paths straight" (Proverbs 3:5-6).

C. The Benefits of Submission

1. Freedom. There is freedom in knowing that you can trust Jesus with your husband. You do not have to be responsible for the decisions he makes. This is not your responsibility.

2. Intimacy. A woman who trusts her husband will often find a deeper intimacy and friendship with him. No longer is there competition, but unity.

3. Spiritual growth. There is an increased reliance on God, knowing that you may not always like the decisions that are being made but that you can trust Him to work through them even if they are the wrong decisions. As you look to Christ and trust Him through loving submission to your husband, you will have the opportunity to mature in your faith as you see God work in your marriage.

4. Safety. There is protection as you live in obedience to Christ.

V. Submission can be distorted.

A. Involuntary Submission
Submission is not something your husband forces on you. Submission is what you do in obedience to God. It is voluntary.

B. Male Domination
This happens when a husband asserts his will without regard to his wife's spiritual equality, her rights, and her value.

C. Negative Feminism
This occurs when women deny male leadership in the home and assert no distinction in roles.

D. Male Passivity
This leaves a vacuum in the home because the husband refuses to take his God-given responsibility of leadership.

E. Submission Dependent upon Agreement
Submission is trusting in Christ even when you don't agree with the decisions being made. Your husband has been given the role of leader. Now let him lead.

F. Submission to All Men
Scripture says, "Wives, submit to your husbands," not, "Women, submit to men."

• • •

In our own home, I had become the leader. I am naturally more assertive, and my husband is naturally more of a peacemaker. As I began to embrace God's design, it was challenging to step back and look to my husband for leadership and then wait for him to take the lead. It was not an easy process, but it brought about the necessary changes that only enhanced our relationship.

All the distortions we've discussed leave sorrow, frustration, and confusion in the home and destroy intimacy, harmony, and unity.

VI. When a Wife Should Not Submit

A. When There Is Physical Abuse
Physical abuse should *never* be tolerated. Seek help from a pastor, professional Christian counselor, or a friend immediately. Leave any physically unsafe marriage environment.

B. When It Involves Sinful Activity
A wife should *never* submit to partaking in sin such as drug use, sexual promiscuity, fraud, deception, cheating, or anything that God has commanded His people not to do.

VII. When the Helper Becomes the Leader

A. When There Is Serious Sin

When a husband gets into trouble and is unable to help himself, the wife must step in and seek that help for him. Drugs, alcohol, and pornography addiction can render a man helpless. As his helper, there is a time when a wife must fight for her man and do whatever it takes to find the help he needs to return to health and wholeness.

B. When There Is Serious Illness

The husband of one of my friends became seriously ill with cancer. As his strength left him, she needed to step in and take over the role of leader.

VIII. Conclusion

God created man and woman with equal value, equal worth, and equality in the sight of God, and yet He gave them different roles. The wife's role is to submit. When the day comes that we stand before the Lord, we will not stand with our husbands. We will stand alone. We are only responsible for our own obedience to God. We are *not* responsible for the way our husband carried out his role.

"Wives, submit to your husbands as to the Lord." It is Christ who is your God. It is Christ who loves you above all. And He will take care of you. This gives you great freedom to be an amazing woman.

Now What?

What were the most important points for you personally in this message, "Dictator or Darling? Submission"?

Homework Day 2

What?

"For you have been called for this purpose, since Christ also suffered for you, leaving you an example for you to follow in His steps, . . . and while being reviled, He did not revile in return; while suffering, He uttered no threats, but kept entrusting Himself to Him who judges righteously. . . . In the same way, you wives, be submissive to your own husbands so that even if any of them are disobedient to the word, they may be won without a word by the behavior of their wives, as they observe your chaste and respectful behavior" (1 Peter 2:21, 23; 3:1-2).

So What?

Submission has become a reviled word. Yet in all aspects of life, there needs to be a leader, one in ultimate charge.

1. Sarah was held up as an example of a woman who submitted to her husband. What was the key to her submission (see 1 Peter 3:1-6)?

2. What role does fear play in your ability to submit with a quiet and gentle spirit? What does God say about fear (see Isaiah 41:10)?

3. How has the culture around you shaped your view of submission (see Romans 12:2)?

Dictator or Darling?

4. When you think of submission, what negative examples come to mind? How about positive examples (see Ephesians 5:21, 24)?

5. Do you have a quiet and gentle spirit? Would your husband and children agree (see 1 Peter 3:4; Proverbs 19:13; 21:9, 19; 27:17)?

6. Are you willing to do what it takes to acquire a quiet and gentle spirit? What specific steps must you commit to in order to live in obedience to Christ in this area (see Proverbs 12:4; 18:22)?

Now What?

Now is the time for some self-examination. Thoughtfully answer the following questions:

1. Do I agree with God that an attitude of submission on my part would benefit our family?

2. Have I taken leadership away from my husband?

3. Does my husband know he is the leader?

4. Do our children know and respect him as leader?

5. Am I willing to do what it takes to be a submissive wife and a loving helper?

6. Am I willing to begin today?

7. If you have found there are changes that must take place for you to have a quiet and gentle spirit and be a submissive and loving wife, write the steps you are going to take to achieve your goal.

Homework Day 3

What?

"Now as the church submits to Christ, so also wives should submit to their husbands in everything" (Ephesians 5:24, NIV).

So What?

1. What was the Proverbs 31 amazing woman's attitude, and how did it help her relationship with her husband? How did it affect her whole family (see Proverbs 31:10-12, 25-30)?

2. Submission involves more than one person. Jesus submitted to God, and the church submits to Christ. We may think we are submitting; however, just as an employee can be convinced he is doing a job well, it is the employer who makes that decision. So the hard part begins. Now is the time to have a very frank and open discussion with your husband, asking him the following questions. Choose the time carefully, when neither of you is tired or stressed but can give each question thoughtful consideration.

   a. What does submission mean to you?

   b. Do you believe I am a submissive wife?

   c. In what areas could I improve?

   d. Can you trust me 100 percent?

   e. If not, in what areas do you find me untrustworthy?

   f. Do I have a quiet and gentle spirit?

   g. Do I undermine your authority?

h. Do you feel I treat you with respect in front of the children?

i. Do you feel confident in your role as leader?

j. As your helpmate, how can I best help you?

Now What?

Your husband may have made observations that surprised you. If changes are required, then make them. If forgiveness is needed, then ask for it. If you have proven to be trust-worthy and have shown love and respect to your husband, then thank God and celebrate!

Let's Fight It Out!

Resolving Conflict

"That the word of God will not be dishonored."
TITUS 2:5

DVD Outline

I. **The Trap of Offense**
   A. Offense requires humility.
   B. Offense requires a heart change.
   C. Offense can produce bitter roots.

II. **The Trap of Unforgiveness: When I Have Offended**
   A. Man's Solution
   B. God's Solution

III. **Escaping the Trap: When I Have Been Offended**
   A. We can overlook the offense.
   B. We must examine ourselves.
   C. What if someone legitimately offends us?
   D. Forgiveness is the cancellation of a debt.
      1. Truths about forgiving
      2. God can use conflict.

IV. **Conclusion**

Discussion Questions

1. How do you resolve conflict?
2. Are there conflicts currently going on that you need to handle?
3. What is difficult for you in resolving conflict?

Homework Day 1

What?

"What causes fights and quarrels among you? Don't they come from your desires that battle within you? You want something but don't get it. . . . You quarrel and fight" (James 4:1-2, NIV).

So What?

Read the following notes from the DVD message "Let's Fight It Out! Resolving Conflict" and answer the "Now What" question at the end.

I. The Trap of Offense

A. Offense requires humility.

Have you ever seen an animal trap? Maybe you have even used one to trap unwanted critters. The idea is to catch the prey. The animal steps in and experiences the pain and frustration of losing his freedom. The animal is still alive, but rendered helpless and desperate. Isn't this a picture of us sometimes? We have an Enemy who seeks to kill, steal, and destroy. He wants to trap us in offenses that render us helpless, desperate, and frustrated.

Have you ever been trapped in a season of hate? I have been married for thirty-two years and am sad to say I have had a couple of them, all as a result of an unresolved conflict—a trap of offense. A trap of offense is when something happens and we get trapped by our hurt, anger, disappointment, resentment, and selfishness. Sometimes it is caused by something little. Sometimes it is a great offense. Regardless, like an animal caught in a trap, we are alive, but unable to get free.

During one of my early seasons of hate, I was feeling hopeless and desperate to fix my husband. I went to a Christian bookstore in search of answers. I came across a book titled *The Power of a Praying Wife*. You may be familiar with this very helpful book. I picked it up, thinking to myself, *Yes, this is the answer. I will pray for him.* I started at the beginning of the book, and the first chapter was already discouraging because it wasn't talking about fixing him at all; instead, it focused on *me*! This is an excerpt from the very first prayer that wives are supposed to pray.

> Lord, help me to be a good wife. I fully realize that I don't have what it takes to be one without Your help. Take my selfishness, impatience, and irritability and turn them into kindness, long-suffering, and the willingness to bear all things. Take

my old emotional habits, mindsets, automatic reactions, rude assumptions, and self-protective stance, and make me patient, kind, good, faithful, gentle, and self-controlled. Take the hardness of my heart and break down the walls with Your battering ram of revelation. Give me a new heart and work in me Your love, peace, and joy (Galatians 5:22-23). I am not able to rise above who I am at the moment. Only You can transform me *[emphasis added].*

Help me to put aside any hurt, anger, or disappointment that I feel and forgive him the way You do — totally and completely, no looking back. Make me *a tool of reconciliation, peace, and healing in this marriage. Enable us to communicate well and rescue us from the threshold of separation where the realities of divorce begin.*[17]

It goes on for two more pages, but I think you get the idea. My eyes were so focused on my husband and his faults that I didn't see my own. As I got really serious about praying this prayer every day, the season of hate ended because God revealed *my* critical spirit, *my* pride, and *my* selfishness. Humility replaced pride and I could apologize for my offenses, which opened the door for healing. In our marriage, we had to learn to deal honestly and realistically with our differences and seek workable solutions. But it started with me—I had to deal honestly with my own faults and my own responses.

Conflict resolution can be summed up in one mighty word: humility. This is humility before God, which means power under control (see James 3:3). Humility says, "I will release the offender into God's hands and give up my right to be offended." This requires the strength of a truly amazing woman. In order to do this, we need to recognize traps that ensnare us and know how to escape those traps.

B. Offense requires a heart change.

Why is it easy to see sin in our churches, neighborhoods, and husbands, but not see it when we look in the mirror? We can be blind to our own sinfulness. We fall for the bait in Satan's trap of offense that imprisons countless Christians and severs relationships. It is sad to see example after example of offense, betrayal, unforgiveness, bitterness, and hatred among believers today.

As I was working on this study, I kept writing the names in the margin of my notebook of believers I know who had offense and are left today with broken marriages, broken friendships, businesses torn apart, brother suing brother, and families hurt and distant. The commands of God have been forgotten. "What causes fights and quarrels among you? Don't they come from your desires that battle within you? You want something but don't get it. . . . You quarrel and fight" (James 4:1-2, NIV).

It is people that will cause the trap of offense, so as amazing women we must be prepared, because our response to offenses will either glorify God or leave us trapped in sin.

PART TWO: Be Amazing in Relationships

A Christian is what she lives, not what she preaches. God's Word must pierce the heart and bring forth the character of Christ when we are faced with offense. Let's start where it really starts . . . the heart!

C. Offense can produce bitter roots.

Jesus likens the condition of our hearts to that of soil. We are to be rooted and grounded in the love of God. The seed of God's Word takes root and grows and produces the fruit of righteousness (the fruits of the Spirit). But if we plant seeds of offense, unforgiveness, and debt (the belief that someone owes us), then another root grows. It is the root of bitterness.

Bitterness is unfulfilled revenge. It results when revenge is not satisfied to the degree we desire. When roots are watered, nursed, fed, and given attention, they increase in depth and strength. The harvest from bitterness is anger, resentment, jealousy, strife, discord, and hatred.[18]

Bitter roots produce bitter fruits! Hebrews 12:15 powerfully says, "See to it that no one misses the grace of God and that no bitter root grows up to cause trouble and defile many" (NIV). When in a dispute, it is our natural inclination to dwell on the words or wrong another committed. But dwelling on them does not resolve anything. The prison of bitterness destroys us from the inside and alienates us from God.

II. The Trap of Unforgiveness: When I Have Offended

A. Man's Solution

A college student named Jesse Jacobs is an example of man's solution when we offend someone. He created an apology hotline. This hotline makes it possible to apologize without actually talking to the person you've wronged. People who are unable or unwilling to unburden their conscience in person can call the hotline and leave a message on an answering machine. Each week numerous calls are logged as people apologize for things from adultery to embezzlement. The creator of the hotline says, "The hotline offers participants a chance to alleviate their guilt and, to some degree, to own up to their misdeeds."[19] To feel better we may not turn to a hotline, but we may turn to our girlfriends or anyone else who will listen. Another of man's solutions is to ignore what we have done.

B. God's Solution

These methods may seem to offer some relief from guilt, but this is not how Jesus instructed His followers to handle conflict. In the Sermon on the Mount, Jesus told us to do the following:

- Take the initiative and go to the offended brother to apologize for the offense (see Matthew 18:15-18).
- In fact, Jesus taught that the problem of human estrangement is so serious that we

should even interrupt our worship to go on a personal mission of reconciliation (see Matthew 5:23-24).

- The Master encouraged His followers to be reconciled with one another eagerly, aggressively, quickly, and personally. A person who refuses to obey the Word of God deceives his own heart.

In my marriage I was offended, but I was also an offender! Are any of your relationships broken or estranged because of something you said or did? Take the initiative and go now and do all you can to be reconciled. Seek to be a peacemaker, "forgiving . . . just as the Lord forgave you" (Colossians 3:13). Live freely from offense and stay out of the prison of bitterness. I can honestly say that my marriage no longer has seasons of hate. We are different individuals who are now quick to listen, slow to speak, and quick to apologize (see James 1:19).

III. Escaping the Trap: When I Have Been Offended

A. We can overlook the offense.

God said, "Above all, love each other deeply, because love covers over a multitude of sins" (1 Peter 4:8, NIV). First Corinthians 13, the Love Chapter, clearly says, "[Love] keeps no record of wrongs" (verse 5, NIV).

In many situations, the best way to resolve a conflict is simply to overlook the offense of others. Proverbs 19:11; 12:16; 15:18; 20:3; 17:14; and 26:17 all confirm that it is to one's glory to overlook an offense. If offenses were overlooked more often, the following statements would be true:

- Marriages would be more peaceful.
- Family issues would be resolved before division takes place.
- Minor offenses would be given to the Lord and immediately forgiven.

B. We must examine ourselves.

Instead, offenses are dwelt on, responses are justified in our minds, our hearts become defensive, and blame follows. Therefore, the first step in any offense is to examine ourselves. I was so quick to want Steve to change that I never looked at myself. Once I did, I saw all kinds of sin. Self-examination helps us do the following:

- See our true condition
- Bring about a change of heart
- Avoid seeing ourselves as a victim

C. What if someone legitimately offends us?

We always have the right to choose our response when we have been offended. I have this habit of saying out loud, "This is a test" when my family members are pushing my buttons.

It reminds me to watch how I respond, and it says to them, "You are pushing my buttons, so change the tactic."

Here are some things to do if someone offends you:

- Acknowledge the hurt.
- If it is appropriate, go to the person who hurt you. The purpose is not for condemnation but reconciliation. Hopefully the person will realize her condition and repent of her sins.
- Peace is restored by an attitude of humility, gentleness, and love. Sometimes the offender may not recognize her condition, repent, or ask for forgiveness. Then it is up to you, as Romans 12:18 explains: "If possible, so far as it depends on you, be at peace with all men."
- Extend forgiveness even in this situation, because refusing to let go of an offense puts you in the trap of unforgiveness, which leads to bitterness in your own heart. It is possible to forgive by releasing the hurt to the Lord. Remember, humility is power under control.
- Some offenses are so great and the wound so deep that it is wise to seek godly counsel.

D. Forgiveness is the cancellation of a debt.

1. Truths about forgiving:

- Forgiving is the capacity, with the help of Jesus, not to be influenced by the offense.
- Forgiving is obedience, allowing grace to flow by the power of the Holy Spirit.
- A person who cannot forgive has forgotten how great a debt God has forgiven her. This is where many believers get trapped today. We want offenders to pay for their sins, but we do not take Jesus' words seriously that if we don't forgive, we aren't forgiven (see Matthew 6:14-15).

2. God can use conflict.

He can uncover sinful attitudes and habits in our lives. He can reveal pride, a critical spirit, and a bitter heart, like He did for me. But if we are defensive, justify our conduct, or blame the other person, then God's conviction cannot do its work. We must choose to submit to God's conviction rather than justify ourselves.

Jesus Himself exhorts us to reconcile, even if the offense was not our fault. It takes spiritual maturity to walk humbly in order to bring reconciliation.[20] We build walls of protection to keep from getting hurt again by the offender. This is a false sense of security. We can ask God to tear down the walls sin has erected and open the way for renewed relationship.

IV. Conclusion

We live differently if there is a goal. A marathon runner doesn't look back where she's been, but instead has the finish line in sight. We would all agree that how we finish this race of life is more important than how we began. Our goal is to recognize and avoid Satan's traps and run with endurance the race set before us so we will hear God say, "Well done, good and faithful servant." Life is short; eternity is forever. Amazing women train to avoid traps and run the race well.

Now What?

What were the most important points for you personally in this message, "Let's Fight It Out! Resolving Conflict"?

Homework Day 2

What?

"A hot-tempered man stirs up strife, but the slow to anger calms a dispute" (Proverbs 15:18).

So What?

1. God can use conflict to uncover sinful attitudes and habits in our lives: pride, a bitter and unforgiving heart, and a critical tongue. Do you struggle with any of these?

2. What are the acts of the sinful nature that affect relationships (see Galatians 5:19-20)?

I once heard conflict defined as "a difference in opinion or purpose that frustrates someone's goals or desires." We are created as unique individuals, so we will have different opinions, convictions, desires, perceptions, and priorities. A conflict is an opportunity to do the following:
- Manage yourself in a way that glorifies God
- Benefit others
- Allow growth in your character

3. Read the following proverbs and record what you learn:

Proverbs 12:16

Proverbs 17:14

Proverbs 19:11

Proverbs 20:3

Proverbs 28:13

Now What?

Have you been guilty of any of the things we just discussed? Do not let pride keep you from seeing and repenting of the trap of offense. Admit specifically and ask for forgiveness. Repent or turn from your sin. Apologize to the person you have offended and then change your behavior.

Homework Day 3

What?

"Be kind to one another, tender-hearted, forgiving each other, just as God in Christ also has forgiven you" (Ephesians 4:32).

So What?

Christians are the most forgiven people in the world; therefore, we should be the most forgiving people in the world. *The American Heritage Dictionary of the English Language* says that to be forgiven and be reconciled means "to reestablish friendship between; to settle or resolve." Forgiveness is an active process that involves a conscious choice and a deliberate course of action. Forgiveness is not forgetting but rather choosing not to think or talk about what others have done to hurt us. Remembering what Jesus did to purchase our forgiveness should be our greatest incentive for releasing others.

1. What lesson can we learn from God's dealings with us (see Psalm 103:8-10)?

2. Read Psalm 37:1-15.

a. What does this psalm warn you *not to do*?

b. What does it instruct you *to do*?

c. What comforting promises does it provide?

3. What good can God bring about if you respond to your conflicts in a biblical manner?

Now What?

1. We need to learn that offense blocks spiritual growth, but obedience takes us to a deeper relationship with the Lord and with others. What do you need to confess today that will move you toward greater spiritual growth and obedience in regard to an offense?

2. Who do you need to forgive today?

3. If you are having trouble forgiving others, make a list of the sins God has forgiven you.

Got Kids?

How to Love Them!

Michele Helms

"That the word of God will not be dishonored."

TITUS 2:5

DVD Outline

I. **Parenting is intentional.**

    A. Be intentional: motherhood is a high calling.

    B. God's view: children are a blessing.

    C. Role Problems

        1. You are not their best friend.

        2. You are not a dictator.

    D. Biblical Roles for Parents

        1. Discipline

        2. Disciple

            a. The Word

            b. Prayer

II. **Parenting requires communication.**

    A. Talk and listen.

        1. Avoid monologues.

        2. Be a safe placc.

        3. Have rules.

    B. Affirmation and Encouragement

        1. Affirmation and encouragement are areas that have been distorted by our culture.

        2. When and how to encourage and affirm

            a. Encourage character.

            b. Encourage achievements and appearance.

            c. Encourage gratitude.

III. **Parenting requires a great marriage.**

    A. Put your husband first.

    B. A great marriage is the greatest gift you can give your children!

IV. **Conclusion**

Discussion Questions

1. Which do you find the most difficult when it comes to your children: discipleship, encouragement, or communication? Why?

2. What are some ways that you have been intentional about putting your marriage first?

Homework Day 1

What?

"Older women likewise are to be reverent in their behavior, not malicious gossips nor enslaved to much wine, teaching what is good, so that they may encourage the young women to love their husbands, *to love their children,* to be sensible, pure, workers at home, kind, being subject to their own husbands, so that the word of God will not be dishonored" (Titus 2:3-5).

So What?

Read the following notes from the DVD message "Got Kids? How to Love Them!" and answer the "Now What" question at the end.

I. Parenting is intentional.

A. Be intentional: motherhood is a high calling.

We have been talking about how influential women are, and this may be true no more than in their role as mother. I have five children, and it is hands down the hardest job I've ever had and the most rewarding. An amazing woman must be intentional. We can't just ask God to make our children godly without expecting to do any work ourselves. We seem to understand this in the physical world. We wouldn't simply stand on a treadmill and beg and plead with God to make us fit and then get frustrated when He didn't. On the contrary, we would understand that we have to turn the thing on and work hard! Oftentimes, though, we do not understand this truth in the spiritual world. God doesn't just sprinkle fairy dust. Instead, He gives us a very clear command:

> "The LORD our God, the LORD is one. You shall love the LORD your God with all your heart and with all your soul and with all your might. And these words that I command you today shall be on your heart. You shall teach them diligently to your children, and shall talk of them when you sit in your house, and when you walk by the way, and when you lie down, and when you rise. You shall bind them as a sign on your hand, and they shall be as frontlets between your eyes. You shall write them on the doorposts of your house and on your gates." (Deuteronomy 6:4-9, ESV)

Now, that is intentional! This passage first of all says that we, as the parent, must love the Lord with *all* our heart. We cannot teach and model what we are not living! Then these verses say that we must teach our children to love the Lord God in *everything, all the time*—morning until night, as we talk, and as we walk. Our love for the Lord should be present in our actions and evident in our homes.

We live in a culture where parenting has been reduced to providing care, hoping the children will "turn out okay" and being satisfied if they are good, productive members of society. We should want *more*! We should want Christ-honoring warriors who have the tools needed to influence the world.

B. God's view: children are a blessing.

How do we view our children? We are told in Psalm 127:3 that "children are a gift of the Lord." If we view our children as true blessings or gifts from the Lord, it will change how we approach our relationship with them. Let's say I have always dreamed of taking a vacation to Hawaii, and finally, after many years of saving, my husband surprises me with the trip. I am so excited and can hardly wait, but before we even leave I start complaining about the time we have to leave to get to the airport. Then I complain about the weather on one of the days and the fact that the food just wasn't what I had expected. I somehow always manage to throw out the words, "But I am so blessed to have gone," in the middle of my grumbling. At some point you might doubt if I really am grateful for the trip. If we are not careful, we will do this with the blessing the Lord gives us in children.

C. Role Problems

The culture today may regard children as accessories, idols, or impositions, leading to a skewed view of a parent's role:

1. You are not their best friend.

Have you ever heard a mom say about her young daughter, "We have such a good relationship; we are best friends"? While we are to be friendly to our children, we are *not* their best friend! We lose God-given authority and respect when we try to be their best friend, and we become powerless enablers.

2. You are not a dictator.

Or there is the opposite problem. Maybe the role of strong disciplinarian sounds familiar. This position can lead to dictatorship. Kids desperately need discipline, and we are going to talk more about that later, but when a parent's role becomes that of a screamer or a tyrant whose motto is "my way or the highway," a dictator mentality might have taken over.

D. Biblical Roles for Parents

The biblical view would be that of a shepherd/mentor. That is a relationship with many layers. It is a parent who disciplines, disciples, affirms, encourages, protects, teaches, and counsels, just to name a few of the roles.

PART TWO: *Be Amazing in Relationships*

1. Discipline

   We are going to devote most of the next session to this subject.

2. Disciple

   "Watch over your heart with all diligence, for from it flow the springs of life" (Proverbs 4:23). Our children's behavior, and ours for that matter, is a reflection of the overflow of our heart. If we are only interested in changing bad behavior, we will never get to the heart. To really help children, we must be concerned with the attitude of the heart that drives the behavior. We should take every opportunity to point them to Jesus. Our love for Him should be naturally overflowing in all areas of life. We should teach them to love God's Word and to pray in all things.

   a. **The Word.** We started reading Bible stories to our children as soon as they were old enough to listen, and we continue now to discuss biblical principles. We want them to see the Bible as exciting and active, and we also want them to see Jesus and His Word as a place to run to when they are afraid, worried, or in trouble and as a place to look when they are thankful and joyful. We should be training them to be on their own. As parents, our job is to prepare them for adulthood, so we should train them to ultimately cling to Jesus. Eric and I don't want our adult children to depend on us but solely on Christ.

   b. **Prayer.** The Bible tells us, "Do not be anxious about anything, but in everything, by prayer and petition, with thanksgiving, present your requests to God (Philippians 4:6, NIV). Prayer is our way to communicate with the Father and for us to be still and let Him communicate with us. My prayer for my children has always been that they would desire a close, intimate relationship with Him. A big part of knowing Him is talking to Him and learning to listen to His promptings, encouragements, and corrections.

   When our children were little they would have bad dreams, as all children do. They would come into our room, sometimes quietly, sometimes crying and panic stricken. Eric and I would always do the same thing. We would take them in our arms, hold them tight, and pray out loud for them. We would then walk them back to their bed, tuck them in, and sometimes pray for them again. Five children with the same outcome: At some point they would wake us up and say, "Can you pray with me? I'm having bad dreams." And then there would come a time when we would wake up in the morning and they would say, "I was having bad dreams and I lay in bed and talked to Jesus." It is rewarding to see my children walk with the Lord (see 3 John 4).

   Many parents have tried to give the job of discipleship to churches, pastors, youth ministers, and teachers. But it is our God-given responsibility and privilege to disciple our own children. Certainly the church is a part of spiritual growth in our children, but we are held accountable for teaching them to love the Lord with all their hearts. An amazing woman receives a great blessing and joy when she actively teaches and trains her children.

II. Parenting requires communication.

A. Talk and listen.

Communication is so important in child rearing. It requires us to effectively convey our words, and it also demands that we listen to and understand our children.

1. Avoid monologues.

What parents call communication with their children is often a monologue on the part of the parent. The parent shares her own view on the matter but never tries to understand the children's view. Matthew 12:34 says, "For the mouth speaks out of that which fills the heart." If we want our children to have a heart change and not just a behavioral change, we must take time to listen. Do not allow them to communicate by arguing or manipulating. Teaching children how to express their thoughts in a respectful way is a lesson they not only need now but will need for the rest of their lives.

2. Be a safe place.

The foundation of communication starts at a young age. If we want our preteen and teenage children to communicate with us, they need to know that we are a safe place to come. That doesn't mean that parents always agree with them, and it certainly doesn't mean that we fix their problems. However, they need to know they can come to us without us overreacting, teasing, or being sarcastic. We must listen when they are talking about silly things so they know we will listen when it is serious.

We talk all the time around my house. We talk about hopes and dreams, fears and failures. No subject is off-limits and no question is silly. I am always the last one to bed and it is super tiring, but I think it is so important as kids move into the later teen years. Teenagers talk more after dark. I do not know why, but it is true! Usually when they come in they need to exhale, and most of the time, if you wait until the morning you will have lost the moment. So take a nap later if you need to, but stay up and listen.

3. Have rules.

We have rules about how and when certain questions are appropriate. We do not allow teasing from siblings about what someone else is sharing. Words are powerful, so we do not allow name-calling, shouting, or bullying.

PART TWO: Be Amazing in Relationships

My kids will tell you that one of the things I repeated when they were young was, "If you don't have something nice to say, then don't say anything at all." Now that they are older, I ask, "Is that encouraging?"

We are instructed in Ephesians 4:29, "Do not let any unwholesome talk come out of your mouths, but only what is helpful for building others up according to their needs, that it may benefit those who listen" (NIV). This starts with us! We can't expect our children to speak respectfully if their example is disrespectful talk and behavior from us toward our husband and others.

B. Affirmation and Encouragement

1. Affirmation and encouragement are areas that have been distorted by our culture.

Kids are being taught that they are number one in all things, there are no losers, and they are never wrong! This is far from a biblical view of encouragement. Hebrews 3:13 says, "But encourage one another day after day, as long as it is still called 'Today,' so that none of you will be hardened by the deceitfulness of sin."

In Scripture we are told over and over again to encourage others, which means "to inspire with courage." The reason for encouraging our children is not to make them self-absorbed people, but rather to help them combat the Enemy, to point them toward the Savior, and to show them how to be encouragers for others.

2. When and how to encourage and affirm:
   a. Encourage character.

   First and foremost, encourage your children in character issues, such as hard work, kindness, giving, graciousness, honesty, and so on. So many times we get busy correcting and we forget to look for ways to encourage. Sometimes it is just a passing comment, such as, "Wow, you are doing a great job keeping your room clean."

   Sometimes it leads to a whole conversation: "I saw that you helped your sister even though it wasn't your job. That was really an unselfish thing to do. Did you know that it pleases Jesus when we are unselfish? I noticed what you did today, but even if I didn't see you, the Lord always does, and He is the One you want to please!"
   b. Encourage achievements and appearance.

   When a man tells one of my girls she is beautiful someday, it will not be the first time she has heard those words. Since my daughters were little, their daddy has often told them they are sweet and beautiful. We tell our boys they are strong and handsome. The Bible certainly uses such adjectives to describe physical beauty and ability. The problem comes when the only compliments we give our children are focused on their outer appearance. When this is the case, we build self-absorbed children and young adults who believe that the world revolves around them.

c. Encourage gratitude.

Every sin comes back to pride, which manifests itself in selfishness and ingratitude. I have found that there are two ways to build gratitude. First, we must teach our children to be generous. When we are giving of our time and talent, we are learning to be selfless. Second is to teach and model thankfulness. A thankful heart always leads to gratitude.

III. Parenting requires a great marriage.

A. Put your husband first.

Outside of pointing them to Jesus, the best thing we can give our children is a strong, God-centered marriage. When asked by one of my children, "Why does daddy get more bacon than I do?" I replied, "Because he is here to stay and you are just passing through!" We need to openly show affection to our husband. Our children need to know that we cherish the relationship we have with our husband. Even the best marriages go through rough patches, some much more than others, but we should never pass that along to our children. We should not belittle, argue with, or make fun of our husband, even if it is initiated or reciprocated by him. Remember, we stand before the Lord alone.

Oftentimes parents, especially mothers, put children before their husband. Start teaching your children early and in little ways. For example, when you and your husband are talking and they interrupt, you might say, "Remember the rule. Mommy and Daddy are talking, and you must wait a few minutes." This shows them that Daddy is important to you and that your relationship comes first.

B. A great marriage is the greatest gift you can give your children!

Date! Yes, children can be left with a sitter. It is vitally important that you work hard on your marriage for your children's sake. Getting away is a time to reconnect and enjoy each other. If money is tight, trade out with another couple and take a picnic to the park! It is worth every bit of effort. When our children were little we would often put them to bed early and have an in-home date night. Eric would get a to-go meal for us to split. I would light candles, set the table, and put on the music. It was deliberate!

IV. Conclusion

Parenting is not a 100-yard dash; it is a very long and rewarding marathon with many peaks and valleys. We must be intentional in our own walk with Jesus and in our efforts to guide our children to love the Lord their God with all their heart, soul, and mind. Remember, amazing women know they are raising warriors!

Now What?

What were the most important points for you personally in this message, "Got Kids? How to Love Them!"?

Homework Day 2

What?

"Children are a gift of the LORD, the fruit of the womb is a reward" (Psalm 127:3).

So What?

Do you view your children as a blessing or a curse? It overwhelms me to think that the God who made the universe, set the stars in position, and holds the ocean in place wants to bless me! God said that children are a blessing. He didn't say sometimes they are a blessing or some of them are and some of them are not.

When I was a young mother and was feeling very overwhelmed, one of my good friends confronted me about my time with the Lord. I told her I read my Bible and prayed at night but felt as though it had become a box to check off my to-do list rather than a rich, intimate time. She challenged me to start getting up ten to fifteen minutes earlier and to spend that time in prayer and Bible reading. Believe it or not, I protested, saying, "I'm not a morning person. I can't focus first thing. I am too sleepy." At her insistence I did it, and how glad I am that I listened to her advice. I still do my studying at night, but my attitude changed when I started giving Him the first of my morning. My focus is different and my outlook is clearer. I take time to thank Him for the blessing of children and I pray for my husband. I encourage you to do the same. Wake up a few minutes earlier and spend some time with the Lord.

1. What does God's Word say to children (see Ephesians 6:1-3)?2. What does God's Word say to parents (see Ephesians 6:4)?

2. Before we can teach our children, what are we commanded to do (see Deuteronomy 6:4-5)?

3. What else must be true before we can teach our children (see Deuteronomy 6:6)?

PART TWO: Be Amazing in Relationships

4. Summarize what these verses say to you.

Now What?

Knowing how to be an amazing parent starts with knowing God's Word and spending time with Him in prayer.

1. Do you pray specific prayers so you would know if they were answered?

We must move from "bless our children" prayers to praying for specific needs, such as, "Lord, please let (*name*) come to know you personally. Hold (*name*) close so he stays on Your path today and all his life. Give (*name*) wisdom to see that You are real and that Your Word is of utmost importance to him. Help (*name*) to hear and obey Your voice today. Keep (*name*) from bad company or influences. Guard his mind and keep his body from evil. Help me to know how to discipline (*name*) with affection so he learns to obey.

2. Do you pray for your children's future mates and their marriages?

3. Do you pray they will get caught every time they disobey you or any other authority?

4. Make a prayer journal (it can be a simple notepad). List each member of your family and the things that cause you concern now and for the future. Pray specifically and consistently until God answers. Do this for the next month and see what a great work God will do in your home!

Homework Day 3

What?

"Train up a child in the way he should go, even when he is old he will not depart from it" (Proverbs 22:6).

So What?

God's Word teaches us how to be amazing parents, and as such, one of our roles is to teach our children God's Word. We are to train them in God's way, not in what seems right to us, so they will not depart from it. How will you know God's ways? By knowing and applying the principles or truths of His Word and by spending time in prayer.

1. When and where should you teach and talk to your children about God's Word (see Deuteronomy 6:6-7)?

   This shows the intentionality of teaching our children to love the Lord, morning until night.

2. List the places these commandments should be visible (see Deuteronomy 6:8-9).

   These verses are physical and outward. Notice it does not say to put these things on your children but to put them on yourself and your home. Yet another charge to live this out ourselves first!

3. How are you doing in starting your day with God's Word on your heart so it is there to teach your children? What changes will you make?

Now What?

Training is hard work, and we must be deliberate about it. Now that you have read and studied Deuteronomy, think about areas in your own life and in your children's lives that need some deliberate work.

1. List some behaviors of your children that you know need to be addressed.

2. How will you approach these issues and make changes? Remember, amazing women know that the goal for all of our parenting is ultimately to teach our children to "love the Lord with all their heart."

Session 16

Got Kids?

How to Love Them!, Part 2

Michele Helms

"That the word of God will not be dishonored."

TITUS 2:5

DVD Outline

I. **Introduction: Biblical Mandate for Parenting**

    A. Ages 0–6: Establish who is in control.

    B. Ages 6–12: You are a teacher.

    C. Ages 12–18: You are a coach.

    D. Age 18 and over: You are a friend.

II. **Discipline**

    A. Discipline with affection.

    B. Do not tolerate bad behavior.

    C. Discipline disobedience.

    D. Do not discipline childishness.

III. **Responsibility and Respect**

    A. Teach good manners.

    B. Teach responsibility.

    C. Do not be afraid to say "no," "not right now," or "wait."

    D. Do not make excuses for your children.

IV. **Conclusion**

Discussion Questions

1. What is the most important principle God has given you today in regard to shepherding your children into adulthood?
2. When and why is it hard to say no?
3. Do you see the purpose of discipline as behavior modification or as reaching the heart of your children? What needs to change?

Homework Day 1

What?

"Older women likewise are to be reverent in their behavior, not malicious gossips nor enslaved to much wine, teaching what is good, so that they may encourage the young women to love their husbands, *to love their children,* to be sensible, pure, workers at home, kind, being subject to their own husbands, so that the word of God will not be dishonored" (Titus 2:3-5).

So What?

Read the following notes from the DVD message "Got Kids? How to Love Them!, Part 2" and answer the "Now What" question at the end.

I. Introduction: Biblical Mandate for Parenting

We live in a culture where discipline, training, and correction have been replaced with over-indulgence, entitlement, and selfishness. The amazing woman lives in a way that is counter-cultural and accepts the biblical mandate for parents. The Bible says, "Train up a child in the way he should go" (Proverbs 22:6). Oftentimes parents think of discipline as a negative consequence for a bad behavior. Certainly that is a part of discipline, but a better way of thinking might be corrective training that pushes children toward an intimate relationship with the Savior. Training takes much more time and intentionality than behavior modification.

A. Ages 0–6: Establish who is in control.

These years are vitally important. It is the time to establish who is in charge and who is to be respected—YOU ARE! Authority is set by a certain expectation of behavior. My motto during these years is, "If it won't look good on a teenager, then it shouldn't be tolerated in a two-year-old." What do I mean by that? No one wants a whiny, lying, selfish, or disrespectful teenager or young adult, so we should not tolerate such behavior in our toddlers. Children do not just magically wake up one morning with stellar character. It takes intentional parenting!

B. Ages 6–12: You are a teacher.

These ages are full of opportunities to teach life lessons and continue to point your children toward Jesus. The foundation should have been laid in the early years, so it is now a building process. If authority has not been established, then some foundation work will need to be done. Children want to know where the boundaries are and if we are going to enforce them. It is during these years that I tried to impress on my children that even if I didn't catch them in their sin, they hadn't really gotten away with it because God sees it all!

C. Ages 12–18: You are a coach.

From the earliest age we should be teaching our kids to love Jesus, but it is during this stage that most kids begin to own their relationship with the Lord. It should begin to make sense to them that the reason for obedience is because they want a right relationship with Him. My prayer for my children is that ultimately their motivation to obey will be to please Jesus with their lives.

Not too long ago I stood in the kitchen looking up at my very tall teenage son who is stronger and faster than I am. He doesn't have to obey. He could make our home hell or could simply walk away from me, and there would be nothing I could do physically to stop him. But he doesn't. Why? Because we established a long time ago who was in charge! He respects and honors me, and he would tell you that I treat him fairly and respectfully as well. This relationship didn't just happen; it has been intentional.

During this age, choose your battles. If there is an area that involves character, then you should be willing to "die on that hill." But if not, you might need to step back. My sixteen-year-old son decided to grow his hair out to donate to locks of love. He has curly hair, so he now has a giant Afro. It is not my personal preference. But is it sinful? Is it worth causing friction in our relationship? No.

I have seen many parents try to micromanage their children at this age. I am certainly not advocating disobedience, but I am saying that you should look carefully at the things you are saying no to and having endless discussions about. If it is a character or sin issue, then tackle it. If it isn't, then let it go!

While these years can bring challenges, they do not need to be feared. These years can be a rewarding and delightful time. We have lowered our expectation for this age group in our culture. We expect teenagers to be rude, disrespectful, rebellious, and lazy. RAISE THE BAR! Expect hard-working, obedient, respectful, and disciplined young people, and they will blow you away as they strive for excellence.

D. Age 18 and over: You are a friend.

Remember that ultimately we are raising children to leave and start their own lives. This is not the time for micromanagement. Keep in mind that most young adults will make choices we may not agree with, but that doesn't necessarily make them wrong. Don't panic! Just pray for your young adults as they navigate newfound freedoms and choices. Pray that they will run to Jesus just like you taught them to! Enjoy them and the young adults they have become. Continue to encourage them and tell them how much you love them and pray for them in their struggles.

If you have children this age living at home or for whom you are paying college tuition, then you still have the authority to set some rules. If your adult child chooses not to abide by your rules, they have that right, but they will have to take ownership of those choices. Make it clear that you will not financially support sinful behavior. If they choose to continue in ungodly behavior, they have chosen to leave and support themselves.

II. Discipline

A. Discipline with affection.

My parents believed in discipline but were never harsh or unkind. They had a few offenses that were not tolerated, such as lying, bullying, and a sassy mouth. I remember one such offense when I was sitting in my room waiting for my mother to come and administer discipline. Her door was cracked, as was mine, and I could see her down on her knees praying before she dealt with me. I am forever grateful that they taught me lifelong principles and disciplines.

Just like when children are young, there is never a reason for hatefulness, screaming, or guilt. It is always ironic when I see a parent speaking hatefully to a child with statements such as, "You're being a brat!" It just doesn't make sense to tell them how disrespectful they are while we are screaming and being hateful. When God corrects His children, it is always for the purpose of restoring our fellowship with Him, which has been broken because of our disobedience. Oftentimes parents discipline because they are annoyed or tired. Raising godly children is hard work, but amazing women do not become weary in training them to become all they can be for the kingdom of God.

Once the issue has been addressed and the appropriate punishment given, fellowship should be restored. Therefore, do not keep bringing up the same issue over and over again. That certainly is not how God deals with us. When parents do this, the child always feels guilty, and given enough time the child will always respond badly because he thinks it is what the parent expects.

B. Do not tolerate bad behavior.

Most parents don't mean to tolerate bad behavior; they just haven't thought through their actions. Let me give you an example of what I mean.

Example 1: A child walks into the kitchen while her mom is cooking and in her most whiny voice says, "Mommeeeeeeeeee, I want juuuuuiiiccce." Her mother reaches into the refrigerator and hands the child the juice cup while sternly saying, "Do not whine!" Mom thinks she has handled her child's whining because she told her to stop. But in reality, she really just reinforced the behavior because she gave her what she wanted.

Example 2: Let's take the same situation, but this time when the child asks for the juice in her whiny voice, her mom looks at her and says, "Oh my goodness, do we whine in this house? Is that the way you should ask for your juice? Why don't you try that again?" If the child complies, then Mom says, "Oh, that is much better. Here you go." If the child does not comply, then Mom says, "You are still whining. This is how you should ask." Mom then models what this should sound like ("May I have some juice please?"). The point is that the child does not get what she wants until she asks correctly.

Do you see the difference? There is no yelling on the mom's part, but the child will eventually get the picture that whining will not get her what she wants! You also see that example 2 takes more time and effort than example 1. However, the payoff is huge!

Whether it comes from a toddler or a teenager, disrespectful behavior should not be tolerated. This includes demanding, whining, being hateful, or having a pouty attitude. When we give our children what they want, even if we think we are addressing the behavior through our words, which oftentimes includes yelling, we are actually tolerating and reinforcing that poor behavior.

C. Discipline disobedience.

Direct disobedience should always be addressed and never tolerated. Children should never be allowed to tell the parent they will not do whatever is asked of them. Children should not slam doors, roll eyes, stomp off, or talk back. They will try, some of them more than others, but we must deal with this behavior every time! I suggest that you start discipline with words. Let's say you ask a young child to pick up his toys and he says no. Walk over to him and gently say, "You may not tell mommy no. Please go pick up the toys right now." If he obeys with a good attitude, then you are finished. If he does not obey or has a disrespectful tone or attitude, then you are not finished! This goes for an older child as well. Calm communication about why a particular behavior isn't acceptable and what the consequence will be if the child disobeys is always the place to start. If the child chooses to disobey, then the parents must follow through with punishment. Always tell your children what the Bible says about their particular sin. This is important so that as they get older they understand that their disobedience isn't about their parents' rules but about what God says.

So many situations can be avoided just by having intentional conversations about what is expected of your children. I always try to stay a step ahead of behavior by giving warnings. For instance, this is a conversation that my older kids could recite verbatim because I still have younger kids who need reminding, so the older ones have to endure the forewarning: "We are going to Mr. and Mrs. Smith's home for dinner. Boys, make sure that you shake Mr. Smith's hand. I do not know what Mrs. Smith is cooking. You will eat it! You will not whisper in my ear and tell me that you do not like it. Do not do all the talking at the table;

it is rude. Ask others questions. When you are finished eating thank Mrs. Smith. Do not wander in their home. You may only go where you are instructed to go. When we are leaving, thank the Smiths for having us. Does everyone understand?"

Sometimes my reminder comes in the form of a positive statement and then a question: "I love that you are coming to the store with me. It is fun to spend time with you. We are only here to buy the things on my list, so are you going to beg for things? Are you going to help me find the things on my list?"

Keep it simple! There should be certain clear directives about what is expected, but don't overcomplicate things.

D. Do not discipline childishness.

Watch out for ridiculous expectations, such as expecting a toddler to sit at the dinner table quietly for forty-five minutes after dinner is over while adults are talking. Give some thought to taking young children to the store when it is clearly past their bedtime, and don't be surprised when they are crying.

Kids are messy and clumsy (and sometimes so am I!). Don't confuse disobedience with just being a kid. Throwing a ball in the house and breaking a vase is a common example of something a child might do. The issue is throwing the ball, not breaking the vase, but many times parents don't deal with the disobedience until it has a negative effect such as a broken vase. Kids spill things, knock things over, track things in . . . the list goes on and on! Beware! This gets worse during the preteen and early teenage years, especially for boys. Think puppy dogs whose feet and ears are too big for their bodies! Take the time to teach them to clean up their messes. Let them know that we *all* break things on occasion. But don't scream and yell at them because they have accidents—some more than others!

III. Responsibility and Respect

A. Teach good manners.

From the earliest years we should be teaching our children manners, respect, and common courtesy:

- Teach them to say please and thank you . . . every time!
- Teach them the proper way to interrupt. When my kids were little, I taught them that if I was talking to another adult, they were to put their hand on my shoulder and wait. I would reach up and pat their hand so they knew I was aware of them. As soon as there was a break in the conversation I would say "excuse me" to the other adult and then turn to the child and say, "Thanks for the way you interrupted; how can I help you?" If they ran in and interrupted incorrectly, I would turn to them and say, "Is that the way we interrupt?" Then I would resume my conversation and make them interrupt correctly.

Got Kids? (Part 2)

- Teach them when it is acceptable to use their cell phones, electronics, and earphones. It is rude to have these items out at the table, while in a conversation with others, or in a public setting such as school or church. We must examine our own influence and then be the gatekeeper for our families. It always makes me sad to see a young mother at the park pushing her child on the swing while she is deep in conversation on her phone. We have a strict rule at our house that during dinner there are no devices and no television. We also strictly limit the time allowed on the computer, games, and devices, and when it is bedtime, all devices go off. All electronic devices go in a basket before the kids reach the dinner table and before they go to bed.
- Teach them to say "I am sorry" when they are wrong or have offended someone. We must model this as parents.

B. Teach responsibility.

Kids should start at a young age with chores and responsibility. If a child is old enough to dump out a basket of toys, they are old enough to put it all back. The first six years are a real teaching time as far as chores are concerned. You must work alongside them until they know how to do certain tasks. Tell them how proud you are of a job well done. Then, as children get older, you should add to their responsibilities. Make a list for them to put in their room with their responsibilities for each day written out. There should be consequences for not doing these things. If they do a sloppy job, they should be asked to redo the task. If they do a good job, they should be praised.

My husband and I do not give our kids allowances for doing chores, such as keeping their room clean, doing their laundry, helping in the kitchen, taking out the trash, and cleaning the bathroom. Those are just a part of being in a family. Because we do not just hand them money for their whims, we have a list of age-appropriate jobs they can do to earn money. Don't underestimate what your kids are capable of doing. Here are some examples of extra chores kids can do to earn money:

- Clean the baseboards in a room
- Clean the inside of the car
- Clean the ceiling fans
- Plant flowers
- Take down and clean blinds
- Clean the refrigerator
- Pull weeds in flower beds
- Touch up paint on doors
- Wipe down kitchen cabinets
- Scrub outdoor entryways

C. Do not be afraid to say "no," "not right now," or "wait."

Parents seem to be afraid to say "no" or "not now" to their kids. They have bought the lie that if they tell them no, then the child might rebel or hate them. So many parents want their children to fit in, so they say yes to things that are completely inappropriate. Most of the time I try to help my children understand the reason behind the decision, but sometimes the decision can't be explained. I have said on several occasions, "I know you do not understand why we said no, but do you know us to make rules for the sake of making rules or to purposefully wreck your life? Then you're going to have to trust me on this one."

D. Do not make excuses for your children.

We live in a culture where personal responsibility has been replaced with the blame game and entitlement. If we make excuses for our children's behavior and let them make their own excuses, they will never take personal responsibility for anything. Children should be taught that they are responsible for their own actions and reactions.

IV. Conclusion

I think about parenting like a big open field, and right in the middle is a fenced area. Within that fenced-in area, there is great freedom, but outside the fence is restricted. Why? Because there are landmines hidden in the ground. I give my kids freedom to make choices within certain parameters, and I extend those parameters with age and proven responsibility. I do not keep them from the big field because I am mean or stuffy but because I know there are unseen landmines outside the boundaries. The Enemy is really good at making the big field look super enticing and like "real" freedom, but it isn't. It's a trap. If you can help your children see the traps and embrace the freedom that is theirs in Christ, you will give them a lifelong gift.

One passage that has meant so much to me is in Nehemiah. God called Nehemiah to rebuild the wall in Jerusalem, and he was busy doing what God called him to do. Sanballat wanted him to come off the wall to meet him. He was persistent, sending messages five times. Each time he asked Nehemiah to come down, and every time Nehemiah gave the same answer: "I am doing a great work and I cannot come down. Why should the work stop while I leave it and come down to you?" (Nehemiah 6:3).

Parenting is really just a season in your life. It is hard work, but the rewards are enormous. Parent with the end in mind instead of considering it a daily drudgery. There are many things competing for your time and attention, but an amazing woman is an amazing mom. Keep your focus! You are doing a great work!

PS: A Word to Mothers of Adult Children

By Eleanor Lewis

I heard a great illustration that parenting is like riding in a rowboat in the ocean. When the children are eight and put their arms in the dark, dangerous water, you can tell them to stop or pull them out of danger. When they are eighteen they can jump in the water, and you have to watch them struggle against the sharks and dangerous current and pray they will want to get back in the boat.

Some of you may feel you have failed as a parent. Perhaps you accepted Christ when your children were older, you didn't know God's Word, or your husband had a different philosophy, so looking back now, you feel you didn't do it right. Or perhaps you did it right to the best of your ability and your children still have jumped out of the boat. What then?

1. Confess if necessary and forgive yourself.

If specific failures come to mind, confess them once. God says, "If we confess our sins, He is faithful and righteous to forgive us our sins and to cleanse us from all unrighteousness" (1 John 1:9). Therefore, you only confess a sin once. The second time you are reminding God of something He says He has forgotten! After confessing, forgive yourself because God has.

2. Love but don't enable.

Know that adult children may jump out of the boat and there is nothing you can do to stop them. You can love them where they are without a condemning attitude, just as God loves you. He convicts but never condemns. However, don't confuse loving with enabling. Don't finance, endorse, or provide help that in any way enables their sin.

3. Pray more and say less!

Generally speaking, adult children don't want, nor do they listen to, a parent's advice. You may offer it if given the opportunity, but if it is rejected, pray more and say less!
  a. Pray they will want to get back in the boat.
  b. Pray for brokenness. This is difficult because we may be more concerned that they are happy than holy, but godliness requires brokenness.

We raised our son right. He accepted Christ at age four and lived a godly life. Yet he had his terrible twos in his late twenties. Success tempted him to go apart from God's ways. It was a painful time. When a child stumbles, it humbles a parent! But it was good because God used this pain to make me more Christlike. God will use all your pain for good as well.

4. Trust that God is able.

He can "make up to you for the years that the swarming locust has eaten" (Joel 2:25). Conviction came on my son in a day, but it was God's doing, not ours. My son got back in the boat and now lives to keep others from jumping ship. Don't underestimate the power of a loving God!

Now What?

What were the most important points for you personally in this message, "Got Kids? How to Love Them!, Part 2"?

Homework Day 2

What?

"Correct your son, and he will give you comfort; he will also delight your soul" (Proverbs 29:17).

So What?

It is our job as parents to train our children to obey. Obedience requires a yielded spirit. We are training them to obey us so they will obey God. They must learn there are consequences for disobeying us and God. They also must learn that all of life isn't necessarily fun and that they must sometimes do things they don't like to do (such as practicing, homework, or chores).

Parents are to discipline their children, but we recoil at the word, thinking of abuse or something negative or harsh. Yet God says discipline is crucial because, according to *Strong's Concordance,* it means to "correct, train, instruct."

1. The first time the word *discipline* is used in the Bible is in Deuteronomy 4. How does God as our Father discipline (correct, train, and instruct) us (see Deuteronomy 4:36)?

2. What is true if we don't listen to God's words of discipline or if our children don't listen to ours (see Proverbs 15:5)?

We see that God first disciplines, teaches, or corrects through words. We want our children to so love us and the Lord that it only takes a word to correct them.

3. Parents sometimes fear disciplining because they don't want to damage their children's self-esteem. However, esteem doesn't come from the self. What will cause your children to despise themselves (see Proverbs 15:32)?

PART TWO: Be Amazing in Relationships

4. What can a child avoid if a parent disciplines and the child listens (see Proverbs 13:18)?

5. What can a child gain if a parent disciplines and the child listens (see Proverbs 19:20)?

Now What?

You can't control what goes on in the world, but in many ways you can control what happens in your home, at least as far as it depends on you. You can choose to teach and correct your children with kindness and gentleness, saying no to things your kids think they need or deserve. You can choose to have joy and to point your children toward Jesus in everything!

One important aspect of parenting (teaching or instructing) is the art of listening (not just hearing) and talking. When your children get older, especially late high school and college, you should be doing a lot of listening and praying and less talking. When you look at the way Jesus interacted with people in the Bible, you see that He asked questions. We should learn from Him! You need to learn the art of asking your children questions for many reasons:

- To get to know them and their hearts
- To hear their dreams
- To find the real motivation behind their thoughts and actions
- To help them make decisions themselves
- To build trust with them

Your assignment today is to ask your kids some questions and then to listen! If you don't have children, ask questions of those you come in contact with today.

Homework Day 3

What?

"Foolishness is bound up in the heart of a child; the rod [staff] of discipline will remove it far from him" (Proverbs 22:15).

So What?

When your children are obedient, acknowledge it, and when they disobey, discipline to correct them. Remember, the shepherd uses the rod (staff) to protect his sheep from enemies or danger. That is what we are doing when we correct or train our children. We are guarding them from danger. We are not disciplining out of anger or frustration, but, like that loving shepherd, we are gently guiding our child onto God's safe path. Children must learn to receive punishment as from a parent who truly loves them and wants their best. This will teach the children to take responsibility for their own actions before God when you are no longer in the picture.

Eli was a priest in Israel whose sons were "worthless men; they did not know the LORD" (1 Samuel 2:12). We are told they took for personal use the sacrifices given to God and "thus the sin of the young men was very great before the LORD, for the men despised the offering of the LORD (1 Samuel 2:17).

They also "lay with the women who served at the doorway of the tent of meeting" (1 Samuel 2:22). The Lord's words to Eli may prick your heart. God said to this parent, "Why do you kick at My sacrifice and at My offering which I have commanded in My dwelling, and honor your sons above Me?" (1 Samuel 2:29).

1. Why was God about to judge Eli's house (see 1 Samuel 3:13)?

2. What convicting words! Do you allow your children to do things you know are not pleasing to God because you honor or fear them above God (or perhaps just want them to be happy or be your friend)?

PART TWO: Be Amazing in Relationships

3. List all you learn about the Lord's discipline, a parent's discipline of their children, and the result of discipline in Hebrews 12:5-11.

Now What?

Write a prayer about what God has said to you about discipline. It could include the following:
- Repentance that you have fought against God's discipline of you
- Repentance that you have not understood the need to discipline (correct/train) your children or had the right goal for them
- Thanksgiving that God hasn't allowed you to get away with your sin
- Request that God won't allow your children to get away with their sin
- Request for wisdom regarding how to discipline/correct/train your children as a shepherd does his sheep

Be Amazing in the Home

Desperate Housewives

Keeper of the Home

Linda Sweeney

"That the word of God will not be dishonored."

Titus 2:5

DVD Outline

I. **Are you a desperate housewife?**
   A. Introduction: No Place for Desperation
   B. "Just a homemaker?"
   C. God created the home.
   D. The home is a haven.
   E. The Woman's Role in the Home
   F. We can't do it all.

II. **CEO of the Home**
   A. Who is in charge?
   B. But what if I don't like the job?
   C. Attitude is a choice.
      1. Feeling unappreciated?
      2. Feeling overwhelmed?
      3. Feeling discontented?

III. **The keeper of the home guards the gate!**

Discussion Questions

1. How do you view your role as "homemaker"? Have you come to appreciate it more over the years? If so, what made that happen?

2. How has comparison hurt your contentment in regard to your role at home?

Homework Day 1

What?

"Older women likewise are to be reverent in their behavior, not malicious gossips nor enslaved to much wine, teaching what is good, so that they may encourage the young women to love their husbands, to love their children, to be sensible, pure, workers at home, kind, being subject to their own husbands, so that the word of God will not be dishonored" (Titus 2:3-5).

So What?

Read the following notes from the DVD message "Desperate Housewives: Keeper of the Home" and answer the "Now What" question at the end.

I. Are you a desperate housewife?

A. Introduction: No Place for Desperation

Desperate Housewives is a great title for a movie or reality television series because it accurately describes the feelings some women have for their role as a homemaker. God calls women to be and to do many things, but to be desperate is *not* one of them!

The dysfunctional home I grew up in was dark, fearful, and not the kind of home I wanted when I became a wife. God's Word presents a pleasing and positive picture of home because it is so important in not only our family but also our society! We've learned in this study that when we use God's Word as our guide, every area of our lives works better, including our home. These commands are from God Himself, and because our personal helper is the Holy Spirit, there's no place for desperation! As a result, *every Christian woman can be a theologian, so every Christian home is a refuge, and thus, every community is blessed.* That's a tall order, but it's from God. An amazing woman can have an amazing home, but that has nothing to do with its size or location. Every home will look different and will be unique because God made us all different and unique.

Titus 2:5 includes "workers at home" on the list of things older women are to encourage younger women to be.

B. "Just a homemaker?"

It seems to me that when women who do not work outside the home are asked the question, "What do you do?" there's often a hesitation and perhaps even a fear when they respond. The phrase "just a" is frequently attached to the answer: "I am just a homemaker, just a wife, just a mother," and so on. I'm not sure exactly when this began, but I think we need to eliminate this phrase from our descriptions of who we are, regardless of our set of circumstances. Often women who work at home feel they have nothing exciting, interesting, or worth sharing because they aren't what the world deems "professional." Because they may not bring home a regular paycheck does not mean what they do isn't worth more than most firms could pay! Can I hear an "amen"? I want to interject another thought here. If you are a woman who works outside your home, and many do today, I salute you! Frankly, I don't know how you do it. I do know from my own experience in this area that it is difficult at best!

The popular advice columnist Ann Landers (if you are too young to know who she is, don't tell me) has printed some really good and quite sensible articles over the years. In 1988, she printed in her newspaper column the job description of "Just a Housewife," which was sent in by one of her readers. Here is that description:

I'm a wife, a mother, a friend, a confidant, a personal advisor, lover, referee, peacemaker, housekeeper, laundress, chauffeur, interior decorator, gardener, painter, wall paperer, dog groomer, veterinarian, manicurist, barber, seamstress, appointment manager, financial planner, bookkeeper, money manager, personal secretary, teacher, disciplinarian, entertainer, psychoanalyst, nurse, diagnostician, public relations expert, dietician and nutritionist, baker, chef, fashion coordinator, and letter writer for both sides of the family. I am also a travel agent, speech therapist, plumber, and automobile maintenance and repair expert. And during the course of my day I'm supposed to be cheerful and look radiant and jump in bed on a moment's notice. I figure it would take over $75,000.00 a year to replace me! Now what do I get out of my job in the absence of a salary? Joy, happiness, hugs, kisses, smiles, love, self-respect, and pride in knowing that I've done a full day's work to ensure the physical and emotional well-being of those I love! Now if you still want to classify me as "just a housewife," go ahead![21]

Being a homemaker is probably the highest calling women have, as well as the most difficult. Titus 2:5 is evidence that encouragement is needed. We know that times have changed and today more women than ever before are juggling both home and career. There are also many single moms having very difficult times. If you know one, do everything you can to encourage and help her.

C. God created the home.

We read in Genesis that the home in the beginning was a perfect garden that didn't need a roof or walls. The way I imagine it, food was provided and the climate was ideal, with no rain or ultraviolet rays to worry about. No clothes were needed (think of the advantage of that—none to pick up, wash, iron, fold, or put away . . . paradise indeed!). The animals were vegetarians, not meat eaters, and posed no threat.

After the Fall, and as time went on, families lived together as units in tents that could be easily moved. When God gave the children of Israel the Promised Land, He also gave them houses that they could not claim they'd built or supplied. Having these homes was God's gift to them. Therefore, it's safe to say that God intends for our homes to be seen as a gift or blessing. Most women understand this as they have also been given natural "nesting" instincts.

Go back with me to Eden and remember that Adam and Eve were created differently and were given different roles. Adam was already working there when God wanted him to have a companion, a "helper suitable for him" (Genesis 2:18). At this point, God created Eve. This, of course, was the first home, and she was the first homemaker!

D. The home is a haven.

After the Fall sin entered the picture, and when people came home tired from trying to grow crops in rocky, hard, weed-infested ground, the home was a haven. But how can a home be a peaceful refuge? "But as for me, the nearness of God is my good; I have made the Lord GOD my refuge, that I may tell of all your works" (Psalm 73:28). "God is our refuge and strength, a very present help in trouble (Psalm 46:1). According to *Strong's Concordance,* the word *refuge* comes from the Hebrew word *makh·as·eh',* which means "shelter from rain, storm, danger, or falsehood." God is our refuge and we are safe in Him. His plan is that our homes will provide safety for all those who dwell there.

After a long, hard day, who doesn't want to enter the door of a refuge! Ed told me when we were discussing this topic that his most favorite time of the day is getting safely back to our home, finding me there in charge of a nice dinner, and enjoying a well-ordered, peaceful place where he can relax. He further stated that everyone needs a refuge: a place of order, peace, and security. How's that for helpful input on our subject, as well as proving my point! You've gotta love it when things come together so well!

E. The Woman's Role in the Home

I looked at the phrase "workers at home" from Titus 2:5 in several translations and found the following:

- KJV: "keepers at home"
- AMP: "homemakers"
- NIV: "busy at home"

The MacArthur Study Bible has these words: "Keeping a godly home with excellence for one's husband and children is the Christian woman's nonnegotiable responsibility."[22] This means we are to do this whether we like it or not! It's our job description.

The helper (woman) was understood to be "the keeper" of the home. Some women did work outside the home and were very entrepreneurial, like the amazing woman in Proverbs 31. This woman worked both inside and outside her home to provide the very best for her family. Everything she did was done with excellence! We never see her being lazy but always rising early and turning in late.

My grandmother had a saying I loved hearing and believe totally: "A man's work is from sun to sun, but a woman's work is never done!" Can't you identify? We try to accomplish all we can, and because of that, our goals are at times unrealistic. Not meeting them causes us great frustration. This can make us feel desperate, and perhaps like a failure, but neither is God's plan!

F. We can't do it all.

There's a lie out there telling us we can and must do it all! That's wrong! One of the things that works for me and gives me great freedom is making a list of the many things I *need* to accomplish in a given day, as well as the things I *want* to get done that day. Then I pray over the list. My thinking is that God will help me do what He sees as important or necessary, and what is left over are tasks I didn't need to do, at least that day. This keeps me from suffering guilt over an incomplete list.

Life has "seasons," and I would submit to you that we can't do it all and aren't supposed to because we all have different seasons for getting things done. For instance, there are things we should not even try to do when we have small children at home, including some church work we may be offered. It took me a long time to realize that when someone representing the church asked me to do something, it wasn't necessarily God asking me. I had to pray about my response and ask my husband for his opinion (and abide by what he said). I personally believe that if women sought the advice of God and their husbands, they would spend more time at home and be able to accomplish more on their list! I've finally learned that Ed sees firsthand what overloading myself can do to our family life! When he says "no" or "not now," I now know he's not being ornery or contrary; he's protecting me and my time. We would all do well to listen to our husbands.

There are some seasons when women may need or desire to work outside the home; however, remember that God's Word is our guide because it is truth always! When Ed and I were first married, I had a rather impressive job that offered many accolades, opportunities for learning, and a good bit of travel. My mother wanted to watch our daughter when she was born, which made continuing to work a definite option. I loved my job, so I became a homemaker, mother, and career woman all in one. After I became pregnant with our second child, my mother resigned! I tried to keep going the way I had been, with two very unhappy children. I shed tears every day when I left them crying at the door of the day care. I was miserable all day and could hardly wait to pick them up. I'd see them all but hanging out the door looking for me and then jumping for joy when they recognized my car!

PART THREE: Be Amazing in the Home

After a while, it just wasn't working. The children were upset and sick a lot, I was miserable, and our home wasn't the refuge it should be. Every waking moment was spent getting ready for the next workday, and I was tired all the time. Can you relate? Finally, my husband stepped in and actually called my boss to resign for me just in case he tried to sway my decision. It was hard! Our income was cut in half and I was scared. I also missed feeling so important and taking those exciting trips, but looking back I would not change a thing, except that I'd have quit sooner. God provided what we needed, and I was able to stay home and raise my children. I love hearing them tell of their special memories of our time at home together. They never speak about the things they didn't have. Interesting, isn't it?

II. CEO of the Home

A. Who is in charge?

Here's a new thought: when Paul gave instructions regarding young widows who were remarrying and becoming managers of the house (see 1 Timothy 5:14, NIV), the Greek word he used was *oikadespoteo,* which *Strong's Concordance* says means "to be master of a house; to rule a household; manage family affairs." In other words, we women are the CEOs of our homes! Our husbands are the owners/presidents, but we are the ones in charge, not of our husbands, but of the house and all that goes on there.

This does not mean we spend large sums of money on projects, decorating, and so forth without discussing it with our husbands. However, it does mean we get to pick and present the décor. We get to schedule our days, shop for our groceries, and cook the meals. You should want to prepare meals that are favorites for family members, especially your man! There's real truth in the saying, "The way to a man's heart is through his stomach." At my house, I know this is so!

B. But what if I don't like the job?

If you don't know how to cook, learn. In two weeks we will get some practical help on planning and preparing menus. Also, in an age of technology, there is a wealth of information from simple to gourmet at your fingertips. Since there are so many resources to help you in the home, there are no excuses. You could also find a mentor and ask her to help you learn and love to cook! Here's a thought: why not ask God to give you a love and ability for your role in the home? If you don't like to cook, pray that God will give you the desire and joy in doing it because it is part of the job description. We as a society eat out far too often, and Robin will give us reasons why eating at home is beneficial.

Also, if my husband asks me to pick up his dry cleaning or to straighten up the clutter because he doesn't like the house messy, I should find the time to do it. I am reminded on those days when I have to tell him I forgot that I always seem to find time to do the things I want to do! And I'm supposed to be his helper!

The secret to being a Proverbs 31 amazing woman is found in Colossians 3:23-24: "Whatever you do, do your work heartily, as for the Lord rather than for men, knowing that from the Lord you will receive the reward of the inheritance. It is the Lord Christ whom you serve."

Remember the cartoon drawing on how to love your husband? We must remember it is Jesus we love and serve, and this applies to our job as homemakers too.

C. Attitude is a choice.

1. Feeling unappreciated?

If you are feeling unappreciated because you are working hard and no one is calling you blessed, remember that it is the Lord you are serving, and He notices.

So much about being a keeper of the home is an attitude choice! Did you hear that? You can choose your attitude! Realize you may have to wait a long time for sweet, appreciative, affirming words, but if you listen quietly, you may hear God's still, small voice saying, "Well done, good and faithful servant!" (Matthew 25:23, NIV).

You might also hear, "And let us not be weary in well doing: for in due season we shall reap, if we faint not. As we have therefore opportunity, let us do good unto all men, especially unto them who are of the household of faith" (Galatians 6:9-10, KJV). And, "For do I now persuade men, or God? or do I seek to please men? for if I yet pleased men, I should not be the servant of Christ" (Galatians 1:10, KJV).

2. Feeling overwhelmed?

Our biggest problem in this area is that we're so busy with work and everything else that often our families get only "the leftovers." If doing things outside your home takes away from your inside priorities, don't do them! Learn to say no. That's a powerful little word. We need to become acquainted with it! And remember, "I can do all things through Him [Christ] who strengthens me" (Philippians 4:13).

3. Feeling discontented?

One attitude we all need is contentment. We need to replace discontentment with the attitude of gratitude. We should be grateful for all we've been given and stop looking at what it seems others have that is better. Paul said, "I have learned to be content in whatever circumstances I am" (Philippians 4:11).

It took me awhile, but eventually I learned this lesson. Early in my married life, the kitchen window over my sink looked out through my carport to the house on the corner. It really was prettier than mine; I liked the design much better. One day the "perfect family" who lived there began to add on to it! They were getting a master suite (which was unheard of in that day and neighborhood). This was on top of the wife being movie-star beautiful and dressing like a fashion model. Did I mention that her kids were adorable too? I'd wash dishes and think, "Why does she have so much? She doesn't even go to church!" I wasted a lot of time looking out my window grumbling and disregarding all my blessings. I had a faithful husband; sweet babies, whom I was able to stay home with and raise; and a cute and very adequate house, which I was able to decorate. One day I realized that all that glitters is not gold. There was heartbreak under the roof of my neighbor's home. Her walls came tumbling down, and I learned a very valuable lesson. I had been selfish, ungrateful, and discontent. When comparison begins, contentment ends.

III. The keeper of the home guards the gate!

Remember that as CEO you are the gatekeeper of your home. You are to guard what comes in. However, it is also imperative that most things stay private within the home, so you also guard what goes out. To guard the gate is important.

When the Great Wall of China was built for the purpose of keeping out that country's enemies, it seemed like a sure thing. No construction has ever equaled this tall, fortified, magnificent wall. The idea was good and most likely would have worked except for the corruption of the gatekeepers who took bribes to let in the armies of the enemy. The job of "gatekeeper" is crucial!

Being a homemaker and gatekeeper is a blessing, privilege, and great responsibility. If you see it from God's view you will never say you are "just a housewife, homemaker, and mother," and you will be content with all that God has generously given you. Your attitude toward your husband and children will reflect your gratitude. To learn contentment we must "in everything give thanks; for this is God's will for you in Christ Jesus" (1 Thessalonians 5:18). There is even the possibility that one day you will hear your family call you "blessed." An amazing woman reigns well in her home and is a trusted gatekeeper.

Now What?

What were the most important points for you personally in this message, "Desperate Housewives: Keeper of the Home"?

Homework Day 2

What?

"Whatever you do, do your work heartily, as for the Lord rather than for men, knowing that from the Lord you will receive the reward of the inheritance. It is the Lord Christ whom you serve" (Colossians 3:23-24).

So What?

In Titus 2:5 God tells older women to encourage the younger women to be "workers at home," which is also translated, "homemakers," "keepers at home," and "busy at home." Your life as a woman isn't just about loving your husband and children in the ways we've studied; it is also about running an efficient, organized home. However, isn't this really a way to love your husband and children? Our love for each family member spills over into making the home a safe refuge—a secure, peaceful place in the midst of a sometimes crazy world. Christian homes should be the place each family member longs to be, a refuge where love abounds, special memories are made, and joyful, tender care is displayed. It doesn't take earthly riches to accomplish this.

1. What does the role of a "homemaker" or "worker at home" look like in your house?

2. Titus 2:5 says we are to "keep"—the root word of this is "guard"—our home. First Timothy 5:14 says young widows are to remarry and "keep house." *Strong's Concordance* says to "keep house" means to be "master or head of a house, to rule a household, manage family affairs." Why are you to be the CEO and guardian of your home (see 1 Timothy 5:14)?

3. What does the Enemy or "thief" want to do (see John 10:10)?

4. Where is the Enemy (see Genesis 4:7)?

Now What?

It is clear there is danger outside our gates and our role as gatekeepers of the home is important.

1. What are the dangers a broken gate poses to your family?

2. What area of your gate has a break or is broken down?

3. What is your action plan to be a trusted gatekeeper of your home? In other words, what can you do to make your home a refuge or safe place?

Homework Day 3

What?

"In everything give thanks; for this is God's will for you in Christ Jesus" (1 Thessalonians 5:18).

So What?

As Christian women, we are to be content as we perform our role as "workers at home." That does not mean we will jump for joy at the mere thought of cleaning toilets, mopping floors, vacuuming, and dusting! It does mean we will find happiness in being God's woman in the home.

Our responsibility is not only to our family members but to God. Remember, we are to obey God "that the word of God will not be dishonored" (Titus 2:5).

1. What is a desirable attitude to possess in our role at home, and what do you learn about it in the following verses?

Philippians 4:11-13

1 Timothy 6:6-8

Hebrews 13:5

Now What?

For being such blessed people, why are we so discontent? Ask God to reveal any area in your home life or in your role as keeper of the home where you have expressed discontentment.

1. List anything God brings to mind.

2. What is the source of your discontent? Confess it if necessary.

3. What impact does your discontentment have on other family members?

4. Contentment ends when comparison begins! What have you compared your life to that brought you discontentment?

5. "In everything give thanks; for this is God's will for you in Christ Jesus" (1 Thessalonians 5:18). Make a list of what you are grateful for.

Clear the Clutter and Create the Comfort

There's No Place Like Home

"That the word of God will not be dishonored."

TITUS 2:5

DVD Outline

I. **Introduction: Home is a refuge.**

II. **Heart of the Home**
   A. Home: A Peaceful Dwelling Place
   B. Home: God-Honoring, Welcoming, and Comfortable

III. **The Stress of Mess**
   A. Why do we have so much stuff?
   B. Why do we let clutter and mess take over the house?

IV. **Clear the clutter.**
   A. Gather sorting materials before starting.
   B. Next is the time to sort and organize.
   C. Assess the mess: why are items out of place?
   D. Common Overlooked Sources of Clutter

V. **Clean the room.**
   A. Have a cleaning tote.
   B. Wash, dust, and vacuum everything.
   C. Make a cleaning plan.

VI. **Keep it clean.**
   A. A Place for Everything and Everything in Its Place
   B. Making Some Changes

VII. **General Organizational Tips**

VIII. **Create the comfort.**
   A. Welcome Home: The Entryway
   B. Cozy Living Space
      1. Furniture
      2. Pillows and blankets
      3. Books
      4. Pictures
   C. Restful Bedrooms
      1. Mattress pads
      2. Sheets
      3. Pillows and pillowcases
      4. Bed coverings
      5. Maintain cleanliness.

PART THREE: Be Amazing in the Home

D. Let there be light.
   1. Table lamps
   2. Lampshades
   3. Lamp locations
   4. Dimmers
E. Finishing Touches
   1. Flowers and plants
   2. Natural light
   3. Candles
   4. Magazines
   5. Music

Discussion Questions

1. What is your biggest challenge to keeping a clean and organized home?
2. What is the first area you need to tackle in your home?
3. Think about some of the homes you have been in that give you the feeling of restoration. What made those homes comfortable?

Homework Day 1

What?

"But all things must be done properly and in an orderly manner" (1 Corinthians 14:40).

So What?

Read the following notes from the DVD message "Clear the Clutter and Create the Comfort: There's No Place Like Home" and answer the "Now What" question at the end.

I. Introduction: Home is a refuge.

My parents divorced when I was a young child, and life was full of strife and struggle. At Christmastime, my mother would drive my brother and me from the mid-Atlantic to Atlanta to visit my grandparents. This was before video chatting, e-mail, and unlimited long distance, so it could have been awkward with relatives we visited only once a year. But my grandparents' home exuded love and was so warm and welcoming that the distance that existed in our relationship quickly melted away. It was not the décor or the fact that it was clean and tidy that was so welcoming, but rather it was the special touches that made us feel wanted.

Their home was a refuge for us, a place to recharge. The challenges of this world leave us weary and drained. Jesus tells us that we "are not of the world" (John 17:14), yet we are still burdened by the stress of the day. Our home should provide a sense of relief for our families—a refuge. The world is becoming increasingly hostile, and we need a place where we can let down our guard, take off our armor, and relax.

II. Heart of the Home

A. Home: A Peaceful Dwelling Place

Isaiah 32:18 states, "My people will live in peaceful dwelling places, in secure homes, in undisturbed places of rest" (NIV). Isaiah was telling God's women of the reward that awaited them when complacency ended and the righteous returned to God. This type of home, described by God, is a reward for righteousness! If we are living by the Holy Spirit, our homes should reflect that peace and rest. Let's look at this verse a little more closely:

- Peaceful dwelling places: When we purposefully fill our home with warmth and affection, it promotes peace for our family members.

- Secure homes: When we start applying the concepts we have learned in our lessons about kindness, loving our husbands, and parenting, then our family will feel safe and loved.
- Undisturbed places of rest: When we create an environment that comforts our family and restores their energy, peace, and perseverance, then they are ready to face the wearisome world once more.

B. Home: God-Honoring, Welcoming, and Comfortable

As women, we are to create a house that is a welcoming, loving, and comfortable home. However, the skills of homemaking did not come naturally for me. When I was first married, we had a small house, but I didn't follow my mom's example of good housekeeping. The truth is our home was a wreck. We lived less than ten minutes from my husband's parents, and they would often stop by without notice. I was embarrassed by the mess, so each week-end, after working all week, we would clean a week's worth of dishes, laundry, and mess. We would put away all the misplaced items from downstairs, many times into a cardboard box just to get it out of sight. The public areas in our house were then presentable, but don't look upstairs! By the following Friday, it would be a wreck again. This was our routine for years.

Several years later, after moving to Georgia and having a baby, we had more stuff and a bigger mess with less time. I knew I had to do something when my aunt came for a visit with her new video camera. I cleaned in my usual fashion, getting the downstairs presentable by shoving everything into my room. During her visit, I went upstairs to change my daughter's diaper, and my aunt followed me with her camera. I was mortified! The bedrooms were a wreck. The bathrooms were a wreck. I was a wreck.

III. The Stress of Mess

"For God is not a God of disorder but of peace" (1 Corinthians 14:33, NIV). When our homes are out of sorts, we are not reflecting the orderliness of God and our homes may not be peaceful. If we want a home that reflects our relationship with God, establishing order is a good place to start.

Clutter is like a snowball rolling down a hill. The farther it goes, the bigger it gets. It starts with an item or two out of place and before long (sometimes overnight) it multiplies and grows, taking over the entire house.

For my family it starts with the mail. If it is not dealt with daily, it piles up. That pile is followed by others: the laundry, the coats, the dirty dishes. I began to notice that the messier the house got, the harder it was to relax, and the harder time my kids had focusing on school. I was uncomfortable by the mess but couldn't seem to change the pattern. I had to address my heart issue first.

A. Why do we have so much stuff?

When homes have more stuff than we can store or use, we should look for reasons:

- Greed: we want new, better, and more.
- Sentimental: we are trying to save every memory.
- Indecisive: we can't decide what to do with stuff, so we never part with it in case we might need it in the future.

B. Why do we let clutter and mess take over the house?

There are times in life when our circumstances prevent us from keeping the house in order. However, if the mess is a chronic situation, we can ask God for possible reasons:

- We are lazy and just don't feel like dealing with it.
- We are too busy; our home is not a priority but an afterthought.
- We don't understand the value a clean home can bring to our families.

Once a woman desires a home that would please God, it is time to get to work clearing the clutter, cleaning the home, and creating a comfortable environment. So how do we get a clean and organized home? It can be overwhelming if it does not come naturally.

IV. Clear the clutter.

Proverbs 31:27 says an amazing woman "looks well to the ways of her household." Creating an orderly house begins one room at a time. Work only on that room until it is done, even if it takes several days or weeks. Be patient. It took awhile to become a mess, so it will take awhile to organize it. Remember, there is "a time to keep and a time to throw away" (Ecclesiastes 3:6).

A. Gather sorting materials before starting.

You will need three containers (boxes, bags, trash can, or hamper): one for garbage, one for charity/yard sale items, and one for displaced items. Clearly mark each container.

B. Next is the time to sort and organize.

This process could take a long time depending on the level of clutter. Do not get discouraged or move on to another room until this is done. Set manageable stopping points so it is easy to pick up where you left off. Make it fun by setting a timer and racing yourself, invite someone to work with you, or turn on music and jam along as you go. I work well with an incentive, a small treat to enjoy when I am done with a room. Think of a way to keep motivated to finish the job.

As you decide whether each item is worth saving, consider the following questions:

- Do you have more than enough for your family (such as ten travel toiletry bags or fifteen baskets)?
- Is it something you want to save? (Word of caution: every item has a memory associated with it, but you can't save every memory.)
- Could someone else benefit from it?

Put things in the proper container: garbage, charity/sale, or displaced.

- If it belongs in the room you are working in, put it away.
- If it belongs in another room, put it in the displaced container, and when that is full, take it to its proper place.

C. Assess the mess: why are items out of place?

For example, why are there always coats on the living room chair? Possible answers:

- There's no room in the coat closet.
- The coat closet is not near the family entrance.
- You are leaving again soon and will need it.

D. Common Overlooked Sources of Clutter

- Interrupted projects left on tables, such as craft projects, puzzles, or games: use roll-up mats to keep puzzles intact, and use baskets or bins to store unfinished craft projects or games.
- Jumbled computer or appliance wires: hold these together with twist ties, put all cables in a decorated shoe box with holes cut for the wires, or hide them behind a plant.
- Too many magnets and papers cluttering the refrigerator: time to purge!
- Movies and games: use a storage bin or basket.
- Cleaning products left out where they were used: put them away.
- Piles on the floor because the items have no place to go: designate a place for each item.
- Exercise equipment: use a decorative basket or bin to store.
- Trash or things that could be recycled: put them into the appropriate bin.
- Clean clothes in the wrong place or dirty clothes needing to be laundered: put them away or in the laundry.
- Books and magazines: use a basket to display or throw them away.

Items that are being stored for a future reason should be labeled with the contents, the recipient, and when the person should get it. For example: "Granddaughter—When Married." Move the box to a permanent storage location as soon as it is full.

V. Clean the room.

Now that the clutter is gone, it is time to clean. Work around the room, staying in one area until it is done.

A. Have a cleaning tote.
Bring a tote, bucket, or pocket apron filled with cleaning supplies into the room. It should contain glass cleaner, soap scum remover, furniture polish, dust cloths, and whatever else you might need for that particular room.

B. Wash, dust, and vacuum everything.
Clean everything from highest to lowest: light fixtures, doors, knobs, mirrors, all flat surfaces, walls, baseboards, and everything sitting out. Vacuum last.

C. Make a cleaning plan.
Make a schedule to keep it clean. The bigger the mess, the longer it takes to clean. If you are unable to clean the entire house at one time, schedule different rooms on different days, such as bedrooms on Mondays, bathrooms on Tuesdays, and so on.

VI. Keep it clean.

A. A Place for Everything and Everything in Its Place
We have spent a great deal of effort organizing and cleaning the room. Now we need to reduce the chance of messy buildup reoccurring. You have heard the saying, "A place for everything and everything in its place." The hard part for me was that after I came up with a new way to organize, my family could not follow it, and before I knew it, the house was a mess again. I had to come up with a way that would work for my family—accessible and easily understood. I trained my kids to not put anything down for "just a minute." By insisting on them putting their belongings away immediately, we made huge strides in keeping our home clutter free. I trained them by placing their misplaced item in "quarantine." In order to get it released, they had to do a chore for me. It was an effective lesson.

B. Making Some Changes
It is time to solve the problem of why the mess was there in the first place. Here are some possible problems and their solutions:
- If coats always pile up on the living room chair, is it because the coat closet is too full? Then clean out the closet, leaving only jackets worn daily. Is it because the coat closet is too far from the family entrance? Then hang a coat rack near the entrance.

- If shirts destined for the cleaners end up on the floor, place a bag or different hamper next to the laundry hamper.
- If the kitchen counter always has groceries sitting out, is it because the cabinet is too full? Do you need storage outside of the kitchen? Is there a corner in the basement or another closet you can use for lesser used items? Do you have outdated food? Toss it. Do you have food your family doesn't use? Donate it.

We recently remodeled our kitchen by refinishing our cabinets, and I took the opportunity to reassess the items I stored in my kitchen. Our cabinets were always overflowing. We just didn't have enough room. Our daughters have grown older and the toy closet in the next room was no longer needed, so we decided to convert the toy closet into a pantry. It has made it much easier to see what we have and choose what we want. I love it.

VII. General Organizational Tips

By understanding why the mess occurs, we can prevent it from happening again. On pages 276–278 there are "Extra Tips for Room-by-Room Organization" to help you get started. There are also great ideas in magazines and on the Internet that can inspire us to solve our family's unique organizational challenges.

Every cabinet and closet does not need to be filled with matching interlocking containers to keep our homes organized, even though it looks really nice. The goal is to be able to retrieve items easily and, more importantly, put them away.

- Group like items together. Use baskets, boxes, or plastic bins.
- If you need to stack items, put them in a container that you can easily pull out.
- Label everything. A printed label makes it look official and is fun to use.
- Take a picture of an organized cabinet or closet and tape it to the inside door. This will remind the family of what the space should look like.
- Provide a supply list of consumables in the pantry, laundry room, or linen closet for your family to check off when something is needed.

VIII. Create the comfort.

As a homemaker, we are responsible for keeping our home orderly and making it comfortable. The Bible uses the word *comfort* many times, implying we need it. According to *Strong's Concordance,* the word *comfort* means to "strengthen, give hope, console, and lift the spirit." There are practical things we can add for the comfort of those who live in our home and those who visit. Every home should be a refuge, a warm, cozy place where our families can retreat from the world and receive the most rest possible.

We read in Numbers, "How fair [pleasing, delightful] are your tents, O Jacob, Your dwellings, O Israel!" (24:5). Clearly, the Bible does not go into how to decorate our homes, but this verse seems to suggest that they are to be attractive. Look around and think how you might make your family more comfortable and your home warm and inviting.

A. Welcome Home: The Entryway

Coming home is shifting from the public world to the private world. We are "putting down our armor" and coming to our safe place. The area between the world and the home is the entryway. It might be that area right past the front door that houses a coat closet, or it could be the door the family uses most. It is helpful if this area has the necessary things that make that transition easy. Here are a few items you may want to include:

- A coat closet, a coat stand, or hooks on the wall for storing coats
- A table with a lamp and a mirror over it
- A place for school books and briefcases
- A basket for mail, keys, and cell phones
- A basket for umbrellas

B. Cozy Living Space

All rooms should be comfortable, for the family and for living, not a showcase or a museum. Make choices that accommodate your family's personality.

1. Furniture
   - Furniture comes in all styles, but not all furniture is comfortable.
   - Choose stuffed furniture that is comfy and inviting.
   - Straight-back chairs can be moved easily for conversation.
   - Suiting our family's lifestyle, we like a coffee table we can put our feet on without worrying about damaging it.

2. Pillows and blankets
   - Throws are soft, warm, small blankets that should be within easy reach, such as over the arm of a chair or the back of the couch.
   - Make sure there are plenty of throws for everyone and keep them handy in a basket.
   - Decorative pillows are not only inexpensive decoration but also add comfort.

3. Books
   - Books should be easily accessible.
   - Arrange bookcases with some books standing up and others lying down with something interesting resting on it, such as a photograph or knickknack.
   - A reading nook practically oozes comfort with a soft armchair, side table, reading lamp, and footrest. This is the perfect place to disengage from the world.

4. Pictures
- Pictures of the family add warmth and character to a home.
- Children love to have pictures of themselves around the house.
- However, it can be overdone with lots of pictures on every wall.
- Beware of huge portraits that say "look at me."

C. Restful Bedrooms

One-third of our life is spent in bed. Our bedrooms are our most private space and should be for comfort. The bedroom should be a place for rest and relaxation. Ironing boards, office work, and crafts should be kept for other rooms.

1. Mattress pads
- Thick mattress pads add extra comfort.
- The mattress pad is for protection and hygiene. You can't wash your mattress but you can your mattress pad.

2. Sheets
- 100 percent cotton sheets wear the best and are cool in summer and warm in winter.
- Egyptian cotton or pima cotton sheets are the softest.
- Sheets made of a cotton-polyester blend will not wrinkle but are not as soft and may pill.
- Have two sets of sheets per bed so you can make the bed as one set is washing.

3. Pillows and pillowcases
- Two pillows per person offer support for sleeping or sitting up in bed.
- Pillowcases are inexpensive and protect pillows.

4. Bed coverings
- Blankets and quilts come in all shapes, sizes, and weights.
- Bedspreads cover the bed during the day and offer beauty and neatness.
- A coverlet for the foot of the bed welcomes a restful nap at any time.

5. Maintain cleanliness.
- Make the bed daily.
- Wash the linens weekly.
- Wash the mattress pad and pillowcases monthly.

D. Let there be light.

A well-lit room looks warm and welcoming, especially with the array of lightbulb choices available today. Natural lightbulbs fill the room with a soft glow, while a three-way bulb offers the flexibility for soft to bright task light.

1. Table lamps
   - Ceiling lights can be harsh and glaring.
   - Table lamps provide cozy light while making it comfortable to read.
   - Lamps can be inexpensive and match any décor.
   - Old lamps take on a new look with a can of paint and a new shade.

2. Lampshades
   - Tinted or parchment shades provide cozy light.
   - Pure white shades provide a more modern light.

3. Lamp locations
   In addition to having a lamp at every reading spot, add ambience to the following:
   - Kitchen counters
   - Bathroom vanities
   - Fireplace mantels
   - Front hall table
   - Bedside tables
   - Ledges or bookshelves

4. Dimmers
   Dimmers reduce the harshness of overhead lights, especially in dining rooms and bedrooms.

E. Finishing Touches

There are many little touches we can add to our home to make it welcoming. Realtors know this and "stage" homes. These touches help prospective buyers feel comfortable enough to want to buy.

1. Flowers and plants
   - A bouquet of fresh flowers adds beauty and may last up to two weeks if the water is kept clean.
   - Green plants last for years with proper care and add warmth and interest.

2. Natural light
   - Sunlight adds good cheer to any room.
   - Make it a habit to open the shades first thing in the morning.

3. Candles
   - Scented candles add a wonderful aroma and soft light.
   - Scented candles can interfere with the taste of food, so choose unscented ones for the dining table.
   - Candles are inexpensive enough to use for every evening meal.

4. Magazines
   - Well-chosen magazines can add interest and coziness to a home.
   - They can be attractively displayed on a table or in a basket.

5. Music
   - Whatever the mood we are trying to set in the house, music can help make it.
   - Quiet, soothing music is a calming balm.
   - When working, put on music with a jazzy or uplifting beat.

Here's a comfort tip: turn off the television! Turn it on for special programs you enjoy, but do not let the television stay on all day.

As the keepers of our home, we have the privilege of making a place that our families choose to linger and friends are at ease. When the surroundings are clean and orderly, it is much easier to relax and enjoy your home. The effort we spend in creating a comfortable environment refreshes our family's spirits, consoles their hurts, renews their resolve, and restores their strength. Our homes then reflect the secure home and peaceful dwelling place for undisturbed rest that God describes in Isaiah 32:18. That is why an amazing woman keeps her home!

Now What?

What were the most important points for you personally in this message, "Clear the Clutter and Create the Comfort: There's No Place Like Home"?

Homework Day 2

What?

"Unless the LORD builds the house, they labor in vain who build it" (Psalm 127:1).

So What?

As keepers of the home, how we keep our homes is a choice. An orderly home is the goal. However, once we decide to create a neat and organized home, it is easy to become overwhelmed and discouraged when we first get started.

1. Read Philippians 4:13. What encouragement does this verse give you if you are struggling?

2. Read 1 Corinthians 14:40. What does this verse say about how things should be done?

3. What does God say about how we use our time? Are there ways we can be more effective in our home (see Ephesians 5:15-16)?

4. How are we to do our work (see Colossians 3:23)?

Now What?

1. Enter each room of your house and write down what is out of place and why. Determine what could be done to prevent it in the future. Do you need decorative storage baskets, a coat rack, a key rack, or anything else?

2. Which room are you going to clean up the clutter in first? Gather the supplies. Now begin! Remember to keep focused on one room at a time, stop at a logical time or place, and make it fun and manageable.

Homework Day 3

What?

"My people will live in peaceful dwelling places, in secure homes, in undisturbed places of rest" (Isaiah 32:18, NIV).

So What?

God repeatedly speaks of comfort and rest in His Word, indicating how much we need it. On many occasions, it is God Himself who offers the comfort. We know from our own experience that in times of sorrow, frustration, or disappointment, comfort can come in many forms.

Remember, the word *comfort* means "to strengthen, give hope, console, and lift the spirit." Expanding our understanding, *comfort* also means to lessen pain, grief, or loneliness. If our homes are a place of refuge, a place that offers shelter and safety, then comfort and beauty should be part of the environment.

1. List the different sources of comfort in the following verses:

   Psalm 23:4

   Psalm 119:50

   Psalm 119:76

   2 Corinthians 1:3-4

Now What?

Take time this week to study your home. Are there any changes you would like to make to ensure greater comfort for your family? Consider the following questions:

1. Are the beds comfortable and beautiful? Would a thick mattress cover, throw, or pillows help?

2. Is the lighting good in every room? What can you do to improve it?

3. Are the rooms user-friendly? If not, what is needed to make them so?

4. Are the rooms free of unnecessary clutter? Have you done the homework for day 2?

5. Create a list of the changes you would like to make and schedule time to make them.

Tip: Sleep in your guest room for one night. Make sure you have provided for your guests' needs and comfort in both their bedroom and bathroom (pillows, toothpaste, extra blanket, good lighting, bedside table with tissues, and so on). Before guests arrive, make sure the bed is made with clean sheets.

Extra Tips for
Room-by-Room Organization

KITCHENS:

- Use drawer dividers for utensils.
- Use bins to corral unstructured items, such as bags of snacks or pasta.
- Use a lazy Susan for hard-to-reach areas.
- Store similar foods together in the cabinet and the refrigerator.
- Store items by purpose (example: all bakeware together or all food storage together).
- Use rubberized shelf liners that grip the items. This ensures you are purposely moving items instead of sliding them around.
- Establish work zones for food preparation, cleaning, cooking, and so on.
- Minimize the amount of small appliances left on the counter. Only those used daily should remain. Store appliances that are used weekly in a convenient cabinet and those used once a month or less in an out-of-the-way area.

BATHROOMS:

- Use trays or baskets to corral toiletries used every day.
- Use drawer dividers for toiletries or grooming tools.
- Use baskets or bins to store items under the sink. This makes it easier to bring them up to eye level to find what you are looking for.
- Fold all towels the same way for a uniform fit.
- Put spare toilet tissue in a pretty basket or box, either open or lidded.
- If cabinet space is sparse, install shelves.
- Store spare consumables in another area of the home if space is limited.

BEDROOMS:

- Use under-the-bed containers for items such as spare sheets or blankets, off-season clothing, or other storage items that need to be accessible.
- Store clothes by type and, for added organization, by color (for example: all shirts together sorted by color).
- Put most frequently used items in the most accessible drawers.
- Use drawer dividers for small items.
- Use a large basket to hold decorative pillows when the bed is in use.
- If you don't have a bookshelf, use a drawer of a bedside table or a basket to hold reading material.
- Install hooks on the back of the door for robes or clothes you are wearing again the next day.

LIVING AREAS:

- Have a place nearby for frequently used items, such as games.
- Have a storage place that is easily accessible for the media remote—a cute chest on the coffee table, a basket, or an end table drawer.
- Use baskets or decorative bins to store items on a bookshelf.
- Use drawers or baskets to hold media, such as movies or games. Remember to sort before you store!
- Use a magazine rack or baskets under the end tables or coffee table for newspapers or magazines.
- If toys are a part of your living, consider a toy cabinet with shelves. Toys can be stored in bins by type.

OFFICES:

Storing Paperwork:

- Find a method that works for you—traditional hanging folders, notebooks, open trays, or a paperless storage method.
- The key to successful paper handling is being able to retrieve it when it is needed. Use very descriptive labels such as "Takeout Menus" or "Items to Research in the Future." Then put every piece of paper away immediately.
- File everything alphabetically or by similar function, such as all monthly bills in one section, possibly with their own color tabs.

Mail Handling:

- Handle it once.
- Bring it in and shred or recycle the junk mail.
- Process all remaining mail.
- File bills into a "Bills Due" folder, file items you need to discuss with your spouse in a folder with his name, and so forth.

GARAGES AND BASEMENTS:

- Store similar types of items together (for example: all garden tools together or all car care items together).
- Use large tubs or bins to hold sports equipment.
- Use shelves to store bulky items such as coolers or holiday decorations.

OUTSIDE:

- Use a waterproof bin to store lawn furniture cushions or children's toys in an out-of-the-way location.
- Create a "parking lot" for children's outside toys.

· · ·

The purpose of home organization is to eliminate the piles of stuff that regularly accumulate (aka, clutter) and to make sure that every family member is able to easily retrieve items and, more importantly, put them away. There are times when life becomes very busy and we are not able to devote as much attention as we'd like to keeping the home. But if we are sufficiently organized before those times hit, we will be able to maintain our home with minimal effort.

PART THREE: Be Amazing in the Home

What's for Dinner?

Menus and Food Preparation

Robin Rosebrough

"That the word of God will not be dishonored."

Titus 2:5

DVD Outline

I. **Why Menu Preparation Is Important**
   A. Take the "Mastering Your Menu" test.
   B. Benefits to Preparing Meals in Advance
   C. Meals should always be more than just food.
   D. Roadblocks to Being Prepared
      1. Time constraints
      2. Inexperience
      3. Fatigue
      4. Laziness

II. **The key to success is planning.**
   A. Choosing Food
   B. Think seasonally.
      1. Winter
      2. Spring
      3. Summer
      4. Fall

III. **Practical Applications**
   A. Well-Stocked Pantry, Refrigerator, and Freezer
   B. Organization
   C. Cooking Tips

Discussion Questions

1. What is your roadblock to nightly food preparation?
2. Do you take advantage of cooking seasonally, utilizing God's creation in variety, color, and texture?
3. What is one thing you learned that you can go home and put into practice?

Mastering Your Menu Test

Month by Month

1. Do you know what you are having for dinner tonight?

   Yes _____   Score 5 points

   No _____   Score 1 point

2. How many times do you eat out each week? (average)

   1–2 times _____   Score 5 points

   3–4 times _____   Score 3 points

   5–6 times _____   Score 1 point

3. How many times do you go to the grocery store each week?

   1–2 times _____   Score 5 points

   3–4 times _____   Score 3 points

   5–6 times _____   Score 1 point

4, When was the last time you had guests for dinner?

   Past week _____   Score 5 points

   Past month _____   Score 3 points

   2 mo/longer _____   Score 0 points

5. How often do you sit down as a family for dinner?

   5–7 days a week _____   Score 5 points

   3–4 days a week _____   Score 3 points

   0–2 days a week _____   Score 1 point

Homework Day 1

What?

"Day by day continuing with one mind in the temple, and breaking bread from house to house, they were taking their meals together with gladness and sincerity of heart, praising God and having favor with all the people" (Acts 2:46-47).

So What?

Read the following notes from the DVD message "What's for Dinner? Menus and Food Preparation" and answer the "Now What" question at the end.

I. Why Menu Preparation Is Important

There is a saying that goes, "Some people eat to live and some people live to eat." I am definitely in the "live to eat" category. I grew up in a big Italian family where food was a big deal. We did all our socializing over food. We would sit at the table for hours, and food was always present. I don't remember a time that my relatives were not prepared to put something on the table in front of us. In my own home there are just two of us now, but I still enjoy cooking; however, it does take time. And you have to spend time to save it. Planning not only saves time but also eliminates stress.

A. Take the "Mastering Your Menu" test.

Take the "Mastering Your Menu" test at the beginning of this session. The number of points you earned indicates the following:

- 25 points: Congratulations! You don't need this teaching.
- 16 points or more: You are going to learn something.
- 15 points or less: You desperately need this teaching!

This teaching is twofold:

First, it will demonstrate the importance of planning family meals. Busy schedules of both parents and children make it harder to have family dinners. But you may not be aware of the benefits that come with regularly eating together at the table. Research suggests that having dinner together as a family at least four times a week has positive effects on child development. Family dinners have been linked to a lower risk of obesity, substance abuse, and eating disorders.[23]

Second, it will help you see how a well-stocked pantry, refrigerator, and freezer will allow you to be prepared and to serve others. Disaster and sickness give no warning. I personally experienced this earlier this year when I took a fall and severely injured my foot. Even though I was off my feet for six weeks, we were able to eat for weeks out of my freezer.

My favorite story in Scripture of a woman who was well prepared is the story of Abigail (see 1 Samuel 25). King David and his men were very hungry and they asked her husband, Nabal, to help them. He refused, so David had a plan to kill him. Abigail learned of her husband's foolishness and she immediately took action. She definitely had a well-stocked tent because she fixed two hundred loaves of bread, one hundred clusters of raisins, two hundred cakes of pressed figs, five sheep that were already prepared, and five measures of roasted grain. Due to her preparedness and generosity, she saved her household from disaster.

Having organized lives today may not have such dramatic results as it did for Abigail, but we are to take care of our families. There is a lot of research that shows that the family dinner hour is an important part of healthy living. We can develop both skill and creativity in planning menus and serving well-cooked meals. It helps if we judge this task by the value it has to the family unit.

B. Benefits to Preparing Meals in Advance
There are many benefits to preparing meals in advance:
- It is a stress buster.
- It makes your home more peaceful.
- It cares for family and brings connectedness.
- It helps provide nutritious and balanced food for healthy living. Statistics show that nearly one in five children aged six to nineteen in the United States is overweight. This puts them at higher risk for health problems later in life, including heart disease, high blood pressure, and diabetes, as well as emotional problems. Teaching nutritious eating when they are young encourages healthy eating habits that they will carry into adulthood.
- A big benefit is that you won't gain ten pounds from eating out several times a week like I did when our daughter went off to college! The average restaurant meal has as much as 60 percent more calories than a homemade meal.
- A huge benefit is that teens whose families eat together at least five times a week have a much lower chance of smoking, drinking, and using drugs. Children who eat with their family generally have better grades in school.[24] Also, you and your kids will talk more and therefore you'll be more likely to hear about a serious problem.

C. Meals should always be more than just food.
Meals should be a time of:
- Relaxation
- Family bonding that produces a sense of security and togetherness

- Enhanced communication. By engaging your children in conversation, you teach them how to listen and provide them a chance to express their opinions. This allows your children to have an active voice within the family.
- Expressing loving care in the home.

This shows how very important this task is! Eating well is one of life's important and enjoyable experiences, so we need to be willing to devote time and energy to it.

When our daughter was in high school, I decided she needed some practice in the kitchen. So we told her she would begin once a week to plan, shop for, and prepare a meal. Her response was resistant, but she took on the task. At the beginning, she was more cautious about choosing her menu, but as time went on, she became more comfortable in the kitchen and her menus became more challenging. It proved to be good training. Today she is married and is a mother, and she plans and prepares meals for her family daily. She constantly tries new recipes (she has good eaters) and is not intimidated in the kitchen.

Train your children to assist in the kitchen. Teach them to set the table and to help with preparing the meal. Even young children can mix in a bowl or make a salad. This training will help develop future cooks!

D. Roadblocks to Being Prepared
1. Time constraints: "I don't have time."

So often this is the case with our busy schedules. This is why meals aren't on the table at home and takeout becomes an option.

2. Inexperience: "I don't know how."

Today there are so many resources that give even the least knowledgeable cook the ability to show her family care by providing healthy meals. The Internet is a wealth of information.

3. Fatigue: "I'm just too tired!"

This one can get any of us. But a well-stocked freezer helps!

4. Laziness: "I just don't want to."

If this one is your issue, you need an attitude change! Remember, attitude is a choice.

II. The key to success is planning.

A. Choosing Food
Food should be chosen for its nutrition value but also to give variety and interest to meals. It should be chosen to give pleasure, to bring cheer after a hard day, or to comfort others in pain. Meals should be varied and show imagination. Variety makes food more interesting to cook, as well as to serve and eat.

God created things for us to enjoy richly. He designed us with taste buds, a delicate sense of smell, and a sensitive appreciation and response to texture and color. Eye appeal (we do eat with our eyes first) as well as taste should be remembered when preparing food. This is true if you are cooking for two or twenty-two.

Plan meals that that are more extravagant for celebrations: successes of family members, birthdays, good news, and answered prayers.

You don't need an extravagant food budget to serve food with variety and good taste.

B. Think seasonally.

1. Winter

From hearty root vegetables to bright sweet citrus, winter produce offers a surprising range of flavors. Get inspired by what is available.

Winter vegetables include squashes (butternut and acorn are my personal favorites). You can stuff either of them for a meal, or you can turn them upside down on a cookie sheet and roast them. An excellent way to prepare butternut squash is to cut it up, put it in an aluminum foil pocket with butter and brown sugar, and bake it. It is delicious served with barbecue. Other vegetables in season are parsnips, sweet or white potatoes, brussels sprouts, beets, and turnips, which are delicious cut up in one-inch squares and roasted in a high-heat oven coated with extra-virgin olive oil, salt, and pepper.

The obvious comfort foods of winter are soups, stews, and chili. This becomes a complete meal when served with a side salad and warm bread. It warms the soul. The options are numerous as to what kinds of soups and chili to make. Always make big pots so you can freeze some (think preparedness). Soup is the best way to empty your produce drawer. Remember, "waste not, want not" as you think creatively. Maybe the recipe doesn't call for green beans, corn, or cabbage, but you have it in your vegetable bin. Throw it in the soup. You can do the same with frozen vegetables that have a little bit left in the bag. You have to think outside the box, or recipe.

Other comfort foods that are good winter choices are chicken pot pie, meatloaf, and casseroles. These are robust, hearty, and will stay with you on cold winter nights.

2. Spring

As the weather warms, there are vegetables that start to become abundant and less expensive. Asparagus and peas top the list and are delicious served alongside ham.

This is also a good season for brisket, flank steak, and hamburgers, all inexpensive cuts of meat that with some preplanning and marinating can be delicious.

Seafood is wonderful in the spring, and the price comes down. Tilapia is a very mild fish that is inexpensive and can be grilled or pan sautéed and used in fish tacos.

Pastas are also good in the spring as main dishes, topped with vegetables and sauces that please even children.

3. Summer

This is the most abundant season with the largest variety of produce. You can make meals with vegetables in season.

This is also a great time to make full use of a grill. You can even grill vegetables. Eggplant, zucchini, squash, onions, mushrooms, asparagus, and peppers all grill beautifully with a little olive oil, salt, and pepper brushed on them. They can be made ahead and served cold. Make extra and use them the next day over a salad.

Frittatas (an egg dish with vegetables) are a fast way to use leftover vegetables and are a good source of protein.

A fun meal to make is pizza, where each family member makes his or her own. Grocery stores sell premade pizza dough in the bakery section. It's easy and as good as homemade. Again, think outside the box!

Salads can be a main dish when served with three ounces of protein. Start with two cups of shredded lettuce per person. Add one cup of fruits or veggies per person, such as edamame, avocado, broccoli, zucchini, cucumber, carrot, peppers, snow peas, red onion, celery, artichoke hearts, peaches, strawberries, raspberries, blueberries, apples, pears, mandarin oranges, dried apricots, or cranberries. Next add protein. This can be cheese (blue, feta, parmesan, cheddar, or mozzarella), chicken, shrimp, grilled salmon, bacon, tuna, diced ham, deli turkey, or flank steak. Finally, give it some crunch: toasted nuts, sunflower seeds, croutons, or french fried onion rings.

Tip: When fruits and vegetables are so inexpensive, freeze them for the winter. Berries, corn, and green beans are all wonderful frozen and hold up well in recipes.

4. Fall

As the weather begins to turn cooler, leave the lighter fare and move to a little bit more substantial cooking.

Pork roast is my first thought in the fall, marinated and served with roasted root vegetables.

Pumpkin can be used in a multitude of ways, such as soup, muffins, or bread. Think more than dessert for this nutritious vegetable.

Meatloaf, stews (including Brunswick stew), roasted chicken or turkey, and pot roast are all good fall menus.

III. Practical Applications

A. Well-Stocked Pantry, Refrigerator, and Freezer

Let's shift to a well-stocked pantry as it relates to preparedness and the ability to serve others. Seasons of life, sickness, injury, accidents, and death do not give warning. You should have on hand items to enable you to throw together a meal for your family or for someone else's in a day's notice. If you have to run to the grocery store more than once a week, it is costing you valuable time and money. The goal is to be able to prepare a meal with what you have at home or to pull an already prepared meal out of your freezer.

In a few weeks, Michele will teach you how to stock your cupboards and freezer using coupons and weekly specials.

Here are a few suggestions for being prepared:

- Cook simultaneously. When making meatloaf, make two and freeze one. All soups and chili can be frozen, so make big pots. When I make spaghetti sauce, I make a huge pot and freeze it in multiple containers. I always have sauce in the freezer.
- Leftover pork roast or beef roast can be shredded for barbecue a few days later. Repurpose what you cook, and it will make a completely different meal a few days later.
- Leftover rice and mashed potatoes can be thrown into soups or stews. Bigger is better! When you cook rice, cook double and freeze it or use it in another recipe. Or you can make an entire meal of fried rice by adding meat and vegetables.
- When you buy rotisserie chicken, buy two and cut one up to freeze. You then have meat ready for a casserole or a soup. You've saved time by thinking ahead.
- With one rotisserie chicken you can make a casserole, fried rice, or chicken salad; add it to a salad; shred it for tacos, enchiladas, or quesadillas; add it to soup, stew, or chili; or add barbecue or hot wing sauce and serve on top of a baked potato.
- Embrace convenience. Stores are full of shortcuts: pizza dough, chopped-up veggies, bagged salad, chopped garlic, and quick-cooking grains, just to name a few. While they cost more, they are time savers, so you are paying for that convenience.
- Keep healthy snacks on hand. Stock fresh fruit, nuts, and low-fat cheese for kids to snack on after school.

B. Organization

Here are some tips for effective organization:

- Drawers and cabinets should be arranged for faster, more efficient preparation of food.
- Get rid of clutter on your kitchen counters; you need the room to work.
- Spices are best laid out in a drawer in alphabetical order. Be sure to keep them away from heat.
- Organize your grocery list by category, such as dairy, produce, meat, frozen foods, and so on. This saves time while shopping.
- Plan a menu choosing dishes that complement each other in both taste and color. Start with a main course and then plan the rest of the menu around it. Magazines and cookbooks give complete menus.
- Find a go-to source for recipes. The Internet is a wealth of information. Several magazines offer "super-fast recipes."

C. Cooking Tips

- Use the Crock-Pot. Put everything together before leaving in the morning and come home to a delicious cooked meal.
- Always line your baking sheets with aluminum foil so you never have to wash the pan.
- Always keep lemons on hand. A squeeze can be added to soups and stews at the end of their cooking time to brighten the flavors.
- The most important key ingredient is salt. Kosher is my choice.
- Good wine vinegars, fresh squeezed lemon or lime juice, coffee (which intensifies chocolate), and fresh herbs are wonderful additions to foods and add a big punch of flavor.
- Larger, tougher cuts of meat such as brisket, chuck roasts, and bottom round work best with moist heat methods such as braising or stewing.
  - ★ *Braising* (cooking in a small amount of liquid at a low temperature) helps moisten meat and soften collagen fibers.
  - ★ *Stewing* is similar, but smaller pieces of meat are immersed in liquid and then slow-cooked. When done, let the meat rest ten minutes to reabsorb its juices and then slice thinly across the grain to further tenderize.

Don't let the demands and challenges of your life keep you out of the kitchen. Aim for variety, creativity, and nutrition to prepare meals your family will enjoy eating. Abigail was prepared, and it prevented disaster for her entire household. We can be prepared to show our family love and security by providing for their basic needs. Don't let the chaos of life keep you from being a worthy keeper of your home. An amazing woman plans well to take care of her family.

Now What?

What were the most important points for you personally in this message, "What's for Dinner? Menus and Food Preparation"?

Homework Day 2

What?

"Give us this day our daily bread" (Matthew 6:11).

So What?

The Lord's Prayer reminds us of our constant dependence on God for everything we need to sustain us. Cooking for our families is more than just preparing food. Mealtimes can foster communication and bonding and show love and care. They provide a feeling of connectedness, as well as nutrition and basic needs. Planning ahead has many benefits, including reducing stress and creating a peaceful home.

Bread was the primary food of people in Bible times. Bread has special significance in the Bible—it represents the sustenance of life in the world. It was regarded by Jews as a gift from God.

1. What principles or lessons can we learn for our family mealtimes from Jesus' attitude and actions in Matthew 14:15-20?

Jesus always thanked the Father before eating to acknowledge that everything comes from God alone. We need to begin each meal by thanking God as well.

2. What do we learn from the Proverbs 31 woman regarding food (see verses 14-15)?

With proper planning and the use of our freezer, we can provide for our family's needs quite easily; therefore, we are without excuse.

Now What?

This will be a practical lesson. Print a calendar off the computer, create one on paper, or use the "Meal Planner" on page 293 to plan your menus for one week. First, place your family's schedule on the calendar. Highlight the nights that will be a mealtime challenge because of schedules. You might choose a Crock-Pot meal here. Next, decide your source for recipes. You can choose family favorites, cookbooks, or the Internet. As you plan, simultaneously make a grocery list (see "Weekday Meal Plan and Shopping List" on page 294). Remember to cook extra to freeze or to share with another who is in need or crisis.

Now that you know how to plan a menu and are prepared with the necessary food, enjoy the task! Think creatively and use variety! And remember, "Man shall not live on bread alone, but on every word that proceeds out of the mouth of God" (Matthew 4:4).

Homework Day 3

What?

"Our people must learn to devote themselves to doing what is good, in order that they may provide for daily necessities and not live unproductive lives" (Titus 3:14, NIV).

So What?

Eating well is one of life's important issues, so we need to be willing to devote time and energy to it. Scripture has lots of lessons on the importance of preparedness, and planning and cooking for our families and others should be at the top of the priority list. Having plenty for our loved ones makes us amazing providers.

1. Summarize what these proverbs from *The Message* say it takes to provide meals for our families.

   a. "Hard work always pays off; mere talk puts no bread on the table" (Proverbs 14:23).

   b. "A commonsense person lives good sense; fools litter the country with silliness" (Proverbs 13:16).

2. What did God tell Noah to do before the flood (see Genesis 6:21)?

   Throughout the Bible, the Lord gives examples of keeping one's pantry stocked. Noah was told to take every kind of food that would be eaten and store it away for his family and the animals.

3. Another example is the story of Joseph. What did God, speaking through Joseph, tell Pharaoh to do (see Genesis 41:25-30, 35-36)?

Pharaoh had a dream about seven lean cows and seven fat cows. The Lord used Joseph to prepare the entire country of Egypt for a famine that would not occur for seven more years. In these preparations of stocking up, not only was Egypt saved, but the nation of Israel was also rescued.

4. What was Nabal's attitude toward feeding strangers in need (see 1 Samuel 25:9-11)?

Abigail had a foolish husband named Nabal (his name means "fool"). Abigail was prepared when she heard her husband's life was in danger. She was able to save her household through the hard work of preparing food. If there is profit to you in your toil to organize and produce a well-cooked meal every night, let us begin like Abigail with a well-stocked pantry, refrigerator, and freezer.

Now What?

1. In order to prepare, you need an inventory of what you already have. Start with your pantry and compare it to the pantry list in your workbook (see pages 299–300). Make a list of items you need to add to your pantry. Each week, add a few of these items to your shopping list.

2. Next, take an inventory of all meat, vegetables, and prepared meals in your freezer (see page 301).

3. What is an action step you will take this week to be prepared?

Meal Planner

Week _____

Sunday

Main Course

Cookbook   Page

Vegetable

Dessert

Notes

Monday

Main Course

Cookbook   Page

Vegetable

Dessert

Notes

Tuesday

Main Course

Cookbook   Page

Vegetable

Dessert

Notes

Wednesday

Main Course

Cookbook   Page

Vegetable

Dessert

Notes

Thursday

Main Course

Cookbook   Page

Vegetable

Dessert

Notes

Friday

Main Course

Cookbook   Page

Vegetable

Dessert

Notes

Saturday

Main Course

Cookbook   Page

Vegetable

Dessert

Notes

Special Ingredients

☐

☐

☐

☐

☐

☐

☐

☐

Weekday Meal Plan and Shopping List

Menu	Produce	Dairy & Refrigerated	Meat, Poultry, & Fish	Frozen	Dry Goods & Miscellaneous

Recipes

Hodgepodge Soup

1½ pounds ground beef
1½ cups chopped celery
¾ cup chopped onion
1 clove garlic, minced
3 10 oz. cans Campbell's condensed minestrone soup

1 30 oz. can baked beans in tomato sauce
3 cups water
1 teaspoon dried oregano
1 tablespoon Worcestershire sauce

In large pot, cook beef, celery, onion, and garlic until the beef is browned. Add soup, beans, water, oregano, and Worcestershire sauce. Bring to a boil, reduce heat, cover, and simmer for 20 minutes. Season with salt and pepper to taste. Serves 10.

Marie's Cornbread

1 stick butter, melted
1 8 oz. container sour cream
2 eggs, slightly beaten

1 8.5 oz. can whole corn
1 8.5 oz. box Jiffy corn muffin mix

Preheat oven to 400 degrees. Grease an 8 x 8 baking dish. In a bowl, mix butter, sour cream, eggs, corn, and muffin mix. Pour into baking dish. Bake 25–30 minutes. Serves 9.

Shrimp & Grits Casserole

1 cup grits—cooked until stiff
2 cups Monterey Jack cheese
1 cup sour cream
½ cup sautéed onions

½ cup chopped parsley
1½ cups cooked shrimp
1 cup thin-sliced Andouille sausage

1. Fold all together with 1 cup of the cheese. Reserve the other cup to sprinkle on top.
2. Bake uncovered at 350 degrees for 30 minutes. Serves 6. (Can prepare ahead and refrigerate.)

Hot Chicken Salad

(Taken from *Southern Living*)

3 cups cooked chicken

2 cups chopped celery

1 cup green pepper

1 medium onion, chopped

1 can water chestnuts, sliced or chopped

1 stick butter, melted

1 cup cooked rice

1 can cream of mushroom soup

1 teaspoon lemon juice

1 cup Helmann's mayonnaise

1 cup sliced almonds

Mix all together and place in casserole dish. Bake 30 minutes at 350 degrees. Then add one cup sliced almonds mixed with butter to top of the casserole and bake 10 more minutes.

Cranberry Chicken

1 can whole cranberries

1 small chopped onion

¾ cup orange juice

¼ teaspoon cinnamon

¼ teaspoon ginger

6 boneless chicken halves

1. Whisk whole cranberry sauce to make it liquid from its congealed state. Combine with spices, onion, and orange juice in a saucepan and bring to a simmer.
2. Flour chicken and brown in small amount of oil. Place in baking dish.
3. Pour sauce over chicken. Bake at 350 degrees for 35–40 minutes.
4. Serve with wild rice and fresh steamed green beans.

Crock-Pot Roast

1 rump roast

1 can cream of mushroom soup

1 cup red wine

potatoes, carrots, parsnips, onions

1. Place all the ingredients in your Crock-Pot in the morning.
2. Mix the wine with the soup and pour over the meat and vegetables.
3. Put the lid on and cook on low for about 8 hours.
4. Serve with warm bread.

Crock-Pot BBQ Sandwiches

1 Boston butt pork roast
1 large onion, peeled and cut into chunks
1 bottle Bull's-Eye BBQ sauce
sandwich rolls

1. Place roast in Crock-Pot with the onion and cook it all day on low.
2. When close to serving time, remove the roast and pull off fat and bone. Shred the meat and place it back in the Crock-Pot with the BBQ sauce.
3. Slightly warm the rolls and serve with meat.
4. Any extra can easily be frozen for another meal.

Cheese & Pasta in Pot

1 8 oz. package shell macaroni
2 pounds lean ground beef
2 medium onions, chopped
1 clove garlic, crushed
1 14 oz. jar spaghetti sauce

1 16 oz. can stewed tomatoes
1 3 oz. can sliced mushrooms
1½ pints (24 oz.) sour cream, divided
8 oz. sliced provolone cheese
12 oz. sliced mozzarella cheese

1. Cook macaroni according to package directions, drain, rinse, and set aside.
2. In a large frypan or dutch oven, sauté together the meat, onion, and garlic. Drain off any excess grease.
3. Add the spaghetti sauce, tomatoes, and mushrooms and simmer for 30 minutes.
4. In a large greased casserole, layer as follows: ½ pasta shells, ½ meat sauce, ¾ pints (12 oz.) sour cream, provolone cheese, and the remainder of the pasta, meat sauce, and sour cream. Top with sliced mozzarella. Cover and bake at 350 degrees for 40 minutes. Remove the cover and continue to bake until cheese melts and browns slightly. Serves 8–10.

Orange Cream Salad

1 20 oz. can pineapple tidbits
1 16 oz. can peach slices, drained
1 11 oz. can mandarin oranges, drained
2 medium bananas, sliced
1 medium apple, chopped

1 3.4 oz. package instant vanilla pudding
1½ cups milk
⅓ cup frozen orange juice concentrate
¾ cup sour cream

1. In large salad bowl, combine fruits and set aside.
2. In small bowl, beat pudding, milk, and orange juice for 2 minutes.
3. Add sour cream and mix well.
4. Spoon pudding over fruit and toss to coat.
5. Cover and chill for at least 2 hours. Serves 8–10.

Mixed Green Salad

¼ cup red wine vinegar

1 tablespoon Dijon mustard

1 tablespoon fresh thyme

¾ cup olive oil

2 5 oz. bags mixed greens

7 ounces dried cranberries

1½ cups glazed pecans or walnuts

1 5.5 oz. log goat cheese, crumbled

1. Whisk vinegar, mustard, and thyme in a small bowl and add oil. Season with salt and pepper.
2. Mix greens, cranberries, and pecans in a large bowl and mix in enough dressing to coat.
3. Sprinkle with cheese.

Crock-Pot Mac and Cheese

1 stick butter, cut into chunks

2 12 oz. cans evaporated milk

3 cups milk (I use skimmed)

1 teaspoon salt

4 eggs

4 cups grated sharp cheddar cheese (about 16 ounces)

2 cups grated medium cheddar cheese (about 8 ounces)

16 oz. box macaroni (uncooked)

1. Place butter in the Crock-Pot insert and melt in the microwave. Twirl melted butter to coat sides of insert and add all milk, salt, and eggs. Whisk lightly to mix eggs with the milk. Add grated cheese and macaroni (without cooking). Mix well and cook for 3–4 hours on low.
2. You can easily make half of this recipe for a small Crock-Pot.
3. If you do not have a removable insert, butter the Crock-Pot before adding melted butter and remaining ingredients.

Nonperishable Pantry Items

Spices and Seasonings
- [ ] Adobo
- [ ] Balsamic vinegar
- [ ] Basil
- [ ] Bay leaf
- [ ] Beef bouillon granules
- [ ] Cayenne pepper
- [ ] Celery seed
- [ ] Chicken bouillon granules
- [ ] Chili powder
- [ ] Chili spice blend (homemade)
- [ ] Chives
- [ ] Cider vinegar
- [ ] Cilantro
- [ ] Cinnamon
- [ ] Cooking sherry
- [ ] Cumin
- [ ] Curry powder
- [ ] Dehydrated onion
- [ ] Dill
- [ ] Dry mustard
- [ ] Dry red wine
- [ ] Garlic powder
- [ ] Garlic salt
- [ ] Good Seasons Italian dressing mix
- [ ] Ground ginger
- [ ] Hot sauce
- [ ] Italian seasoning
- [ ] Ketchup
- [ ] Lemon pepper
- [ ] Liquid smoke
- [ ] Marjoram
- [ ] Nutmeg
- [ ] Onion powder
- [ ] Onion soup mix
- [ ] Oregano
- [ ] Paprika
- [ ] Parsley
- [ ] Pepper
- [ ] Poppy seed
- [ ] Ranch dressing mix
- [ ] Red wine vinegar
- [ ] Rice vinegar
- [ ] Rosemary
- [ ] Salt
- [ ] Sesame oil
- [ ] Taco seasoning mix
- [ ] Tarragon
- [ ] Thyme
- [ ] Vinegar
- [ ] White cooking wine
- [ ] Worcestershire sauce

Baking Needs
- [ ] Almond extract
- [ ] Baking powder
- [ ] Baking soda
- [ ] Biscuit mix
- [ ] Bread crumbs (regular and Panko)
- [ ] Bread flour
- [ ] Confectioners' sugar
- [ ] Corn meal
- [ ] Cornstarch
- [ ] Corn syrup
- [ ] Evaporated milk
- [ ] Flour (all-purpose and self-rising)
- [ ] Honey
- [ ] Jell-O packages (miscellaneous sizes and flavors for fruit salads)
- [ ] Nonstick cooking spray
- [ ] Olive oil
- [ ] Olive oil spray
- [ ] Rolled oats
- [ ] Stuffing mix
- [ ] Sugar
- [ ] Vanilla extract
- [ ] Vegetable oil
- [ ] Wheat berries (for grinding and making bread)

Beans
- [ ] 15 bean soup mix
- [ ] Pinto beans
- [ ] Black beans
- [ ] Kidney beans
- [ ] Lentils
- [ ] Red beans
- [ ] White navy beans

Fruit
- [ ] Pineapple, crushed
- [ ] Raisins/Craisins

Miscellaneous
- [ ] Coffee
- [ ] Croutons
- [ ] Graham crackers
- [ ] Peanut butter
- [ ] Taco shells
- [ ] Tea bags

Pasta and Rice
- [ ] Egg noodles
- [ ] Elbow macaroni
- [ ] Fettuccini
- [ ] Linguini
- [ ] Rice (brown, calrose, instant, white, wild)
- [ ] Rice noodles
- [ ] Shells (jumbo, medium)
- [ ] Vermicelli
- [ ] Yellow rice packets
- [ ] Wild rice packets

Vegetables (Canned)

- [ ] Cut corn
- [ ] Creamed corn
- [ ] Green beans
- [ ] Mushroom pieces
- [ ] Peas
- [ ] Pimientos
- [ ] Roasted red peppers
- [ ] Rotel (diced tomatoes and green chiles)
- [ ] Tomatoes (crushed, diced, sauce, and paste)
- [ ] Water chestnuts, sliced

Other Canned Goods

- [ ] Beef broth, several cans
- [ ] Chicken broth, several cans
- [ ] Coconut milk (for Thai dishes)
- [ ] Cream soups
- [ ] Enchilada sauce, red and green
- [ ] Green chiles, diced
- [ ] Salsa
- [ ] Spaghetti sauce

Paper and Plastic

- [ ] Heavy-duty foil
- [ ] Parchment paper
- [ ] Plastic baggies (freezer and storage, all sizes)
- [ ] Plastic wrap
- [ ] Roasting bags, turkey size
- [ ] Wax paper

Refrigerator & Produce Items

Many of the items listed will vary based on your preference. Some of them will be used regularly in menus (like cheese—but you may prefer one type of cheese over another), but some are just items to keep on hand for your own use, such as condiments like salad dressings and relish. Stock what you use regularly and ignore the rest.

Cheese

- [ ] American cheese slices
- [ ] Cottage cheese
- [ ] Feta cheese
- [ ] Shredded cheese (cheddar, mozzarella, Parmesan, Mexican blend; can also be frozen)
- [ ] Velveeta cheese (store brand unless it is on sale)

Condiments

- [ ] Barbecue sauce
- [ ] Dill pickle spears
- [ ] Fruit preserves (100% fruit)
- [ ] Hot sauce
- [ ] Lemon juice
- [ ] Lime juice
- [ ] Mayonnaise
- [ ] Salad dressing
- [ ] Salad peppers or relish
- [ ] Soy sauce/tamari
- [ ] Teriyaki sauce
- [ ] Yellow mustard

Dairy

- [ ] Butter
- [ ] Buttermilk
- [ ] Cream cheese
- [ ] Eggs
- [ ] Milk
- [ ] Plain yogurt
- [ ] Sour cream

Meat

- [ ] Bacon or bacon bits
- [ ] Deli meat (various kinds for sandwiches)
- [ ] Pepperoni

Miscellaneous

- [ ] Crescent roll dough (for last-minute meals with a crust)
- [ ] Whole wheat tortillas
- [ ] Yeast

Produce

- [ ] Carrots
- [ ] Garlic cloves
- [ ] Green bell peppers (1–2 depending on the season)
- [ ] Lettuce leaves
- [ ] Mushrooms
- [ ] Onions (a bag)
- [ ] Salad mix
- [ ] Apples
- [ ] Bananas
- [ ] Grapes

Freezer Items

Most of these items are based on your preference. Some of them will be used regularly in menus (like ground beef, cooked chicken, and cooked onions), but some are just items to keep on hand for your own use, like frozen vegetables for soups and side dishes. Most families choose to adjust these items based on their preference, so do not stock up on vegetables that your family does not like just because they are on our list.

Fish
- ☐ Baby shrimp (for stir fry or fried rice)
- ☐ Tilapia (bags of individually frozen fillets)

Frozen Fruit
- ☐ Bagged berries, miscellaneous (for smoothies)

Frozen Vegetables
- ☐ Asparagus
- ☐ Breaded okra
- ☐ Broccoli cuts
- ☐ Cauliflower
- ☐ Edamame
- ☐ Hash browns
- ☐ Mixed vegetables (for fried rice, soups, and casseroles)
- ☐ Okra (not breaded)
- ☐ Peas
- ☐ Peas and carrots
- ☐ Shoepeg corn

- ☐ Stew vegetables
- ☐ Stir fry vegetables
- ☐ Sugar snap peas
- ☐ Tater tots

Meat
- ☐ Beef hot links
- ☐ Beef (ground, roast, stew, and flank)
- ☐ Chicken (whole and breasts)
- ☐ Hot dogs
- ☐ Hot Italian sausage
- ☐ Kielbasa
- ☐ Pepperoni
- ☐ Pork chops

Miscellaneous
- ☐ Miscellaneous meals that have been prepared and frozen
- ☐ Nuts (almonds, pecans, pinenuts, walnuts)
- ☐ Seeds (sunflower seeds, sesame seeds)

- ☐ Puff pastry sheets
- ☐ Shredded cheese (several bags each of mozzarella, cheddar, Mexican blend, and Parmesan)
- ☐ Tortellini
- ☐ Ravioli

Prepared Ingredients
- ☐ Black beans, cooked
- ☐ Buttermilk biscuit dough
- ☐ Chicken, cooked and diced or shredded
- ☐ Ground beef, browned
- ☐ Ham, cooked and diced
- ☐ Meatballs
- ☐ Peppers, chopped and sautéed
- ☐ Onions, chopped and sautéed
- ☐ Prepared chili
- ☐ Prepared spaghetti sauce

The Door Is Open, the Light Is On!

Hospitality

Pat Harley

"That the word of God will not be dishonored."

Titus 2:5

DVD Outline

I. **Introduction**
   A. Hospitality Defined
   B. Biblical Examples

II. **Scriptural Foundation for Hospitality**
   A. God commands us to practice hospitality.
   Principle 1: God commands Christians to habitually show hospitality to brothers and sisters in the faith.
   B. It is part of the role of a woman.
   Principle 2: God sees hospitality as a part of the role of a woman and worthy of honor from the church. Hospitality includes kindness and care to strangers.
   C. We may receive heavenly blessings.
   Principle 3: When we practice hospitality we have the opportunity to receive heavenly blessings, and there is a clear statement that we may even entertain angels unaware.
   D. We are to be hospitable without complaining.
   Principle 4: All hospitality should be done with an attitude of good cheer and no complaining.
   E. Hospitality demands nothing in return.
   Principle 5: Hospitality demands nothing in return. Your reward is not on this earth, but there is a promised reward reserved for you that is eternal.

III. **Stumbling Blocks to Hospitality**
   A. Pride
   B. Fear
   C. Disobedience/Laziness
   D. Inexperience
   E. Being Overextended

IV. **Benefits of Being Hospitable**
   A. It can offer care and comfort to the hurting and brokenhearted.
   B. It can be a great tool to reach your neighbors for Christ.
   C. It can provide help for those with physical needs.
   D. It can provide special ministry to women.

V. **Final Thoughts on Hospitality**
   A. The Role of Food
   B. What It Will Cost You

C. What You Will Gain

D. What You Don't Need

E. What You Need

Discussion Questions

1. What are some specific ways people have made you feel cared for and wanted in their homes?

2. Have you ever experienced "negative hospitality" (for example, words or actions that made you feel unwelcome)? If so, what was that like?

3. What are some of the stumbling blocks you deal with when it comes to hospitality?

4. What would have to change for you to be more hospitable?

Homework Day 1

What?

"Be devoted to one another in brotherly love; give preference to one another in honor; not lagging behind in diligence, fervent in spirit, serving the Lord; rejoicing in hope, persevering in tribulation, devoted to prayer, contributing to the needs of the saints, practicing hospitality" (Romans 12:10-13).

So What?

Read the following notes from the DVD message "The Door Is Open, the Light Is On! Hospitality" and answer the "Now What" question at the end.

I. Introduction

When my beloved and I came to Christ, we had been married ten years. Christ saved us from ourselves and a lot of misery. He totally changed our lives and immediately put us in a strong Christian community. We were surrounded with mature believers who had so much to give in terms of service to Christ, but we felt we had nothing. One night we were talking about how we might serve. We had little money, so our meager tithe seemed so small. We knew nothing about the Bible, so teaching was out of the question. But we did have an empty bedroom. So that night we gave that bedroom to God and asked Him to use it for His glory. God took us at our word and began to bring people to our home, our table, and that bedroom. We began to understand why He commands His people to practice hospitality.

A. Hospitality Defined

What is the definition of hospitality? The *Oxford American Dictionary* says, "It is the friendly and generous reception and entertainment of guests." Biblically, it is meeting the needs of strangers and Christian friends alike, even our enemies. It is bringing others into our homes, feeding them, and offering fellowship. The Greek word is *philoxenia,* which simply means "the love of strangers."

B. Biblical Examples

There are many examples in the Bible that demonstrate the practice of hospitality. Here are just a few:

- Abraham saw three strangers coming his way as he sat at the door of his tent. He jumped up and ran to meet the strangers, bowed at their feet, and asked them to

PART THREE: Be Amazing in the Home

stay for a while. He brought water to wash their feet and offered a restful place for them to relax. He then had an extravagant meal of bread cakes made of fine flour, choice beef, curds, and milk. He showed them true hospitality (see Genesis 18:1-8).

- Mary and Martha welcomed Jesus into their home, providing good food and a listening ear (see Luke 10:38-42).
- On two occasions Jesus took care of the needs of thousands of His guests by providing a fish dinner (see Matthew 15:38; Luke 9:14; Mark 8:9; John 6:10).
- After the Resurrection, Jesus welcomed the surprised disciples around the campfire and fixed them all breakfast (see John 21:7-14).

II. Scriptural Foundation for Hospitality

A. God commands us to practice hospitality.

"Be devoted to one another in brotherly love; give preference to one another in honor; not lagging behind in diligence, fervent in spirit, serving the Lord; rejoicing in hope, persevering in tribulation, devoted to prayer, contributing to the needs of the saints, practicing hospitality" (Romans 12:10-13).

The *New Living Translation* states Romans 12:13 this way: "When God's children are in need, be the one to help them out. And get into the habit of inviting guests home for dinner, or, if they need lodging, for the night."

Principle 1: God commands Christians to habitually show hospitality to brothers and sisters in the faith.

My mother was a remarkable person. She grew up in the South and from the time she was born she lived in a home that had a maid. After she married my father, she also had a maid. She did not cook. She did not clean the house.

Then, when my mother was thirty-three, my father was transferred from Wilmington, North Carolina, to the small town of Ludington, Michigan. It had harsh winters, the population was less than ten thousand people, and it was one hundred miles away from a city. There was no household help available. And yet Mama took the challenge. She learned to clean a house and cook excellent meals (three times a day), and she opened the doors of her home to others with lavish hospitality.

That "opening of the doors" made an impact. Though our home was small by today's standards, it was truly a refuge for others. My father's boss lived in a new, large house that he and his wife had designed and built, yet as soon as my parents decided to retire and move back to the South, Dad's boss bought that little house before it even hit the market. They moved in as soon as the house was vacant, and at their deaths their daughter became the owner. Another family friend loved the house so much that she asked for first refusal if it was ever put up for sale again. I think it wasn't the house itself they all loved . . . it was the spirit of hospitality my mother showered upon all who entered that made them want to be there.

Today in our rushed life, the world is still hungry for that place of refuge and for people who really care about others. Those are the people who are willing to sacrifice their time, resources, and talents to bring comfort, good cheer, and fellowship to others. In the midst of this hunger, God commands His people to be hospitable.

B. It is part of the role of a woman.

"A widow is to be put on the list only if she . . . [has] a reputation for good works; and if she has brought up children, if she has shown hospitality to strangers, if she has washed the saints' feet, if she has assisted those in distress, and if she has devoted herself to every good work" (1 Timothy 5:9-10).

Principle 2: God sees hospitality as a part of the role of a woman and worthy of honor from the church. Hospitality includes kindness and care to strangers.

These verses in 1 Timothy put the greater responsibility on the woman. Remember that the Greek word used for a woman's role is *oikadespoteo,* meaning she is the CEO, the manager of the home.

Mrs. Cory was a widow friend of my family when I was growing up. When my beloved and I were close to our wedding date, she invited us over so she could see the ring and hear all about the wedding plans. We so enjoyed her company. As the afternoon moved on we got up to leave, but she invited us to stay for supper. She left the room for about five minutes and came back for more conversation. Ten minutes later she left again and soon emerged from the kitchen with three trays containing plates of Noodles Alfredo with shrimp and a slice of lettuce with a vinaigrette dressing. The Alfredo had been made from a box, and the shrimp came out of a can, yet it tasted as delicious as a gourmet dinner. That was almost forty-five years ago and I can remember those hours and that delicious meal as if it were yesterday. She practiced hospitality and left both of us with a lifelong memory.

C. We may receive heavenly blessings.

"Let love of the brethren continue. Do not neglect to show hospitality to strangers, for by this some have entertained angels without knowing it" (Hebrews 13:1-2).

Principle 3: When we practice hospitality we have the opportunity to receive heavenly blessings, and there is a clear statement that we may even entertain angels unaware.

Several years ago my husband and I signed up to house two folks who were traveling with a choir . . . or at least that is what we were told. When our guests arrived, it was not two but four adults. It was not a choir but missionaries with Jews for Jesus. They drove into our driveway and parked a van with Jews for Jesus written in huge, colorful letters on both sides.

Now, this was a little awkward as we shared our small cul-de-sac with three Jewish families. We had prayed for them for a long time, yet faith and religion were topics that were never discussed. The van stayed in our driveway for about ten days. While we entertained "angels," they educated us about the Jewish faith and helped us better understand our neighbors.

After they left, I was informed that our neighbors were all very angry with us because they believed no Jew would *ever* believe in Jesus. And so it opened a door. It was Christmastime, so we invited them all over for a five-course lavish meal. We also asked Bruce Wilkinson to speak about why Christians celebrate Christmas. It turned out to be a lovely evening that opened doors on both sides. When they left, there was such a sense of love and understanding between us. From then on we could have honest conversations about belief, and we grew to be trusted friends. Did they ever come to Christ? To my knowledge, no. We moved a few years later. But I do believe the strangers were sent by God to open doors that seemed shut tight.

D. We are to be hospitable without complaining.

"Be hospitable to one another without complaint" (1 Peter 4:9).

Principle 4: All hospitality should be done with an attitude of good cheer and no complaining.

We are to cheerfully share our homes with those who need a meal or a place to stay. In Matthew 10:40 we are told that anyone who welcomes a Christian into his or her home is welcoming Jesus Himself. Those who welcome Jesus are welcoming the Father, and if they give a cup of cold water to someone in His name, they will be rewarded (see verse 42).

We had some relatives come to stay with us supposedly for a night or two. But their car broke down and they ended up staying with us for a few weeks. At the same time we had a young couple with a colicky infant living with us. We also had our house up for sale, so it was pretty stressful taking care of everyone, feeding everyone, trying to be a good hostess, and keeping a spotless house. One day I realized I was becoming a complainer, venting to my husband about "those people" who were staying with us. During a quiet time one morning, God directed me to 1 Peter 4:9, which says, "Be hospitable to one another without complaint." No complaining. Serve with joy. It was humbling and helped me change my attitude. In the end, the relatives' extended visit turned into a great blessing for us, and I think we were able to be a blessing to the young couple struggling with their first child. And we actually sold our house!

E. Hospitality demands nothing in return.

"When you give a luncheon or a dinner, do not invite your friends or your brothers or your relatives or rich neighbors, otherwise they may also invite you in return and that will be your repayment. But when you give a reception, invite the poor, the crippled, the lame, the blind, and you will be blessed, since they do not have the means to repay you; for you will be repaid at the resurrection of the righteous" (Luke 14:12-14).

Principle 5: Hospitality demands nothing in return. Your reward is not on this earth, but there is a promised reward reserved for you that is eternal.

When my husband and I were first married, we had a combined income of about $6,500 a year. We were paying for both graduate and undergraduate school, along with housing, food, and the other normal costs of living. We were dirt poor. An older couple we knew would often invite us for a meal. These were not ordinary meals. They were feasts, and after we had eaten twenty-five-cent boxes of macaroni and cheese all week, they were like heavenly feasts. Years later I began to understand why she made so much food. It was for us. She would send all the leftovers home with us! They never mentioned our poverty, nor did we. But they knew and understood our needs, and they quietly, without embarrassing us, did what they could to help.

III. Stumbling Blocks to Hospitality

A. Pride
There really are two types of pride that hang us up.

One type of pride says, "What I have is not good enough for guests." You may think your house is not nice enough, clean enough, big enough, or whatever. Or you may think you don't have the skills to put a meal on the table.

I taught school in the inner city before school lunches were served, so the children went home for lunch. I was frequently invited to have lunch at my students' homes. And this is where I learned what true hospitality is. A cup of tomato soup in a chipped cup and a peanut butter sandwich on a small plate graced with kindness and conversation made a feast to remember. They had little and still lavishly used what they had for me.

Another kind of pride is the opposite. It says, "I don't want to use my stuff because it is too good for guests."

I met a woman who had eighteen sets of beautiful fine china, each set with service for twelve people! When I said she must love to entertain, she replied that she *never* entertained because the dishes were so good she didn't want any of them to get broken. So she kept them safely packed away.

An amazing woman knows that everything she has was given to her by God to be used for His glory and His glory alone! If you have a house, then use it for others. If you have food, then share it often with guests. Be amazing!

B. Fear
Fear is deciding that God is not enough to help you. My husband was an elder at our church, and one evening he came home from an elder meeting where a young man had sought help. The young man thought he was HIV positive and was trying to get out of the homosexual lifestyle. He was terrified and had no place to go. So my beloved invited him to move in with us temporarily. I had some fear but then began to see that God was in control. This young man lived with us for almost two years. An amazing woman has faith, not fear.

C. Disobedience/Laziness
Laziness is disobedience! This basically is saying, "I know what Scripture says, but surely

God doesn't mean that I have to have guests in my home for a meal or the night. God isn't really serious about hospitality, so I will close my eyes to Scripture and simply ignore the command because I don't want to put forth the effort." An amazing woman knows that obedience displays her love for Jesus.

D. Inexperience

Inexperience comes from not having the skills to prepare a meal, set a table, or plan a meal so that everything is ready to serve at the same time. You may have a lack of confidence so you do nothing. An amazing woman knows that learning skills builds confidence.

E. Being Overextended

We fill our lives with so much running around that there is no time to reach out to others. We once lived in a neighborhood where no one opened their homes because they were so busy. Hospitality takes time. An amazing woman uses her time wisely and sets her priorities on the things that are at the heart of God.

IV. Benefits of Being Hospitable

A. It can offer care and comfort to the hurting and brokenhearted.

We had a friend who had become deeply involved in pornography. In despair, he ended up sitting in a truck with a gun, ready to kill himself. My beloved went to him and talked him into putting the gun down and coming home with him. He stayed with us for three months. He needed a safe, supportive, and compassionate environment.

You might have a friend who just found out she has cancer, or one who is battling depression or having marital problems. She may need you to offer the gift of hospitality for the purpose of comforting and supporting her in her time of sorrow.

B. It can be a great tool to reach your neighbors for Christ.

Cookouts are easy, brunches are inexpensive, and people love to come to your house! After church on Sunday is a wonderful time to invite guests over for dinner. Hospitality builds bridges and friendships and opens doors for conversation regarding faith.

C. It can provide help for those with physical needs.

I was in bed with a back injury for several months, and during that time my friends brought their hospitality to me in the form of meals, visits, great books, magazines, and love.

D. It can provide special ministry to women.

You can invite a neighbor for coffee or offer a neighborhood Bible study. There are excellent helps on the Internet for starting a neighborhood Bible study. Remember, above all, an amazing woman is a great listener. Make the conversation about others, become skillful at asking great questions, and show true, heartfelt interest in your guests.

V. Final Thoughts on Hospitality

A. The Role of Food

Part of welcoming people into our home is being prepared to offer them something to drink and eat. It says "welcome" and creates a gracious and warm environment. If the guests are unexpected, then a cup of coffee or tea and a cookie or some crackers is all that is needed. Most cookie recipes freeze well and defrost in minutes, so it is easy to have something special on hand. But a store-bought cookie works just fine. One time when I dropped in on a friend, she made delicious cinnamon toast and tea. It left a lasting and lovely memory.

However, if you are expecting guests, then preparation is required. Nothing says "you are not welcome here" as much as traveling to someone's home and finding that nothing has been prepared for your arrival. With the incredible resources readily available, wonderful food should be waiting for expected guests. The home does not have to be perfect, though it should be straightened and clean. Freshly laundered sheets should be on the guests' bed and their room made comfortable. Groceries should be in the house, menus planned, and some preparation done so the host and hostess are relaxed and free to give full attention to their guests.

Last week Robin gave you some wonderful ideas and recipes. Also, the Internet has fabulous resources for quick, easy, and inexpensive meals that can be prepared ahead of time and put in the freezer. In addition, at the end of this session I have included some of my favorite tried-and-true recipes and menus to help you get started. Food offers comfort. It can be simple because it is your love and care for others that is the centerpiece and the main ingredient to having a home and heart that says welcome.

B. What It Will Cost You
- Money
- Time
- Energy
- Wear and tear on your belongings
- Loss of family privacy

C. What You Will Gain
- Blessings beyond imagination

- Children who learn to serve and share
- Children who develop conversational skills
- Broader interests, deeper friendships, and compassion
- Strengthened faith in God as you see Him answer prayers in new ways
- The privilege of seeing lives change as Christ uses you

D. What You Don't Need
- A bigger house
- Nice dishes
- Expensive food
- A perfect home and family

E. What You Need
- A heart for God and His people
- A willingness to be obedient to His command to habitually practice hospitality
- An open heart and an open door

An amazing woman knows she can have an impact on the world around her by opening the door of her heart and home.

Now What?

What were the most important points for you personally in this message, "The Door Is Open, the Light Is On! Hospitality"?

Homework Day 2

What?

"Be hospitable to one another without complaint" (1 Peter 4:9).

So What?

1. The Bible has a great deal to say about serving others. What can you learn about hospitality from the following stories?

Matthew 25:34-46

Mark 6:30-44

Luke 7:36-50

Luke 10:38-42

Luke 14:12-14

John 2:1-10

John 13:1-17

Now What?

1. Based on the Scriptures you just read and those used in the lecture, what changes do you need to make in order to practice hospitality in a way that would honor God?

2. Discuss with your husband and family (if your children are old enough) ways that you can practice hospitality and what role each person will play. Young children can set the table and clear the dishes; older children can help cook a meal or prepare snacks. Decide how each person in the family can participate. Review with them the Scriptures that show God's desire for Christians to practice hospitality and the principles you have learned in this study.

The Door Is Open, the Light Is On!

Homework Day 3

What?

"But when you give a reception, invite the poor, the crippled, the lame, the blind, and you will be blessed, since they do not have the means to repay you; for you will be repaid at the resurrection of the righteous" (Luke 14:13-14).

So What?

1. Look at the list of stumbling blocks that keep Christians from being hospitable. Do any of these prohibit you from obeying God's command to be hospitable? Once your stumbling blocks are identified, take the necessary steps to overcome them. Think creatively, seeking the help of the Holy Spirit.

Now What?

Now it is time to put what we have learned into practice. Invite someone to your home for a meal or coffee this week. Review some of the recipes Robin has given you or use some of the menus I have included. The Internet has a vast number of quick and easy (or complicated if you enjoy that) recipes and menus to get you started. Set aside time each month for you and your family to invite guests to your home. Be especially mindful of those people God has brought into your life who may need encouragement and who would benefit from being with you and your family.

1. Write out who you plan to invite, what you will serve, and when you will do it this week. Be willing to report back to the class next week.

Menu for Sunday Dinner Entertaining

This is a great menu because almost everything can be made ahead of time, leaving very little preparation on Sunday. Set the table the night before and have the serving dishes you will need out and ready to use. When you arrive home from church, the casserole is hot and ready, and it takes only minutes for the salad and bread. Bon appétit!

Layered Hamburger Bake
Crunchy Spring Salad
Hot Italian Bread
Brownies with Vanilla Ice Cream and Chocolate Sauce

Layered Hamburger Bake

This can be assembled a day ahead and refrigerated until ready to bake. On Sunday morning I put it in the oven before we go to church. Then I set the timer so the oven will turn on while we are in church and the dish will be ready to come out of the oven shortly after we arrive home.

3 cups medium noodles, cooked according to directions
1 pound hamburger
1 15 oz. can tomato sauce
1 teaspoon sugar
½ teaspoon salt
¼ teaspoon garlic salt
⅛ teaspoon pepper
1 8 oz. package cream cheese, softened
½ cup sour cream
3 tablespoons milk
2 tablespoons finely chopped onion
1 10 oz. bag frozen chopped spinach, cooked and liquid squeezed out of it
1 cup shredded cheddar cheese

1. Brown hamburger in skillet and drain off fat. Add tomato sauce, sugar, salt, pepper, garlic salt, and noodles. Set aside.
2. Stir together cream cheese, sour cream, onion, and milk.
3. In a 2-quart casserole, layer half of the ground beef mixture, half of the sour cream mixture, all of the spinach, the remainder of the ground beef mixture, and the remainder of the sour cream mixture. Sprinkle with cheddar cheese. Bake at 350 degrees for 40–50 minutes. Serves 6.

Crunchy Spring Salad

You can make the dressing and toast the ramen noodles and pecans a day ahead of time.

Red Wine Vinaigrette

½ cup vegetable oil
½ cup sugar
3 tablespoons red wine vinegar
¼ teaspoon salt
¼ teaspoon pepper

1. Put the ingredients in a jar and shake it up well.
2. Store in refrigerator. It will keep for one week or more.

Salad

1 20 oz. can mandarin oranges, drained
1 package ramen noodles, broken and toasted (discard seasoning packet)
10 ounces spring salad mix
4 ounces feta cheese, crumbled
1 cup pecans, toasted
½ cup dried cranberries

Mix all together and serve with the dressing. Serves 10 people or more. Halve salad ingredients for fewer guests.

Hot Italian Bread

Slice a store-bought loaf of Italian bread not quite all the way through. Butter one side of each slice. Wrap in foil. This can be done a day ahead. When ready to serve, bake at 350 degrees for about 10–15 minutes or until hot. Serve at once.

Brownies with Vanilla Ice Cream and Chocolate Sauce

Using a brownie mix, make brownies according to the directions. This can be done a day ahead. Cover with foil. When ready to serve, slice brownies into squares, top with a dollop of ice cream, and drizzle a little hot chocolate sauce over the top.

A Simple Brunch for Ten

Celebration Punch
Coffee
Christmas Day Strata
Sour Cream Coffee Cake
Fresh Fruit
Almond Bars

Celebration Punch

(Taken from *Southern Scrumptious Entertains* by Betty Sims)

8 cups cranapple juice
8 cups pineapple juice
1½ cups sugar

2 tablespoons almond extract
2 quarts ginger ale, chilled

1. Mix together the first four ingredients until the sugar is dissolved. This can be done the day before and refrigerated.
2. When ready to serve, add ginger ale.

Christmas Day Strata

(Taken from *Entertaining: Summit Style*)

This can be assembled a day ahead and refrigerated until ready to bake and serve.

6 pieces bread (white or sourdough,
   crusts removed) torn into bite-sized pieces
6 tablespoons butter, melted
8 eggs, beaten
1 cup milk
1 teaspoon dry mustard
½ teaspoon salt
½ teaspoon black pepper

dash of cayenne (red) pepper
3 green onions, sliced thin
4 ounces cream cheese, cut into small cubes
6 mushrooms, sliced
1 medium tomato, chopped
4 ounces grated cheddar cheese

1. Butter or spray with nonstick cooking spray a 13 x 9 ovenproof baking dish.
2. Cover bottom of pan with torn bread. Pour melted butter over bread.
3. Beat eggs in a large mixing bowl, add milk, and mix well.
4. Add mustard, salt, pepper, onions, cream cheese, mushrooms, tomato, and cheddar cheese to mixture. Mix well.
5. Pour mixture over bread. Cover with foil. Refrigerate if not serving immediately.
6. When ready to serve, bake at 375 degrees for 25 minutes.
7. Remove foil and bake an additional 40 minutes. Serve hot.

Sour Cream Coffee Cake

This can be made a day ahead of time. It also freezes beautifully.

1 cup butter, softened

1 cup sugar

2 eggs

1 teaspoon vanilla

2 cups flour

1 teaspoon baking powder

1 teaspoon baking soda

¼ teaspoon salt

1 cup sour cream

TOPPING

½ cup brown sugar

1 teaspoon cinnamon

½–1 cup chopped pecans or walnuts

1. Beat together sugar and butter. Add egg and vanilla. Beat well. Add flour, soda, powder, and salt. Beat well. Add sour cream. Beat until well incorporated.
2. Spread half of the mixture into a tube pan.
3. Combine the brown sugar and cinnamon. Sprinkle half of this mixture over the cake batter.
4. Spread rest of batter, then the rest of the topping. Sprinkle chopped nuts on top.
5. Bake at 350 degrees for 45 minutes. Serves 10–12.

Fresh Fruit

This can be anything you like. Some ideas are melon, berries, sliced oranges, grapefruit, or an assortment.

Almond Bars

These can be made a day ahead of time.

2 sticks butter, softened

1 cup sugar

2 cups flour

1 teaspoon vanilla

1 teaspoon almond extract

1 egg, beaten and divided

sliced almonds

1. Mix butter and sugar with a fork. Add vanilla and almond extract.
2. Mix until moist.
3. Add the flour and *half* of the beaten egg.
4. Mix well. Mixture may be crumbly, but that is okay.
5. Place mixture in a 7 x 11 pan and press down and smooth with hand. Brush on the remaining egg. Sprinkle sliced almonds on top. Bake at 350 degrees for 30 minutes. Cool slightly and slice into rectangles.

Cookies for Coffee with Friends or Drop-In Guests

The following are cookies that I make and keep in the freezer. The recipe makes a lot, and the cookies are very good and keep beautifully. This means I always have something on hand for drop-in guests or treats for kids.

Chocolate Chip Oatmeal Cookies

BEAT WELL:

1 cup butter or margarine	2 cups white sugar
1 cup solid shortening such as Crisco	4 eggs
2 cups brown sugar	2 teaspoons vanilla

MIX TOGETHER AND ADD:

4 cups flour	2 teaspoons baking soda
2 teaspoons salt	1 teaspoon baking powder

Add the following ingredients. (The dough will get thick. If you have a stand mixer, put the dough hook on at this time. If too thick for a hand mixer, then incorporate by hand.)

3 cups quick oatmeal
3 cups Rice Krispies cereal
1 12 oz. package chocolate chips
1½–2 cups chopped pecans or walnuts

1. Drop by spoonfuls onto greased cookie sheets.
2. Bake at 350 degrees for 10–14 minutes.

Show Me the Money

Finances

Traci Martin

"That the word of God will not be dishonored."

Titus 2:5

DVD Outline

I. **Introduction**
   A. There are over 2,000 verses in the Bible related to money.
   B. God's economy is countercultural to the way the world views money.

II. **God's Role**
   A. He owns it all.
   B. All comes from Him.

III. **Our Role**
   A. We are stewards.
   B. We are accountable.
      1. Our use of money reflects our relationship with God.
      2. Possessions compete with the Lord.
      3. Money is time-consuming.

IV. **Our Responsibilities**
   A. Give an offering to the Lord.
   B. Get out and stay out of debt.
   C. Create a spending plan or budget.
      1. What are our goals?
      2. Where is our money going now?
   D. Track expenses.
      1. Computerized
      2. Envelope system
      3. Broad categories
      4. Spending guidelines
   E. Stay on track.
      1. Keep up with tracking.
      2. Do an annual review.
      3. Know your temptations.
   F. Financial Life on One Page (FLOP)

1. In Romans 12:2, we are warned not to be conformed to the behaviors and customs of this world. What financial behaviors of the world are you most tempted to follow?
2. What is the most important thing God has said to you today about your finances?
3. What are some changes God is challenging you to make for your family?
4. What is working and not working for you financially?

Show Me the Money

Homework Day 1

What?

"He who is faithful in a very little thing is faithful also in much; and he who is unrighteous in a very little thing is unrighteous also in much" (Luke 16:10).

So What?

Read the following notes from the DVD message "Show Me the Money: Finances" and answer the "Now What" question at the end.

I. Introduction

When my husband and I were first married, we had no money. We paid for our wedding ourselves, bought a house, and paid for my college tuition. Most of the time, there didn't seem to be enough pennies to scrape together to pay our expenses. We were "ramen noodle" poor, yet we can now look back on that time and laugh at some of the creative ways we managed life. Right after we bought our home, our oven broke. The part we needed to fix it cost almost as much as a new stove, so it remained broken. For years, I had only a toaster oven and a microwave. Then my husband's coworker offered us her old stove when she remodeled her kitchen. Excited at the prospect of cooking a Thanksgiving turkey, we gratefully accepted it. However, there was a problem with it: it was a full-size stove and ours was apartment-size. It wouldn't fit in our kitchen. Not one to let a problem stop us from having Thanksgiving at our house, we connected it directly to the electric box—in the bedroom! We could honestly say we did our best cooking in the bedroom.

Once I graduated from college and started working full-time, our money crunch eased a bit. Unfortunately, neither of us had ever had any money, so we hadn't learned how to manage it. We never really grasped the principles necessary to thrive financially. Our church offered a Bible study on biblical money management, which we eagerly joined. We learned not only the practical methods for handling money but also how we honor God with our finances.

We had no idea that God's Word talks so much about money!

A. There are over 2,000 verses in the Bible related to money.
This includes everything from saving to giving and everything in between. Scripture defines God's economy for us.

B. God's economy is countercultural to the way the world views money.

God's economy is one in which He is at the center of all financial decisions. So today we are going to discuss what God's role is in our finances, what our role is, and how to handle money responsibly.

II. God's Role

A. He owns it all.

In 1 Chronicles 29, King David commissioned his son, Solomon, to build a magnificent temple to the Lord, and he gave many of his own personal resources for the structure. The Israelites followed his example by giving treasures of gold, silver, bronze, iron, and precious stones. David praised God in front of all the people for His greatness, power, majesty, and splendor. As they gave, I am sure David thanked the people for their generosity. But why was he praising God? David answered that question himself:

> For everything in heaven and earth is yours. Yours, O LORD, is the kingdom; you are exalted as head over all. (1 Chronicles 29:11, NIV)

> The earth is the LORD's, and everything in it, the world, and all who live in it. (Psalm 24:1, NIV)

It's all His! From the land to everything in it, from our homes to our 401(k), it's all His! We are all His!

B. All comes from Him.

Recently we updated our kitchen. It had taken a long time and we were near the end of the project as my hubby spent the weekend painting. Monday, he headed off to work and I started the laundry. After a while, I started hearing the sound of water dripping onto my kitchen's new hardwood floors. The fill nozzle on the washing machine, which is located upstairs above the kitchen, had broken and the water never shut off. It poured out, collapsing the ceiling. I have to admit, I cried. Not because of the damage, but because my husband's hard work was wasted. Bill came home to help with the cleanup, looked at the gaping hole above, laughed, and said, "I guess God wants an open ceiling!"

He was right; it is God's washer, God's ceiling, and God's house. All that we have comes from Him, and He is in charge of it all (see 1 Chronicles 29:12). The book of Job tells how Job was sifted by Satan and lost everything he had—his family and his wealth. Yet he fell down and worshipped God. Job understood that we have nothing when we arrive on earth and we take nothing with us when we leave. It is all the Lord's to do with as He pleases. God's role in the realm of finances is simple: He owns it all, and all we have comes from Him.

So what is our role?

III. Our Role

A. We are stewards.

We need to deny our ownership and accept Christ's lordship over our belongings. Luke 14:33 says, "So then, none of you can be My disciple who does not give up all his own possessions." Do we have to give up our belongings to be followers of Christ? No. It is not so much about giving away what we have but about acknowledging that it is the Lord's. It is about making decisions that will honor Him and seeking His wisdom in how we handle our wealth. If we have food on the table and clothes on our back, we have wealth. Our role is stewardship, and according to 1 Corinthians 4:2, "It is required of stewards that one be found trustworthy."

In Matthew 25, the parable of the talents, Jesus told of a master who was going on a journey and entrusted his business to three of his servants. To the first, he gave five talents (which is a unit of money). To the second he gave two talents, and to the third he gave one. The servant with five talents invested it and earned five additional talents. The servant with two talents invested it and also made 100 percent return. The third took his single talent and buried it.

When the master returned, it was time for his servants to account for how they managed his business while he was away. The servant with the five talents shared the news of doubling the investment, and the master was very pleased. He said, "Well done, good and faithful servant! You have been faithful with a few things; I will put you in charge of many things. Come and share your master's happiness!" (verse 21, NIV). The master had the same reaction to the servant with two talents who had also doubled the investment. However, to the servant who buried his only talent, he chastised him as wicked and lazy.

A good steward is not someone who is fearful and unwilling to use what the Lord has given him, but rather someone who will assume the risk for the benefit of the owner. We are to use what the Lord provides for us, not only for our life essentials, but to benefit His kingdom. Our end goal is not to have more money for the sake of more money and a better lifestyle, but to have resources to use for the needs the Lord brings before us. Commentator Ray Stedman said, "It is a temporary vehicle to accomplish permanent good."[25]

B. We are accountable.

We are going to be held accountable for how we handle money, whether we feel we have been given much or little, whether we are neglectful or good managers. It is not how much we have but how we use it. This matters to the Lord for several reasons:

1. Our use of money reflects our relationship with God.

Jesus said, "Do not store up for yourselves treasures on earth, where moth and rust destroy, and where thieves break in and steal. But store up for yourselves treasures in heaven, where neither moth nor rust destroys, and where thieves do not break in or steal; for where your treasure is, there your heart will be also" (Matthew 6:19-21). How we use our money reflects the condition of our heart!

2. Possessions compete with the Lord.

"No one can serve two masters; for either he will hate the one and love the other, or he will be devoted to one and despise the other. You cannot serve God and wealth" (Matthew 6:24). Money is the image of a rival god. We have money to use, but we don't need to chase after it.

3. Money is time-consuming.

"So teach us to number our days, that we may present to You a heart of wisdom" (Psalm 90:12). We spend so much time earning money, deciding how to spend it, and planning savings and investment strategies. We need money to operate in life, and God wants us to come to Him for instructions.

• • •

Several years ago, my youngest daughter wanted to go on a mission trip to Brazil, and being the protective mom that I am, I said she could go but I was going as well. This was our first mission trip overseas and we were excited, but also apprehensive. I had another daughter in college, and this opportunity presented itself just as a recession hit. There was no extra money in our budget, so we had to depend on support from others. It was humbling to ask for money. I thought we should just be able to pay for it. God, oh so gently, revealed my pride to me. You see, other people may not be able to go to a foreign country to teach the gospel, but they can still participate in spreading the gospel by financially supporting others who are able to go.

Our faith grew as God used other believers to fund our trip, and it was just the beginning of how God was allowing us to experience the ways in which His economy works. In Brazil we went to work with a missionary couple who preached the gospel full-time. They rely solely on financial contributions from others for their livelihood and the work they are doing. In one week, we witnessed hundreds of people committing their lives to Jesus Christ. Every single person who helped fund the trip earned an eternal return on their investment.

Now that we understand our role in God's economy, we need to discuss practical ways to be responsible with the money that has been entrusted to us.

IV. Our Responsibilities

A. Give an offering to the Lord.

Leviticus 27:30 talks about giving a "tithe" to the Lord of everything we receive. Tracing the word *tithe* back to the original Hebrew word *ma'aser*, we see that it means "a tenth part." In

Malachi 3:8-10 we are told that we are robbing God if we don't bring the full tithe to Him. Moreover, we are to give the tithe and test Him, as He will pour out a blessing on us until it overflows. Also, our attitude is important: "Each one must do just as he has purposed in his heart, not grudgingly or under compulsion, for God loves a cheerful giver" (2 Corinthians 9:7).

B. Get out and stay out of debt.

Impulsive and reactionary spending is one of the biggest contributors to our household debt problem. Our nations and families are saddled with debt; in fact, we are considered odd if we don't have debt. But the Bible has a different view on this. Romans 13:8 says, "Owe nothing to anyone." And in Proverbs 22:7 we read, "The borrower becomes the lender's slave."

The bigger the debt and the less ability we have to pay, the stronger the oppression. We now owe instead of being free to save, spend, or serve with our money. Additionally, debt presumes that we will continue to earn at the current rate or better and that there will be no illness, accidents, or downsizing. But the Bible tells us, "You do not know what your life will be like tomorrow" (James 4:14).

It is this simple: If we don't have money, we shouldn't spend it. If we owe others money, then we don't have money. It's a simple concept but one that is difficult to live by. If we have debt, eliminating it needs to be the first financial goal we set.

C. Create a spending plan or budget.

We need to know exactly where our money is going and be intentional about it. Many people in our culture, Christians included, live impulsive and reactive lives. We want something and so we buy it without a second thought. Or we don't set aside an adequate emergency fund to cover a broken appliance or unexpected car repair. Everything we do as Christians should bring glory to God. Rarely does that happen with impulsive and reactionary spending.

In Philippians 4:19 we read, "And my God will supply all your needs according to His riches in glory in Christ Jesus." God will provide for us, but we need to be wise with what He provides. Setting financial goals is the first step necessary in creating a spending plan.

1. What are our goals?

"For which one of you, when he wants to build a tower, does not first sit down and calculate the cost to see if he has enough to complete it?" (Luke 14:28). Both you and your husband (if you are married) should take time to thoroughly discuss what you want to do with your money. If you are in debt, the first goal is to get out of it! Perhaps the next goal is a new house, sending children to college, or perhaps funding a ministry. Regardless of what you decide, the goals should not only glorify God but also put you and your husband on the same page.

According to *Money Magazine* (October 2012), "Couples average three money fights a month with common triggers being insufficient savings (32%), unexpected expenses (49%), and differing opinions of 'needs' and 'wants' (58%). Setting goals would help eliminate many of those arguments."[26]

2. Where is our money going now?

In the parable of the talents (see Matthew 25) that we discussed earlier, the servants had to give an account of how they used the money left for them to manage. The next step in creating a spending plan is becoming aware of what we have, what we owe, and where our money goes. You can do this by following these three steps:

    a. Make a list of all your assets.
    b. Make a list of all your debts.
    c. Take a few weeks to track your expenditures.

D. Track expenses.

When we first started tracking what we were spending, my husband was eating lunch out nearly every day at $7–10 a day, which comes to over $1,500 a year. That is a mortgage payment! Coffee shop drinks several times a week came to $720 a year. That buys tires for the car. And my weekly manicures came to $480 a year, which would be enough money to sponsor a needy child.

It is amazing to see how quickly our money disappears and how quickly our little purchases add up to big amounts. This is why it is crucial to track where our money is going.

1. Computerized

There are programs designed especially for tracking budgets, such as You Need a Budget (www.YNAB.com), and comprehensive financial managers, such as Quicken (www.Intuit .com). These are easy to use and will track your finances and give you a clear picture of where your money is going and growing. There are spreadsheet-based programs such as Microsoft Excel that can track expenses with a little bit more effort but at no additional cost if you own Excel. Templates are available on the Internet. Also, there are many good apps for tracking, such as EEBA (www.eebacanhelp.com).

Note: Be wary of using any Internet program that requires any of your personal information to use the application. Financial information should be kept as private and secure as possible. My identity was stolen twice, so be careful! Don't give away your information online.

2. Envelope system

This is a noncomputerized version of expense tracking where you create envelopes for each of your budget categories and fund each envelope with cash. When you spend money, you take it from the appropriate envelope. When the money is gone, it is gone.

My in-laws taught my husband and me to use envelopes to track our expenses. When we got paid, we went to the bank and received cash to stock the envelopes. When we went out to eat, we took the dining out envelope. When we went to the grocery store, we took the grocery envelope. On one particular shopping trip, I needed to buy more than usual because family was coming to town. We were on a very slim budget, so I clipped coupons, planned which stores would give the best deal, and took my calculator to keep a running total. I got excited as it seemed my money was going far. I went to the register to check out, expecting my total to be about $100. It was nearly double that! Somewhere along the line my calculator had reset itself. Because we were on a cash-only basis, I had to put back the extra treats. It was embarrassing, but I could not go over budget.

In these days of direct deposit and plastic cards, how easy it is to slide a card and let the budget slip! Spending cash helps us be intentional about where our money goes.

3. Broad categories

Set up categories to help define your expenses. The fixed expenses, such as mortgage and utilities, will be easy. These are the bills that come due every month and have a fairly consistent payment. The harder categories will be groceries, entertainment, gifts, and the dreaded miscellaneous. These are generally the categories that blow our budget!

- Keep the categories broad, such as household supplies instead of cleaning supplies, paper products, and pet food. We don't need to micromanage our money. We only need to see where it is going.
- Plan on a set allowance. This is a certain amount of pocket money that is not tracked and is used for an occasional lunch or unplanned treat. Always take this in cash because it is easy to spend our allowance over and over again.
- Don't forget to set aside money for infrequent bills such as annual homeowner dues or life insurance premiums. Have an emergency fund for the unexpected repair or medical crisis.

4. Spending guidelines

To have an idea of a reasonable amount to plan for in each category, there are charts available online. Find one that matches the spending categories you set up for your budget. These are to be used as a reference only.

E. Stay on track.

1. Keep up with tracking.

Once you have your spending plan in place, deduct the money you spend from the appropriate category. It is important not to let your receipts pile up.

2. Do an annual review.

Most companies reallocate budget categories and amounts once a year. That is a good rule of thumb for us too. It helps keep our goals in front of us. Tax time can be a good time to do this. Another advantage of keeping track of our spending is that it makes tax preparation go more smoothly.

Reevaluate your spending plan as life circumstances change, such as a job loss or a debt paid off. These require an adjustment to the spending plan.

3. Know your temptations.

If you are an impulse shopper, don't go to the mall, watch shopping channels, or subscribe to prepaid discount websites. You never save money by spending money. Shop with a list and stick with it. Don't shop hungry!

• • •

As new Christians, my husband and I decided to take God at His word and start living according to His financial principles. We were accustomed to spending money on whatever we wanted and had a large amount of debt. We committed to eliminate debt and live within our means. It was not easy. We would make a budget that looked balanced on paper, but something unplanned would happen every month. But God blessed us in unique ways, and because we were earnestly trying to be obedient, we were able to see His activity in our life through our finances.

F. Financial Life on One Page (FLOP)

One final important suggestion: in most families, one person manages the finances and has a better understanding of the overall financial picture. If you and/or your husband were to die, would those left behind know where to find your financial information? Do they know where you bank and how many accounts you have? Do you have insurance policies? With whom? Do you have a retirement account? You get the idea.

Financial Life on One Page (FLOP) is a spreadsheet that lists the pertinent details of all your financial dealings. You can find it online at www.christianPF.com. It contains the name, phone number, web address, and account numbers for each institution. Include the separate location where passwords can be found so those using it have access to web information.

• • •

When we understand God's role as owner and provider of everything and recognize our role as stewards, carrying out our responsibilities can be done with joy. It is hard work to live with a balanced budget, but it is worth it. You may feel that you are so far in a hole that nothing would help. That's a lie that Satan would love for you to believe. He wants you to think that changes aren't necessary or possible. Start with one thing today. Ask God for direction and encouragement as you resolve to commit your ways to Him and as He promises to direct your path.

Amazing women live freely in the area of their finances.

Now What?

What were the most important points for you personally in this message, "Show Me the Money: Finances"?

Homework Day 2

What?

"You were bought with a price; do not become slaves of men" (1 Corinthians 7:23).

So What?

Debt binds us to the lender. In other words, debt enslaves us. An amazing woman knows that Jesus paid the price for our sin and He wants us to be free.

1. What does God's Word say about borrowing (see Deuteronomy 15:6)?

2. Though God was talking to Israel in Deuteronomy 28:12, discuss some of the financial principals we can gain from this verse.

3. What is someone called who is in debt (see Proverbs 22:7)?

Now What?

1. Make a list of all your debts. Looking at your list, are you in debt because of critical life circumstances or indulgences? Seek repentance with God, if necessary.

2. Make and follow a plan to get out of debt as soon as possible.
- Focus your efforts on the debt with the highest interest rate first.
- Pay as much as you can afford, while maintaining a minimal payment on the remaining accounts.
- When the first account is paid off, apply the amount you were paying on it to the account with next highest interest rate.
- Continue until all accounts are paid in full.

List your debts on the chart that follows in the order of the highest interest rates.

STARTING DATE: _____

Creditor	Balance	Interest Rate	Payment	Paid-Off Date

Homework Day 3

What?

"For which one of you, when he wants to build a tower, does not first sit down and calculate the cost to see if he has enough to complete it?" (Luke 14:28).

So What?

We need to plan how to use our resources or they may disappear before we have accomplished our goals. An amazing woman is intentional about how she spends money.

1. What is the benefit of planning (see Proverbs 21:5)?

2. What should we do with our plans (see Proverbs 3:6)?

3. How do our plans move forward (see Proverbs 16:9)?

Now What?

Create a budget. List all money coming into the household and all expenses, both fixed and discretionary. Make sure your spending does not exceed your income.

Family Household Budget

INCOMES

Projected Monthly Income		Actual Monthly Income	
Income 1		Income 1	
Income 2		Income 2	
Extra income		Extra income	
Total monthly income		Total monthly income	

EXPENSES

Housing	Projected Cost	Actual Cost	Difference
Mortgage or rent			
Second mortgage or rent			
Phone			
Electricity			
Gas			
Water and sewer			
Cable			
Waste removal			
Maintenance or repairs			
Supplies			
Other			
Subtotal			

Transportation	Projected Cost	Actual Cost	Difference
Vehicle 1 payment			
Vehicle 2 payment			
Bus/taxi fare			
Insurance			
Licensing			
Fuel			
Maintenance			
Other			
Subtotal			

Insurance	Projected Cost	Actual Cost	Difference
Home			
Health			
Life			
Other			
Subtotal			

Food	Projected Cost	Actual Cost	Difference
Groceries			
Dining out			
Other			
Subtotal			

Children	Projected Cost	Actual Cost	Difference
Medical			
Clothing			
School tuition			
School supplies			
Organization dues or fees			
Lunch money			
Child care			
Other			
Subtotal			

Pets	Projected Cost	Actual Cost	Difference
Food			
Medical			
Grooming			
Other			
Subtotal			

Personal Care	Projected Cost	Actual Cost	Difference
Medical			
Hair/nails			
Clothing			
Dry cleaning			
Health club			
Organization dues or fees			
Other			
Subtotal			

Entertainment	Projected Cost	Actual Cost	Difference
Video/DVD			
CDs			
Movies			
Concerts			
Sporting events			
Live theater			
Other			
Subtotal			

Loans	Projected Cost	Actual Cost	Difference
Personal			
Student			
Credit card			
Credit card			
Credit card			
Other			
Subtotal			

Taxes	Projected Cost	Actual Cost	Difference
Federal			
State			
Local			
Other			
Subtotal			

Savings or Investments	Projected Cost	Actual Cost	Difference
Retirement account			
Investment account			
College			
Other			
Subtotal			

Tithes and Offerings	Projected Cost	Actual Cost	Difference
Church			
Charity 1			
Charity 2			
Subtotal			

Total of all income			
Total of all expenses			

Projected balance (Projected income minus expenses)	

Actual balance (Actual income minus expenses)	

Difference (Actual minus projected)	

Session 22

Bag a Buck!

Time and Money Saving Tips

Michele Helms

"That the word of God will not be dishonored."

TITUS 2:5

343

DVD Outline

I. **Introduction**
   A. Why save money?
   B. Need Versus Want

II. **Ways to Save Time and Money**
   A. Food
      1. Coupons
      2. Meats
      3. Fruits and vegetables
      4. Eggs
      5. Drinks
   B. Gifts
   C. Clothing
   D. Cleaning Products
      1. Laundry detergent
      2. Glass and window cleaner
      3. Disinfectant
      4. Laundry spot remover
      5. Sink and tub cleaner
   E. Home Decorating
      1. Paint
      2. Pinterest.com
   F. Entertainment and Activities

III. **Conclusion**

Discussion Questions

1. Share your best time-saving tip with the group.
2. Share your best money-saving tip with the group.

Homework Day 1

What?

"Go to the ant, O sluggard, observe her ways and be wise, which, having no chief, officer or ruler, prepares her food in the summer and gathers her provision in the harvest" (Proverbs 6:6-8).

So What?

Read the following notes from the DVD message "Bag a Buck! Time and Money Saving Tips" and answer the "Now What" question at the end.

I. Introduction

A. Why save money?

Whatever his or her season of life — single, married, young parent, or empty nester — everyone wants to save time and money. Whether we have great or little resources, we are all called to be good stewards of what God has given us. So let's think of what we could do with extra money:

- Pay bills
- Make it on one income
- Pay off debt — Dave Ramsey says, "Live like no one else so you can give like no one else."
- Help kids with college
- Build an emergency fund
- Go on a vacation
- Go on a mission trip

B. Need Versus Want

"The earth is the Lord's, and everything in it, the world, and all who live in it" (Psalm 24:1, niv). Before we can talk about saving money, we need to distinguish between a need and a want. We are blessed and should be thankful every day! Young adults who have been given every luxury without ever working for it often feel entitled to a lifestyle that has taken their parents twenty-five years to build.

A few years ago I met with a young mom who was pregnant with her second child. She was working full-time and wanted to try to either stay home or go part-time. I asked her to go through her bank statements for four months and make a list of all expenses and then put them into two categories, need and want. When we sat back down together, I was surprised at her "needs" list. It included cable television, manicures, expensive haircuts and color treatments, a large budget for eating out, dog grooming, a large clothes budget, and a hefty landscaping payment. I challenged her to reassess these items because many of them were not needs at all and some could be greatly reduced. She held firm to her list. I walked away thinking that this woman was trading her desire to be with her babies for things that ultimately don't matter.

I know it is not a popular thought, but most of the things we own and the services we enjoy are wants, not needs. Is it wrong to have wants? Absolutely not! Is it wrong to enjoy the blessings the Lord has given us? Absolutely not! But if we really view everything we have as the Lord's (see 1 Chronicles 29:11-13), then we must be willing to praise Him if He chooses not to provide as we think He should. It is easy to say, "Everything I have is the Lord's" when we have abundance, but the true test comes when He asks us to give something away or when He allows us to lose it. Sometimes we think God would never allow what we perceive as bad to happen. But He does! Just look at Job. However, it is always for our good and His glory.

This became a reality for my family five years ago. Now let me be clear: even when the bottom fell out for us financially, we were a long way from needy or poor because at our lowest we were ridiculously rich in the eyes of most of the population of the world! We stepped away from a corporate job with all the benefits into a ministry for at-risk teenagers that was 100 percent reliant on donations. Our income dropped 95 percent overnight and remained that way for two years. I had a choice to make. I could whine and complain about what I didn't have, or I could support my husband and teach my children that our joy was not wrapped up in stuff. Did I do a perfect job of that? No. It was difficult, but the payoff was huge. We all grew in our understanding that contentment does not come from stuff. We didn't sit around and talk about what we didn't have, but instead we made what we did have fun! We ate lots of peanut butter and jelly sandwiches at the park. We went on lots of hikes and bike rides and had late-night story time. I was glad during those months that my parents had taught me that money and things can't buy happiness, and I hope I modeled that for my own children as well.

II. Ways to Save Time and Money

A. Food

1. Coupons

The grocery store can be one of the biggest budget drainers. I have always been frugal. I learned it from my mama. But until a few years ago I hadn't used coupons. I really thought they were mainly for junk food or that I could get the store brand cheaper. A good friend challenged me to use them and then taught me how to do it effectively.

There are many ways to coupon. Some shoppers look for every little savings detail and they save extraordinary amounts of money. With five children, I do not have time for this kind of couponing and Internet scouring. I need to save the most amount of money in the least amount of time.

In a nutshell, couponing works by waiting until an item is on a rock-bottom sale and then combining it with a coupon. There are great free websites that do all the work for you so you do not have to spend time looking through sales flyers. When items my family uses go on sale, I buy several of them. I may not need them that week, but when I do need them, I can just go to my pantry. I buy all toiletries, feminine products, cereals, nuts, pasta, canned and frozen veggies, condiments, and spices for 70 to 80 percent off regular price. Then I add fresh fruit, veggies, meat, and dairy to the things I already have on hand. My savings are huge! Even if you do not choose to use coupons, you can save a great deal of money just by stocking up on items you use when they go on sale.

2. Meat

Another way to save money is by buying extra meat when it goes on sale. Sometimes I just divide it into proper serving sizes and freeze it. Sometimes I cook it all and then freeze it. While this takes a little extra time on the front end, it saves a huge amount of time on the back end.

You can use boiled chicken for all kinds of things, from soups and casseroles to quesadillas. Put the boiled chicken in a freezer bag, cover with broth, push the air out, seal, and label! Then when you plan your menu for the next weeks it is ready to be thawed and used.

When making extra ground beef or turkey, brown without any seasoning and rinse in a colander with hot water to get extra fat out. Then either add to your recipe or measure into a freezer bag, push the air out, label, and freeze. I use this meat for chili, spaghetti sauce, soup, and tacos.

I am always thinking about meals that I can double or even triple and freeze. I collect extra items when they are on sale and then make several recipes. Some suggested foods to make ahead of time are spaghetti sauce, lasagna, casseroles, and even cookie dough. Even cooked bacon freezes well. Just place it on a paper towel in the microwave for thirty seconds to reheat!

We grill a lot, and to save time, I divide raw chicken pieces into serving sizes, put marinade in the freezer bag with the chicken, and freeze it. Once it thaws, it will be ready for the grill. My standard marinade is 1/2 cup Italian dressing and 1/4 cup teriyaki for every four chicken pieces. Most marinades work great when freezing.

3. Fruits and vegetables

Buy seasonal fruits and vegetables. If you have extra fruit that is getting too ripe, freeze it to make a smoothie or bread. We throw away so much food simply because we don't have a plan. Plan to eat first those fruits and vegetables that will go bad, such as berries, bananas, lettuce, peaches, mushrooms, and tomatoes. Save hardier produce like apples, carrots, celery, cabbage, onions, and squash for later use.

4. Eggs

Eggs are inexpensive and packed with protein. Boiled eggs are great for snacks or salads, and they keep in the refrigerator unpeeled for five days.

5. Drinks

Bottled water is a huge expense compared to buying a pitcher for filtering and refilling your own cup. To encourage our kids to drink more water, we let them pick out a fun insulated cup with a straw and tell them that no other beverage can go in except water. It works! Be careful with the amount of unnecessary money spent on juice and other beverages as well. I have a friend whose family gave up bottled water and put the savings from that "sacrifice" in an envelope. When the savings reached $200, which came much more quickly than she anticipated, the family gave a water filtration system to a missionary family in Africa. I love that!

Many beverages such as iced tea and coffee can be made inexpensively at home. Freeze extra coffee in ice cube trays to make fancy coffee drinks. Put the coffee cubes in a blender with milk and your favorite flavoring such as chocolate, vanilla, or almond. Delicious!

B. Gifts

Think about little gifts that can be kept on hand for birthdays, baby and wedding showers, and just for saying "I love you." I have a gift box under my bed that I keep stocked with little things I find on clearance.

Acts of service do not cost money but are wonderful gifts. Teach your kids that gifts do not have to be costly or even material. Whenever my kids ask for ideas for my birthday, Christmas, or Mother's Day, I always include acts of service along with reminders of how much I love their paintings, drawings, songs, and poems.

When Eric and I were first married and had no extra money at Christmas, we came up with the idea of giving service gifts to our parents. We pulled up an entire ivy bed that covered Eric's parents' front yard. We chopped and stacked firewood for my parents. They were all thrilled and we were pleased we had given them presents they enjoyed.

C. Clothing

The best time to buy clothes is at the end of each season when items are on clearance for 75 percent off or more. Be on guard that you do not buy things you will never use just for the sake of getting a deal! Thrift stores, consignment shops, and yard sales are also fantastic places to find deals.

PART THREE: Be Amazing in the Home

D. Cleaning Products

Making your own cleaning products can be a huge money saver and a way of keeping chemicals at a minimum.

1. Laundry detergent

The single biggest money saving tip I have for growing families is homemade laundry detergent. This recipe makes ten gallons for less than two dollars. While this may not appeal to an empty nester, it is a huge savings to families. All supplies can be found in the laundry section of most stores.

> 1 bar Fels-Naptha bar soap
> 1 cup Arm & Hammer washing soda (not baking soda)
> ½ cup 20 Mule Team Borax

Grate soap and combine with 2 quarts of water in a pot. Heat on medium heat until the soap is completely melted. Fill a 5-gallon bucket half full with hot tap water and add washing soda and Borax. Wisk the melted soap mixture into the bucket mixture and continue stirring until the soap is incorporated and the dry ingredients have completely dissolved. Fill the bucket to the 5-gallon mark with water and stir again. After sitting, the mixture will be lumpy and thick. That's okay. This mixture is actually concentrate, so after stirring, fill a smaller container half full with the soap concentrate and add water to fill the other half. Give it a good shake, and it is ready to use!

For a front-loading machine, use ¼ cup (640 loads). For a top-loading machine, use ¾ cup (214 loads).

2. Glass and window cleaner

> 1 cup rubbing alcohol
> 1 cup water
> 1 tablespoon white vinegar

Mix and put into a spray bottle. The key to streak-free glass is to rub until completely dry.

3. Disinfectant

One tablespoon bleach per gallon of water kills all household bacteria and viruses! It does not need to be strong. Mix in a spray bottle and be sure to label it. Use for kitchen sinks, bathtubs, and toilets.

4. Laundry spot remover

    2 cups peroxide

    1 teaspoon Dawn dish soap (the original blue)

    Combine in a spray bottle. This takes out almost any kind of stain!

5. Sink and tub cleaner
    Sprinkle baking soda or Borax instead of other abrasive cleaners for tubs and sinks.

E. Home Decorating
1. Paint

    Even for a person who isn't handy there are many projects that are simple. I love spray paint. It is easy to use, inexpensive, and totally changes the look of things. My daughter recently took down my very dated ceiling fans that still worked perfectly. We spray-painted them and they look awesome! It saved me hundreds of dollars and gave me an easy update. I look for items at yard sales and thrift stores that might look dated or worn but still sturdy. I paint them and have something new for my house or to give away for a fraction of the cost. Paint is a great way to freshen up a room in your house as well. If you feel unsure, start with a small bathroom and you will be inspired! Tutorials can be found on the Internet for step-by-step instructions for almost any project.

2. Pinterest.com

    I love Pinterest! There are so many suggestions for anything you might want to try. I have found so many cute, inexpensive ideas, oftentimes using things I already have around the house. There are great savings in repurposing items for decoration or organization. If you don't know about Pinterest, go to www.pinterest.com. You are in for a treat! Since we are talking about time saving as well, I must say that limits should be set on this and all other media avenues. They can be a destroyer of your time. I once had a mom tell me she was having trouble getting her housework completed because she was so involved with a game on her phone. That is not being a good steward of time.

F. Entertainment and Activities
There are many websites with discount entertainment, dining, and vacations. My family enjoys taking advantage of those on occasion. However, truly some of the greatest memories from my own childhood and with my children have been doing things that didn't involve money or travel. Families need time together. Families need traditions. Here are some suggestions:

- Go to the park and throw a Frisbee around. You can even make up a new game while you are at it!

- Have a water balloon fight.
- Have a picnic by candlelight (or flashlights) in the living room on a rainy night.
- Build a fort with sheets and read a book.
- Turn the music up loud and dance!
- Teach your kids to make mud pies.
- Do you have girls? Have a spa night with manicures and pedicures and maybe even a mud mask!

You get the picture. Slow down, put the electronics away, and make memories.

III. Conclusion

We are all accountable to God for the use of the money, talents, and resources He has given us. I have tried to give you some new ways to think about your responsibility and what you could do with money saved. Will you hear God say, "Well done, good and faithful servant! You have been faithful with a few things; I will put you in charge of many things" (Matthew 25:21, NIV)? An amazing woman is a creative and wise steward of the resources and time she has been given.

Now What?

What were the most important points for you personally in this message, "Bag a Buck!" Time and Money Saving Tips"?

Homework Day 2

What?

"Well done, good and faithful servant! You have been faithful with a few things; I will put you in charge of many things" (Matthew 25:21, NIV).

So What?

God commands us to be good stewards. *Strong's Concordance* says the word *steward* means "the manager of a household or of household affairs; one to whom the head of the house or proprietor has entrusted the management of his affairs, the care of receipts and expenditures, and the duty of dealing out the proper portion to every servant and even to the children not yet of age." In other words, one of our jobs as "keeper of the home" is the responsibility of managing what God owns.

1. List everything that belongs to God according to the following verses:

    Psalm 50:10-12

    1 Chronicles 29:11-12

Our mind-set needs to change from "it is my money" to "it is all God's." With this in mind, you can make a huge impact on your family's budget and be a better steward of what God has supplied by making a few simple changes.

2. What do you learn from the following verses about being a steward of the wealth or talents (sum of money) God gives you?

    Matthew 25:19-29

Matthew 25:37-40, 44-46

Luke 16:10-12

God desires us to be good stewards, and we need to realize that He will judge us according to how we use what He has entrusted to us. Do we even think about this responsibility or take it seriously?

Now What?

Look honestly at what you are spending money on and think about creative ways you can cut costs.

1. Visit a coupon saving website. At the time of this writing, www.southernsavers.com and www.couponmom.com are good ones. Some websites show helpful videos on how to coupon. It may seem overwhelming, but it doesn't take long for the savings to start adding up, and it will be well worth spending a little time and effort. Write down what you learn during this research.

2. List ways you do or can save money. Consider buy-one-get-one-free sales. Stock up when your favorite meat is on sale. If you don't like paper coupons, try using iPhone apps to get weekly ads and store coupons at the stores you frequent. (Big-box stores and groceries have apps.)

Another way to cut costs is to Google recipes for particular meals that you like at restaurants so you can make them much less expensively at home. Try it and see what you find!

Homework Day 3

What?

"The earth is the LORD's, and everything in it, the world, and all who live in it" (Psalm 24:1, NIV).

So What?

Almost everyone can cut $100 out of their monthly expenses just by making a few changes. Ask the Lord how you might spend that money wisely: to put toward debt, help with household bills, save toward a bigger purchase, support a ministry? You might be an empty nester and could donate your savings to a needy family or to your own children.

1. What does God say about giving to others (see 2 Corinthians 8:1-5)?

2. What does this add to your understanding of God's view of giving (see 2 Corinthians 9:6-10)?

I believe that one of the greatest gifts I have given my girls is the ability to save money and look for bargains. They know how to live on very little money and to find their contentment in things that money can't buy. An amazing woman helps her children find contentment in the Lord and not in material things. It starts with you!

Now What?

1. Do you (and your children) know how to shop for a bargain? What do you need to learn in this area?

2. How are you teaching your kids to be good stewards of their money?

3. List some gifts you (and your children) could give that do not cost money.

4. Summarize what God has said to you about being a good steward.

Session 23

Behave!

Etiquette

Robin Rosebrough

"That the word of God will not be dishonored."

TITUS 2:5

DVD Outline

I. **What is etiquette?**
   A. Manners are the result of a kind heart.
   B. Etiquette is an orderly way of doing things; a customary code of conduct of good behavior; kindness applied.

II. **The Top Ten Lost Arts of Etiquette**
   10. Neighborliness
   9. Appropriate Attire
   8. Mealtime Manners
   7. Being a Good Houseguest
   6. Correspondence (Particularly Thank-You Notes)
   5. The Pleasure of a Reply (RSVP)
   4. Arriving on Time
   3. Social Media Etiquette
   2. E-mail Etiquette
   1. Cell Phone Etiquette
      a. Be courteous!
      b. Speak softly.
      c. Be in control of your phone; don't let it control you!
      d. Avoid talking about personal problems on the phone in public.
      e. Do not send text messages when you are in the company of others.
      f. Private information can be forwarded, so don't text it.

III. **Conclusion**

Discussion Questions

1. In the present culture, what are some ways that you have personally observed lost arts of etiquette?
2. What can you do as a parent to train your children in lost arts of etiquette?
3. Why do we need to be in control of our cell phones or smartphones and not let them control us?

Homework Day 1

What?

"And in your godliness, brotherly kindness, and in your brotherly kindness, love" (2 Peter 1:7).

So What?

Read the following notes from the DVD message "Behave! Etiquette" and answer the "Now What" question at the end.

> From all that I had read of History of Government, of human life, and manners, I have drawn this conclusion, that the manners of women are the most infallible barometer to ascertain the degree of morality and virtue in a nation. All that I have since read and all the observation I have made in different nations, have confirmed me in this opinion. The manners of women are the surest criterion by which to determine whether a republican government is practicable in a nation or not. The Jews, the Greeks, the Romans, the Swiss, the Dutch; all lost their public spirit, their republican principles and habits, and the republican forms of government when they lost the modesty and domestic virtues of their women.... The foundations of national morality must be laid in private families. In vain are schools, academies, and universities instituted if those principles and licentious habits are impressed upon children in their earliest years. The mothers are the earliest and most important instructors of youth.
>
> — *John Adams, 1778*

I. What is etiquette?

On a recent trip to visit a friend, I was weary after traveling. I rented a car and drove to her home, arriving in the late afternoon. I noticed several things upon my arrival. No dinner was prepared (we ate out), the sheets for the bed were folded on top of the bed, and the bathroom was not clean. It made me realize the importance showing kindness to others. Do you see why we need to devote a teaching to etiquette? Most of us think of etiquette as manners, but there is a difference.

A. Manners are the result of a kind heart.

B. Etiquette is an orderly way of doing things; a customary code of conduct of good behavior; kindness applied.

Miss Manners has three rules of etiquette: to think of others before yourself; to make others feel at ease; and to be kind. Linda taught us about kindness in session 7, and today we are going to focus on how to live it out.

II. The Top Ten Lost Arts of Etiquette

10. Neighborliness

The Golden Rule says, "Treat others the same way you want them to treat you" (Luke 6:31). If we always did this, it is likely we would not offend others and our actions would be courteous. Here are some things to consider:

- Never intentionally embarrass or criticize another. We must be especially careful of this in our own homes, as well as in our neighborhoods. Use your words to build up, not to tear down.
- Never gossip (see Proverbs 17:9; 18:8, 21; 20:19; 21:23; 26:22).
- Exhibit appropriate personal habits and hygiene.

  I was on a flight from the east coast to the west when I observed something I couldn't believe. A man in the aisle across from me decided to use this downtime to clip his fingernails. My husband performs this act of hygiene when I am away because for some reason it grates on me like fingernails on a chalkboard. And there I was, a captive audience, while this stranger did it right next to me. What really got me was that all his cut nails were ending up on the floor of the airplane and someone was going to have to clean it up—and it was obviously not him.

  I've even seen people floss their teeth in public. We've all witnessed or maybe have even been guilty of some acts of personal hygiene in public. Let's remember that this is best done in private.

- Be considerate of those who serve you.

  I was with a group of women at a restaurant very early in the morning. The waitress came to take our order and was rather curt with us. We complained about her among ourselves after she left but decided when our food arrived to be good Christians and ask how we could pray for her. She told us her husband was suffering from cancer and she had to leave him alone to do this job because there was not enough money to pay their bills. She gratefully held hands with us while we prayed for her. We were all humbled to think we had judged this woman who was suffering so much. We left her a very big tip and learned a valuable lesson in the process. We need compassion for all those who serve us because we do not know their circumstances.

- Avoid road rage in your driving.
- Clean up after yourself.

   How many of you have gone into a fitting room in a store and found it full of clothes strewn in complete disarray? I spoke to a department store clerk as she was cleaning up a room, and she told me most of her work hours were spent cleaning up after others. Doesn't kindness say that if you try something on and don't purchase it, you should return the garment to its hanger and take it to the racks provided?

The following are a few rules for being a good neighbor:
- Know your neighbors.
- Respect their privacy.
- Keep your animals under control in your yard (no barking or litter).
- Keep your yard attractive.
- Don't block driveways.

9. Appropriate Attire

Pat covered modest dressing in session 6, and even though today's culture is *much* more casual than it used to be, there are still rules of dress that are appropriate.

- We should not go out in public in our bedroom wear, nor should we allow our daughters to do so. Nor should we wear in public places such as restaurants the "weary clothes" we lounge in.

   I was in a coffee shop with a friend when a very nicely dressed older gentlemen arrived and sat at the table next to us. In a few minutes, a young man arrived dressed in an oxford shirt, shorts, and flip-flops and joined the older man. We soon realized this was a job interview. My younger friend leaned over to me and said, "He shouldn't have dressed like that!" I've learned that colleges are offering classes on appropriate dress and manners for students before they enter the marketplace. If it is necessary to have classes to teach proper etiquette, it tells us it is not being taught in the home.

- While jeans can be expensive, they are not wedding or funeral wear. It is no longer considered necessary to wear black to a funeral, but choose clothes that are inconspicuous and subdued in color.

- Beware dressing as the trends dictate because sometimes that trend is not appropriate for your body type. The low-rise pant, for example, should not be worn if the top of your panty, or worse, can be seen when you bend down.

8. Mealtime Manners

Being at ease at the dinner table means being able to thoroughly enjoy the company and the cuisine. You want your family and guests to be relaxed while experiencing gracious dining. As meals are social events, it is essential to practice proper manners. This includes setting the table, serving yourself and others, using utensils, and cleaning up. It also can mean dealing with those unexpected dining difficulties, such as specific allergies, unruly children, or guests that overstay. As with any social situation, consideration for those around you can make a world of difference in regard to the outcome.

Here are some dos and don'ts:

- Table manners should be practiced whether alone or at dinner with family members. When always used in private, they will always be used in public.
- If you're having dinner with friends and family, be with them. How many times have you been in a restaurant and witnessed a table where no one is talking to one another because everyone is on the phone or has earphones in his or her ears? We have raised a generation of kids who can't carry on a conversation. Teach your children how to have dinner conversation. Talk about their day, share stories, and ask questions. There is much to be learned at the dinner table.

   My family invited a friend and her husband for dinner. Her husband was going to be out of town and rather than decline the invitation, she substituted her teenage son. The day of the dinner, she called to ask if her son's friend could come also (now there's another etiquette problem). I prepared more food. During dinner we asked the boys many questions about their school and their interests, and every time they answered with a simple yes or no. Throughout the entire meal, they did not make conversation or eye contact. When they finished eating, they went home to play video games. It so discouraged me!

- Slouching, tipping your chair back, talking with a mouth full of food, and looking at your smartphone (or worse, talking on it) are never appropriate.
- As soon as you are seated, put your napkin in your lap; if you must leave the table, put the napkin on your chair. Use your napkin throughout the meal.
- Pass plates of food to your right.
- If a food you don't like is served, simply say, "no thank you." You do not need to express that you don't like it.
- Utensils being used should always stay on the plate and not on the table.
- Place your fork and knife in the four o'clock position on your plate to indicate you are finished eating.
- Set your table. Even toddlers can help set the table. This shows that you are prepared and welcomes family and guests to the dinner table. (See the table-setting diagram on page 372.)

7. Being a Good Houseguest
My experience has been that my best guests are those who have had guests!

Tips for a one-time event (such as a dinner invitation):
- Take a small gift for the hostess.
- Never take your children or another person to an event unless they have been specifically invited.
- Do not overstay your welcome.
- Be on time.

Thoughtful rules for being a good overnight houseguest:
- Let the hostess know when you are arriving and leaving and stick to those times.
- Show gratitude often; no complaining! "A friend loves at all times" (Proverbs 17:17).
- Eat what is served.
- Make the bed in the morning, and on the day you leave strip the bed and put the sheets and towels in the laundry. If the hostess will give you clean sheets, make the bed.
- Clean up after yourself by putting dishes in the dishwasher and not the sink. Help as much as you can. Look for ways to be helpful.
- Make your schedule fit into your hostess's. Don't stay up later than she does and do not oversleep in the morning.
- Don't use too much hot water (no thirty-minute showers, even if you do this at home).
- Don't leave your things around the house.
- Do not listen to the television too loudly.
- Respect the privacy of the hostess. Do not look in drawers or help yourself to things in the refrigerator unless permission has been given.
- Leave nothing but pleasant memories behind.
- Be a blessing to the home you stay in. A small gift brought or sent afterward is a kind gesture. Some ideas are note cards, flowers, a scented candle, or a book the hostess would enjoy. Be sure to write a thank-you note after your stay!

6. Correspondence (Particularly Thank-You Notes)
Phyllis Theroux once said, "To send a letter is a good way to go somewhere without moving anything but your heart."[27] The art of saying thanks in written form is going away. What the postal service calls "household to household" correspondence is less than 1 percent of the 100 billion pieces of first-class mail every year. E-mail has replaced the handwritten note; however, handwritten notes are warmer than other forms of thank-you expressions.

The rule of thumb is that you should send a written note any time you receive a gift and the giver wasn't there to thank in person.

Thank-you notes should be written within two weeks of receiving the gift (except for weddings, which should be within three months). Name the item or favor you are thankful for and highlight why you like it and/or how you are using it. Be sincere in your note.

5. The Pleasure of a Reply (RSVP)

All events require time, energy, effort, and often great financial expense. Therefore, all invitations, no matter what type, should be answered as promptly as possible and definitely by the deadline if one is given. Samuel Ward McAllister, the self-appointed arbiter of New York society in the late 1800s, once said, "A dinner invitation, once accepted, is a sacred obligation. If you die before the dinner takes place, your executor must attend."

- It is incredibly inconsiderate for guests to fail to RSVP.

  Some forget; others procrastinate and then feel guilty, so they delay even longer. When a hostess does not receive an RSVP, it appears that the invitee is simply waiting for something better to come along. A consequence of the failure to RSVP is that relationships often suffer due to the hostess's hurt feelings and frustration.

- If you accept an invitation, only an emergency should keep you away.

  James 5:12 says, "Your yes is to be yes, and your no, no." Just recently I hosted a get-together at the lake for the ladies in my Bible study. Twelve women replied that they were coming. The day before the event, three changed their minds because "something else came up." Unfortunately, if people do not host events where food is offered, they do not realize the lost effort and cost of their declining at the last minute.

4. Arriving on Time

- Fifteen minutes is the appropriate length of time a hostess should delay for a late guest; likewise, don't arrive more than ten minutes early.
- Allow for delays, but if you are unexpectedly delayed, call the hostess to tell her when to expect you.
- Who said fashionably late was appropriate? Lateness is never fashionable; it is rude.

3. Social Media Etiquette

Using your computer to communicate with others involves acting with the same respect and consideration that you use in the nonvirtual world. Human contact still matters, along with what you say and how you say it.

- Oversharing is a problem. Personal problems should be kept offline. "When there are many words, transgression is unavoidable, but he who restrains his lips is wise" (Proverbs 10:19).

PART THREE: Be Amazing in the Home

- Beware of embarrassing photos. Resist the temptation to post every photo from your birthday party, especially those that cast others in an unflattering light.

In addition to being kind, think about safety.
- A teen's social media page is like a diary and is open to hackers and others. Instead of using their real names, have your children use nicknames to maintain privacy. Choose tricky passwords and change them often.
- Restrict access. Keep current with privacy settings and limit to people you know.
- Researchers have found that "Facebook envy" can lead to depression and isolation. Those who spend a lot of time on Facebook are more socially isolated and frequently depressed than those who do not. They are less satisfied with their own lives. Beware of this in your home.[28]

2. E-mail Etiquette

Considerate use of your smartphone or personal digital assistant (PDA) requires utmost responsibility and command of your device. It is often taken for granted that information and communication are always at hand. However, it is also important to know when and where to access it appropriately and, perhaps more importantly, those times and places it is best left alone. "The lips of the righteous nourish many, but fools die for lack of judgment" (Proverbs 10:21, NIV).
- A personal e-mail is like a personal phone call, so don't say anything you wouldn't say on the phone. Always double-check before you hit "send."
- Think about what you are saying. A bad attitude, anger, criticism, sarcasm, and frustration are still palpable via e-mail messages. It's not *what* you say, but what others *hear* you say.
- Be discreet about the messages you send, including forwards. Do not forward chain letters or messages full of inappropriate jokes or pictures.
- Do not check your e-mail in the presence of others. It is rude. Always be aware of who is around you when checking e-mail.
- Using all capital letters equates to shouting.
- Deliver bad news in person or verbally.

1. Cell Phone Etiquette

Cell phones are great; they keep us in touch with friends and family and can be lifesavers in an emergency. However, they can be annoying if not used properly. Today's phones are capable of countless special functions, but remember that basic etiquette still applies. Being aware of who is with you and where you are when receiving a call is important, as well as having an awareness of your volume and tone of voice.

a. Be courteous!

If a phone call will interrupt a conversation or activity, turn your cell phone off. We don't want friends or relatives to think our mobile device matters more to us than they do. If you must take a call, move to a private space and speak as quietly as you can. If you're with a group, simply excuse yourself for a few minutes, saying, "Sorry, I need to take this call. I'll be right back." Then keep the call as brief as possible.

b. Speak softly.

Keep your voice low. For some reason, people's "phone voices" are always louder than the voice they use in normal conversation. Cell phone use should be kept brief and your voice low on public transportation (trains, planes), in hospitals, restaurants, theaters, and at checkouts.

c. Be in control of your phone; don't let it control you!

Taking a call in the presence of another person signals that the person you are with is less important than the person calling. The caller can always leave you a voice mail. Remember, your cell phone doesn't have to be on all the time and you don't always have to answer it immediately. Learn to use your phone's features such as silent ring, vibrate, and voice mail to handle the times when use of your phone would bother others.

d. Avoid talking about personal problems on the phone in public.

Talking about personal problems in public can make those around you feel uncomfortable and can be embarrassing. Make sure you save these conversations for home or another private place.

e. Do not send text messages when you are in the company of others.

If you're having dinner with friends and family, be with them. Just because texting is a quiet activity (unlike a phone call), you're not fooling anyone. The guideline is that you do not text when you are involved in any type of social interaction (conversation, listening in class, at a meeting, and especially at the dinner table). If you really need to communicate with someone who is not at the event — or at the table — excuse yourself and return as soon as you can.

f. Private information can be forwarded, so don't text it.

Don't text anything confidential, private, or potentially embarrassing. You never know when your message might get sent to the wrong person or be forwarded, not to mention if someone finds your lost phone.

III. Conclusion

We live in a culture that has rapidly changing codes of behavior. Can you imagine the impact we could make as believers if we put others before ourselves? "So then, while we have opportunity, let us do good to all people, and especially to those who are of the household of the faith" (Galatians 6:10). Let us make the most of every opportunity to do good to all. Then we will be amazing women who are good examples for others, have godly influence, and make an impact on our world.

Now What?

What were the most important points for you personally in this message, "Behave! Etiquette"?

Homework Day 2

What?

"Treat others the same way you want them to treat you" (Luke 6:31).

So What?

Luke 6:31 is the Golden Rule by which we live. As we review the top ten lost arts of etiquette, go through the following scenarios in light of this Scripture that tells us to "treat others the same way you want them to treat you."

10. **Neighborliness.** A friend shares with you a personal concern about her husband. You leave, telling her that you will pray for them. The following week you are having lunch with some mutual friends and share her concerns with these women. Record what the following proverbs say about gossip (see 17:9; 18:21; 20:19; 21:23).

9. **Appropriate Attire.** You and your fifteen-year-old daughter are shopping for school clothes. She immediately puts on things that are immodest—too low, too tight, too short. When you express your concern, she gets angry. In light of 1 Timothy 2:9, which of the following should you do?
   a. Give in to her anger to avoid conflict and buy her the clothes.
   b. Respond in anger.
   c. Calmly remind her of your responsibility before God to parent according to His Word. Refuse to buy the clothes that are not appropriate.

8. **Mealtime Manners.** Your family goes out to breakfast together. When seated in the restaurant, everyone pulls out his or her electronic device. There is no conversation. What should you do to change this and try to bond your family through communication (see Proverbs 20:11; 22:6)?

7. **Being a Good Houseguest.** Your family goes to your sister's house at the beach for a weeklong vacation. She has labored all day in anticipation of your arrival. You all sit down, the food is served, and your six-year-old announces he doesn't like this food. What can you teach your child in this situation (see Proverbs 16:24; 18:21; 1 Timothy 6:8)?

6. **Correspondence.** Your thirteen-year-old receives a check in the mail from his grandparents. Weeks pass and no thank-you note has been written. As a parent, what is your role (see Proverbs 4:1-2; 1 Thessalonians 5:18)?

Now What?

Based on the verses you just read, what specifically is God asking you to do?

Homework Day 3

What?

"Therefore, as we have opportunity, let us do good to all people; especially to those who belong to the family of believers" (Galatians 6:10, NIV).

So What?

Let's continue our review of the top ten lost arts of etiquette.

5. **The Pleasure of a Reply.** You are hosting an outdoor wedding for your daughter at your home. It will require the rental of tents, chairs, and place settings. The invitations went out six weeks before the event, but two weeks before, only 30 percent of the invitees have responded. Some are waiting to see if they want to come, and some have committed and then changed their minds. As the hostess, what should you do (see Philippians 4:6-7; James 1:5)?

4. **Arriving on Time.** According to Miss Emily Post, an American author famous for writing about etiquette, lateness is rudeness every time. Why is it not okay for you to accept this quality in yourself and others in light of God's command (see Philippians 2:3)?

3. **Social Media Etiquette.** Facebook and other social media forums sometimes read like diaries. You like to share a lot of personal information about your comings and goings, and your contact list is long and distinguished. One of your contacts regularly reads your posts

and begins to get depressed because her life isn't nearly as glamorous as yours sounds. Why is it best not to share so much personal information on this network (see Proverbs 10:19)?

2. **E-mail Etiquette.** Discretion is always best when sending e-mails. Once you hit the "send" button, you can't take back what you have said. It is now a way to communicate bad attitudes, anger, sarcasm, and even frustration without having to have face-to-face interaction. What is the best way to handle an offense that has been inflicted via cyberspace (see Proverbs 12:18; Galatians 5:13-14)?

1. **Cell Phone Etiquette.** You are in the home of a friend, having dinner with ten of your closest friends, when one of the guests receives a phone call on her cell. She answers it while seated at the table and proceeds to have a ten-minute conversation while the other nine guests try to carry on a conversation. What is the appropriate action she should have taken in this situation (see Matthew 7:12)?

Now What?

What attitude or action is God asking you to adopt or change?

INFORMAL

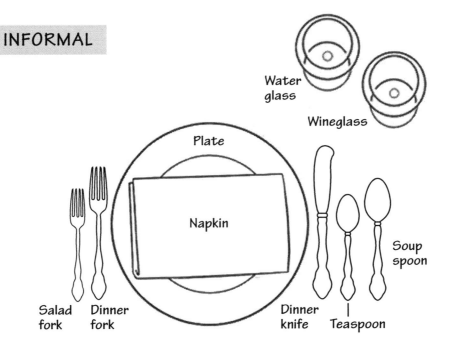

Water glass

Wineglass

Plate

Napkin

Soup spoon

Salad fork   Dinner fork

Dinner knife   Teaspoon

Utensils are placed one inch from the edge of the table

• • • • • • • • • • • • • • • •

FORMAL

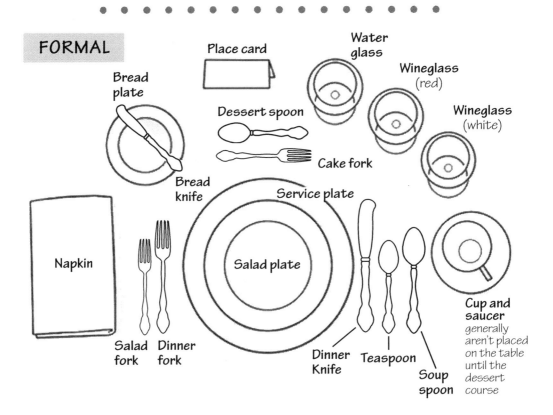

Place card

Water glass

Wineglass (red)

Bread plate

Dessert spoon

Wineglass (white)

Cake fork

Bread knife

Service plate

Napkin

Salad plate

Cup and saucer *generally aren't placed on the table until the dessert course*

Salad fork   Dinner fork

Dinner Knife   Teaspoon

Soup spoon

R U Prepared?

Planning for the Future

Eleanor Lewis

"That the word of God will not be dishonored."

Titus 2:5

DVD Outline

I. **Prepared for the Present**
A. Preparation Defined
B. Prepared for Today

II. **Prepared for the Future: Emergencies**
A. A Safe Place with Emergency Supplies
B. An Emergency "Go Bag"
C. Water
1. Storing water
2. How to prepare your own containers
3. Treating other sources of unclean water
D. Food
1. Emergency food storage considerations
2. Items to store
3. Food storage tips
4. Where to store food
E. Workplace
F. Vehicle
1. Keep your gas tank full.
2. Keep your cell phone fully charged with a car phone charger.
3. Emergency car supplies
G. First-Aid Kit
H. Phones
I. Emergency Heat and Light
1. Light sources
2. Heat sources
J. Thunderstorms
1. To prepare for a thunderstorm
2. If a thunderstorm is likely in your area
3. Avoid the following
K. Fire

III. **Prepared for the Future: Eternity**
A. R U Prepared?
B. A Final Word of Encouragement

PART THREE: Be Amazing in the Home

1. What are one or two things that you are *immediately* going to act on to prepare for a physical emergency?
2. What do you need to do to prepare for eternity?

Homework Day 1

What?

"Strength and dignity are her clothing, and she smiles at the future" (Proverbs 31:25).

So What?

Read the following notes from the DVD message "R U Prepared? Planning for the Future" and answer the "Now What" question at the end.

I. Prepared for the Present

A. Preparation Defined

When I was growing up there was a dangerously sharp curve in the road that was the site of a number of fatal accidents. Someone had written on a rock at the curve, "R U Prepared?" That is actually a good question because we've seen that amazing women consider the future.

According to *Strong's Concordance,* the word *prepare* means "to make the necessary preparations; to get everything ready." The disciples prepared or made the necessary arrangements for the Passover in the upper room. As Robin told us, Abigail was prepared with a supply of food. Jesus says He has gone to "prepare a place for you" (John 14:2).

B. Prepared for Today

Be Amazing has been written to prepare you to be an amazing woman by causing you to think about your role as a woman in a new way. This study, if applied, will equip you to be a more godly, confident woman who makes an impact on those around her. We have seen that God has a high view of women. He desires that older women (and regardless of your age, you are older than someone) are prepared and willing to teach and encourage younger women to have a godly home, character, and relationships.

II. Prepared for the Future: Emergencies

An emergency is defined as a sudden, urgent, usually unexpected event requiring immediate action and a need for help or relief. In the past few years we have had devastating tornadoes covering several states and several very destructive hurricanes. My family personally had broken water lines and twice were without power for an extended time. Jesus said famines and earthquakes will be like birth pangs the closer we get to His return. And we know birth pangs get stronger and more frequent the closer we get to a birth (see Matthew 24:7-8). Therefore, being prepared is important. We can prepare our homes for everyday living, but there are also a number of unexpected emergencies that could occur in the future that we should prepare for:

- Natural disasters:
  - ★ Tornadoes
  - ★ Hurricanes
  - ★ Earthquakes
  - ★ Blizzards
  - ★ Floods
  - ★ Droughts
  - ★ Wildfires
- Manmade disasters or equipment failures:
  - ★ Strikes (food production or shipping strikes that keep food from stores)
  - ★ Power outages (caused by men, nature, or equipment malfunction)
  - ★ Terrorist attacks
  - ★ Water line breaks

If there was an emergency and you had to live for two weeks without electricity, water, or outside assistance, could you do it? Here are some helps for emergency planning.

A. A Safe Place with Emergency Supplies[29]

Have a predetermined safe place: a small interior room with few or no windows. Recently after a hurricane a woman's home was intact but she bled to death because of flying broken glass. Have emergency supplies such as these in your safe place:

- Water: at least one gallon of water per person and pet per day
- Food: at least a three-day supply of nonperishable food
- Moist towelettes for personal hygiene
- Garbage bags/plastic ties for sanitation
- Fire extinguisher
- Wrench or pliers to turn off utilities
- Manual can opener for canned food in case of power outage
- Blankets or sleeping bags
- Sturdy shoes and change of clothing
- Cell phone with chargers, inverter, or solar charger

B. An Emergency "Go Bag"

Put the following in a backpack, bucket, or some other easy-to-carry container to take with you in case you must evacuate. Prepare one bag for each family member and keep it in your safe place. The "go bag" could include the following:

- Flashlight with extra batteries
- Radio: battery, solar, and/or crank (NOAA Weather Radio) with extra batteries. I found an NOAA Weather Radio that runs on electricity, batteries, hand crank, or solar. It also lets you charge cell phones and is a flashlight.
- Whistle to signal for help
- Pocket knife
- Emergency cash in small denominations
- Extra house and car keys
- Dried food containing protein such as nuts and energy bars
- Pet food or infant formula and diapers (if applicable)
- Matches in a waterproof container (or other fire starter)
- First-aid kit (see details in section G)

Other items to consider:

- A FLOP (Financial Life on One Page) kept in a safety deposit box or given to a close family member living in another area could be helpful.
- Copies of important family documents: insurance policies, identification, and bank account records. Keep in waterproof, fireproof, portable container.
- Prescription medications and eyeglasses
- Feminine supplies and personal hygiene items (toothbrush, toothpaste, and so on)
- Mess kits, paper cups, paper plates, paper towels, and plastic utensils
- Bible
- Paper, pencil, books, games, puzzles, or other activities for children
- Unscented household chlorine bleach (nine parts water to one part bleach can be used as a disinfectant and can also be used to disinfect water supply)

C. Water

I have never given much thought to having my home prepared for emergencies because those things happen to someone else! The one thing I have done is store containers of clean water. My husband thought this was a waste of time because "you just turn on the faucet." But one day we had a water line break and help couldn't come for twenty-four hours. When Bob could wash his face, brush his teeth, and have his morning coffee, I was a hero. He now helps fill the jugs!

Water is necessary in any emergency, whether a disaster or a broken water line, as clean drinking water may not be available. Dehydration can cause death in three to five days. Prepare by storing a supply of water that will meet your family's needs for at least three days, and longer if possible.

1. Storing water
   - If you know a potential disaster is coming, fill the bathtub and sinks with water.
   - There is not always warning, so store at least one gallon of water per person per day

for drinking. An additional two to three gallons per day are necessary to cook with and use for personal hygiene.

- Pets need ½ gallon per animal per day. Water is also needed to flush commodes.
- Keep commercially bottled water in its original container and do not open until you need to use it. Observe the expiration (use by) date.
- Do not store where a bottle could leak and cause damage to wood.
- Store in a cool, dark place.

2. How to prepare your own containers
    - **Containers to use:** You can use glass or food-grade water storage containers from a surplus/camping supplies store or plastic two-liter soft drink or bleach bottles. DO NOT use plastic or cardboard milk or fruit juice containers because milk protein and fruit sugars cannot be adequately removed and provide an environment for bacterial growth. Also they can leak. Boxed Mylar pouch water storage kits hold five gallons and can be stacked. Barrels designed for water storage hold five to fifty-five gallons of water but are heavy and need a spout.
    - **Sanitize:** Before filling with water, thoroughly clean the containers with dish soap and water. Rinse completely. Sanitize the bottles by mixing one teaspoon of nonscented liquid household chlorine bleach with a quart of water. Mix the sanitizing solution in the bottle so it touches all surfaces, including the lid. Thoroughly rinse.
    - **Tap water:** Fill the bottle with tap water. If the water has been commercially treated with chlorine by a water utility company, you do not need to add anything else to keep the water clean.
    - **Well water:** If the water is from a well or water source that is not treated with chlorine, add two drops of nonscented liquid household chlorine bleach to the water. Let the water stand for thirty minutes before using. A slight chlorine odor should be noticeable. Water can also be treated with water purification tablets purchased at sporting goods stores.
    - **Date:** Tightly close the container using the original cap. Be careful not to contaminate the cap by touching the inside with your finger. Place the date on the outside of the container. Water that has not been commercially bottled should be replaced every six to eight months. (I replace mine every January and July and use the old water for plants or to flush the toilets. Clean the bottles as described above and refill.)

3. Treating other sources of unclean water
    If you run out of stored drinking water, strain and treat water from one of the following:
    - Water heater
    - Toilet reservoir tank (unless you use toilet tank cleaners)
    - Lakes or streams

Swimming pool/spa water should NOT be consumed but can be used for flushing or washing.

To treat the water, follow these steps:
- **Strain:** Remove large particles of dirt by pouring the water through layers of paper towels or clean cloth (dish towel or clean T-shirt). Then purify the water.
- **Boil:** Bring to a rolling boil for three to five minutes. After the water cools, pour it back and forth between two clean containers to add oxygen back. This will improve its taste.
- **Disinfect:** If the water is clear, add 1/8 teaspoon bleach per gallon of water. If it is cloudy, add 1/4 teaspoon per gallon. Use only regular bleach (5.25 percent sodium hypochlorite), not the "ultra" or "color safe" bleaches. Shake or stir and let stand for thirty minutes. A slight chlorine taste and smell is normal.

LifeStraw is a portable straw that can filter up to 265 gallons of water. More information on water treatment is available at www.RedCross.org.

D. Food

Following an emergency there may be power outages that could last for days, or store shelves may be empty. Stock canned foods, dry foods, and other staples that do not require refrigeration, cooking, much water, or special preparation. Be sure to include a manual can opener and eating utensils. To save money, buy in bulk or purchase food when it is on sale or you have coupons.

1. Emergency food storage considerations
   - Store at least a three-day supply of nonperishable food (several weeks' supply is better).
   - Choose foods your family will eat.
   - Remember any special dietary needs.
   - Choose low-salt crackers, whole-grain cereals, and canned foods with high liquid content.

2. Items to store
   You may already have many of these on hand:
   - Ready-to-eat canned foods such as meats, fruits, vegetables, and soups
   - Protein or fruit bars
   - Dry cereal or granola
   - Peanut butter
   - Honey

- Dried fruit and nuts
- Pasta and rice (requires water and cooking)
- Crackers
- Canned juices, sports drinks, protein drinks
- Nonperishable pasteurized milk or nonfat dry milk (requires water)
- High energy or protein bars
- Food for infants or pets

3. Food storage tips
   - Rotate your stock. Use from the front and replace in back.
   - Mark the "use by" date on all lids with a permanent marker so it can be easily seen. ("Use buy" dates are for taste and nutritional values but do not mean food is spoiled. Foods may spoil before the date if not stored properly or may last well beyond.)
   - Store noncanned food in airtight, pest-resistant containers. These snap-tight containers not only keep crackers fresh but can be used to keep meat or ice cream in the freezer. I do this, and when we were gone for three weeks and had a power outage, I was able to easily throw away the whole container without having to throw away the freezer. In addition, these containers keep bread fresher without that freezer smell. They also keep meat from getting freezer burn.
   - Most canned foods can be safely stored for at least eighteen months.
   - Low acid foods—meat products, fruits, or vegetables—last at least two years.
   - Dry products such as cereal, crackers, cookies, and dried milk and fruits will last six months to one year.
   - After a power outage refrigerated food will keep longer if the door remains shut. Food in the freezer will normally remain safe for two days.
   - Dehydrated or freeze-dried foods have a very long shelf life (twenty-five to thirty years!).

   For more information, check websites such as www.freezedriedguy.com.

   Because my family does not eat much canned food I never had a stocked pantry. However, since I now put the date on the top of the can, I can keep track of the dates and either use the food or donate it to a food bank several months before it expires.

4. Where to store food
   Remember: cool, dark, and dry!
   - Turn a coat closet into storage with shelves floor to ceiling
   - Under a bed in boxes or airtight containers
   - Under pressed-wood end tables with a floor-length tablecloth to hide it

- Use a trash can or bucket full of supplies as a table, put glass or wood on top, and use a cloth to cover
- In the basement, but watch dampness (use a dehumidifier)

E. Workplace

Be prepared with necessities to live twenty-four hours: food, water, medicines. Also have comfortable walking shoes. Keep supplies in a bag that is ready to grab and go in case you are evacuated and have to walk a long distance. Even in the South snowstorms have kept employees in the office overnight. For more information, go to http://www.ready.gov/workplace-plans.

F. Vehicle

If you find yourself stranded, stay in your car, put on your hazards, call for help, and wait until it arrives. If you are in your car during an emergency, close all windows and turn off vents and air-conditioning.

1. Keep your gas tank full.
2. Keep your cell phone fully charged with a car phone charger.
3. Emergency car supplies:
   - Flashlights and extra batteries
   - Jumper cables
   - First-aid items and necessary medications
   - Food containing protein: nuts or energy bars
   - Water
   - Sturdy shoes
   - Rain jacket or coat for cold weather
   - Blankets

Since you do not know where you will be when an emergency occurs, prepare supplies for home, work, and vehicles. To build a disaster supply kit, go to http://www.ready.gov/build-a-kit.

G. First-Aid Kit

Keep all supplies in a snap-tight container with a handle for easy carrying. The week after I took all my first-aid items from two drawers and a closet and put them all in a container that can be carried, I fell up some steps and badly cut my leg. My husband was able to bring the whole supply kit and had everything he needed to treat the wound until I could get to the emergency room.

In any emergency someone may be cut, burned, or suffer an injury. Basic first aid includes:

PART THREE: Be Amazing in the Home

- Sterile dressings and adhesive bandages
- Cleansing/disinfecting products: chlorine, soap, towelettes, hydrogen peroxide, alcohol
- Antibiotic ointment for infection
- Hydrocortisone cream for bites, poison ivy, or rashes
- Burn ointment
- Calamine lotion
- Eye wash solution to flush the eyes
- Tools: scissors, tweezers for splinters/stingers
- Over-the-counter medicine: pain reliever, aspirin, laxative, antidiarrhea medication
- Prescription medications such as insulin, heart medicine, or asthma inhaler

Download a free emergency medical manual to keep in your first-aid kit at www.emergencycareforyou.org.

H. Phones
Cordless phones require electricity; make sure you have a phone that requires no electricity.
- Keep cell phones charged.
- Don't count on your cell phone. Increased traffic can quickly overload wireless capacity.
- Learn how to text. Texting uses a different part of the cell phone network and it might work when voice channels for mobile phones and landlines are jammed.

Register your e-mail address and wireless devices (mobile phones, pagers, and PDAs) to receive e-mail alerts about potential hazards and/or post-disaster information. Go to http://www.weather.com/newscenter/alerts/national/severeWxAlertsNational.html.

I. Emergency Heat and Light
If power is out for an extended period of time, the following are important considerations.

1. Light sources
   - Flashlights (battery, solar, hand crank)
   - Battery LED
   - Candles
   - Oil lamps

2. Heat sources
   - Be sure to have matches.
   - If possible have an outside gas grill (propane) for heating food and boiling water.

My family did not have any heat source but electricity so we purchased an outdoor propane gas grill. We have enjoyed it, and now we have an emergency heating source as well.

- If you have a fireplace keep plenty of firewood on hand (covered), as supplies will deplete rapidly in an emergency. A fireplace can warm your home and heat food.

Warning: To avoid carbon monoxide, use all alternative means of cooking outside your home. Never use a generator, grill, camp stove, gasoline stove, propane, or charcoal burning device inside your home, garage, basement, or any partially enclosed area.

J. Thunderstorms
Do *not* underestimate the danger of thunderstorms.

1. To prepare for a thunderstorm
   - Remove dead or rotting trees and branches that could fall and cause injury or damage.
   - Remember the 30/30 lightning safety rule:
     ★ Go indoors if, after seeing lightning, you cannot count to 30 before hearing thunder.
     ★ Stay indoors for 30 minutes after hearing the last clap of thunder.

2. If a thunderstorm is likely in your area
   - Get inside a home, building, or hard-topped automobile. You may be injured if lightning strikes your car, but you are much safer there than outside. Rubber-soled shoes and rubber tires provide no protection from lightning. However, the steel frame of a hard-topped vehicle provides increased protection if you are not touching metal!
   - If no shelter is available, go to a low-lying open place away from trees, poles, or metal.
   - Secure outdoor objects that could blow away or cause damage.
   - Shutter windows and secure outside doors.
   - Close window blinds, shades, or curtains to protect from shattered glass caused by wind.
   - Unplug appliances and other electrical items, such as computers.
   - Turn off air conditioners. Power surges from lightning can cause serious damage. We have had two very destructive power surges. The first destroyed everything that was plugged in, including the air-conditioning panel, sprinkler system, refrigerator, televisions, clocks, and so on. We then had a whole house surge protector installed, which helped during the second surge but still did not keep all appliances from

being damaged. However, the surge protector company did help pay the damages.

Monitor NOAA Weather Radio, radio, or television for the latest weather forecasts, or download a phone app if available in your state, such as www.ready.ga.gov/mobileapp.

3. Avoid the following:
   - Showering, bathing, and running water. (Plumbing and bathroom fixtures can conduct electricity.)
   - Corded phones except for emergencies. (Telephone lines and metal pipes can conduct electricity.) Cordless or cellular phones are safe.
   - Anything metal: tractors, farm equipment, motorcycles, golf carts, golf clubs, bicycles, and so on
   - Natural lightning rods such as tall, isolated trees or isolated sheds in open areas
   - Hilltops, open fields, the beach, or a boat on the water

K. Fire
   - Identify two ways to escape from every room in your home and practice your plan.
   - Select a safe location away from the home where your family can meet after escaping.
   - Consider purchasing escape ladders for rooms above ground level, have a knotted rope in the closet, or learn how to tie sheets together.
   - If you must exit through smoke, crawl low under the smoke.
   - Feel closed doors before opening them. If they are warm, use your alternate escape route.
   - If smoke, heat, or flames block both of your exit routes, stay in the room with the door closed. Place a rolled towel or blanket underneath the door. Signal for help by waving a brightly colored cloth or shining a flashlight. Call for help if a phone is available.
   - Once you've escaped, stay out!

III. Prepared for the Future: Eternity

A. R U Prepared?
God told Israel there was another preparation necessary: "Prepare to meet your God" (Amos 4:12). Jesus is getting prepared for you; are you prepared for Him? As important as it is to be prepared for emergency situations, the ultimate preparation is for eternity.

Jesus tells us He has done His part. He came and died to pay the wage for our sin of death. Being perfect He had no sin of His own to pay for, so He could pay for ours! He was buried and rose again, defeating sin and death.

He says He has now gone "to prepare a place for you. If I go and prepare a place for you, I will come again and receive you to Myself, that where I am, there you may be also" (John 14:2-3).

Thomas said he didn't know the way to that prepared place. Jesus told him, "I am the way, and the truth, and the life; no one comes to the Father but through Me" (John 14:6).

Remember, the word *prepare* means to make the necessary preparations, to get everything ready. God prepared, or got the world ready, for you in six days, and it is pretty spectacular. Jesus has been gone about two thousand years preparing a place for you, so it must be incredible! In fact, God says we can't even imagine it: "No eye has seen, no ear has heard, no mind has conceived what God has prepared for those who love him" (1 Corinthians 2:9, NIV).

B. A Final Word of Encouragement

Amazing women are theologians, and we want to heed God's warning not to be "always learning and never able to come to the knowledge of the truth" (2 Timothy 3:7). We know God says, "If you love me, you will obey what I command" (John 14:15, NIV). As we obey what we know from this study of Titus 2:3-5, we will become women who are prepared to have an impact on our world because we have these characteristics:

- Sensible: have a sound mind fixed on things above, not on things of the earth
- Kind: in word and deed, resolving conflicts with kindness and caring for others
- Pure: in mind, word, deed, and dress
- Lovers of our husbands: showing them respect and submitting to them as unto the Lord; one with them
- Lovers of our children: training them to be holy
- Keepers of the home: CEOs of the refuge of comfort and safety called home

Applying these truths will not only prepare us for living today but also prepare us for eternity because we will "be found by Him in peace, spotless and blameless" (2 Peter 3:14). We will be amazing women!

Now What?

What were the most important points for you personally in this message, "R U Prepared? Planning for the Future"?

Homework Day 2

What?

"I go to prepare a place for you" (John 14:2).

So What?

The Proverbs 31 woman is an example to us of the advantage of being prepared. To smile at the future as she did, we must prepare by making the necessary arrangements. According to *Strong's Concordance,* in the Old Testament, the Hebrew word for *prepare* is also translated "to make or to produce."

1. What did God make (see Genesis 1:7-12)?

2. What did God ask Noah to make or prepare, and why (see Genesis 6:11-18; Hebrews 11:7)?

God prepared the world for man to live and an ark to save men. *Strong's Concordance* says that in the New Testament, the word *prepare* means "to get everything ready."

3. What does King Jesus say has been prepared for you (see Matthew 25:34)?

4. What two things did Jesus promise His people (see John 14:2-3)?

Now What?

God prepared for us. He is now asking us to prepare.

1. List what God has specifically said you are to do to prepare for your family's physical needs in case of an emergency.

2. What is the most important thing you need to do to be spiritually prepared to meet your God?

Homework Day 3

What?

"Older women likewise are to be reverent in their behavior, not malicious gossips nor enslaved to much wine, teaching what is good, so that they may encourage the young women to love their husbands, to love their children, to be sensible, pure, workers at home, kind, being subject to their own husbands, so that the word of God will not be dishonored" (Titus 2:3-5).

So What?

As we obey what we know from this study of Titus 2:3-5, we will become women who are prepared to have an impact on our world.

Now What?

Let's review what an amazing woman's picture looks like. She is:
- Sensible: has a sound mind fixed on things above, not on things of the earth
- Kind: in word and deed, resolving conflicts with kindness and caring for others
- Pure: in mind, word, deed, and dress
- A lover of her husband: showing him respect and submitting to him as unto the Lord; one with him
- A lover of her children: training them to be holy
- A keeper of the home: CEO of the refuge of comfort and safety called home

1. How have you applied these truths to your everyday life?

2. What changes have you made or are you making?

3. In what areas have you seen progress?

4. What steps are you taking to become a theologian?

5. How has this study encouraged you in your role as a woman?

Congratulations on completing this study!
You are on your way to becoming an amazing woman.

Resources

WEBSITES:
- The Blue Letter Bible: http://www.blueletterbible.org
- Bible Gateway: http://www.biblegateway.com/
- Bible Study Tools: http://www.BibleStudyTools.com

PHONE APPS:

Search the App store for "Bible, Bible reading, or Bible study tools." There are a number of free apps and some that are not free. Try them to see if they are helpful for you. Since I never pay for apps, I have downloaded free ones including the following:

- "Bible is": You can hear the Word spoken as you wait in car pool.
- "Bible" (lifeChurch.tv): Highly rated; many translations and search features
- "Blue Letter Bible": http://www.blueletterbible.org/search.cfm

"ESV+" is not free but has been recommended especially if you are a teacher because it has study notes, Scripture in many different translations, and an area for your own notes. When teaching or studying, if you don't understand a verse, you can swipe to the left, and it gives some commentary. It also has a very fast interface for getting from book to book quickly.

COMMENTARIES:
- Dallas Seminary (John F. Walvoord and Roy B. Zuck, eds.), *The Bible Knowledge Commentary: An Exposition of the Scriptures*
- Charles F. Pfeiffer and Everett F. Harrison, eds., *The Wycliffe Bible Commentary: A Phrase by Phrase Commentary of the Bible*
- Bruce Wilkinson and Kenneth Boa, *Talk Thru the Bible* (concise look at each book)
- Warren W. Wiersbe, the *Be* series (easy to understand from Genesis to Revelation)
- Gordon J. Wenham, J. Alec Motyer, and Donald A. Carson, eds., *New Bible Commentary*
- Kenneth L. Barker and John R. Kohlenberger III, *The Expositor's Bible Commentary* (2 volumes)
- James Strong, *Strong's Exhaustive Concordance of the Bible* (a necessity)

Strong's Concordance and many commentaries are available free on Bible websites such as:

- www.soniclight.com/constable/notes.htm (free downloads of Dr. Thomas L. Constable)
- www.blueletterbible.org/commentaries/
- www.biblegateway.com/resources/commentaries/

STUDY BIBLES:

There are many excellent study Bibles. These are a couple of good ones that I use:

- *Ryrie Study Bible* (NASB)
- *The Nelson Study Bible* (NKJV)

Session 3: Battle for the Mind: Be Sensible *(Sound Mind)*

BOOKS:

- Dr. Linda Mintle, *Letting Go of Worry*
- David Allen, *Getting Things Done*

Session 4: Keep the Main Thing the Main Thing *(Priorities)*

BOOKS:

- Henry Cloud and John Townsend, *Boundaries*

Session 5: What Are You Thinking? *(Purity)*

WEBSITE:

- www.childrensministryonline.com

BOOKS:

- A. W. Tozer, *The Knowledge of the Holy*
- Lawrence O. Richards, *Encyclopedia of Bible Words*

Session 6: You're Going Out in That? *(Modesty)*

BOOKS:

- Wendy Shalit, *A Return to Modesty: Discovering the Lost Virtue*
- Rachel Lee Carter, *Fashioned by Faith* (excellent for teens and their moms)
- Jeff Pollard, *Christian Modesty and the Public Undressing of America*

WEBSITES:

- www.purefashion.com (for teens)
- www.positivelyfeminine.org

Be Amazing

Session 7: **Kindness in a Mean Girl World** *(Kindness)*
CHILDREN'S BOOKS:
- Carol McCloud, *Have You Filled a Bucket Today?*
- Aaron Reynolds, *Tale of the Poisonous Yuck Bugs* (based on Proverbs 12:18)

Session 8: **It's Not All About Me?** *(Others-Centered)*
BOOKS:
- Gary Chapman, *The 5 Love Languages*
- Carol Kent, *Becoming a Woman of Influence*
- Paul E. Miller, *A Praying Life*

Sessions 9–10: **How to Accept Yourself, Understand Others, and Love Them Anyway!** *(Temperaments)*
BOOKS:
- O. Hallesby, *Temperament and the Christian Faith*
- Any book on the temperaments written by Tim LaHaye or Florence Littauer, such as:
  - ★ Tim LaHaye, *Your Temperament: Discover Its Potential* (out of print)
  - ★ Tim LaHaye, *Spirit-Controlled Temperament*
  - ★ Tim LaHaye, *Transformed Temperaments* (out of print)
  - ★ Florence Littauer, *Raising the Curtain on Raising Children*
  - ★ Florence Littauer, *Your Personality Tree*
  - ★ Florence Littauer, *Personality Plus*

WEBSITE:
- Dr. LaHaye's temperament tests are available at www.timlahaye.com.

Session 11: **You Don't Know My Husband!** *(Love Him?)*
BOOKS:
- Eleanor Lewis (Big Dream Ministries), *How to Accept Yourself, Understand Others, and Like Them Anyway!*

Session 12: **It's All About Sex! (Making Real Love)**
BOOKS:
- Linda Dillow and Lorraine Pintus, *Intimate Issues*
- Dr. Juli Slattery, *No More Headaches*
- Linda Dillow, *What's It Like to Be Married to Me?*
- Clifford and Joyce Penner, *The Gift of Sex*
- Linda Dillow and Dr. Juli Slattery, *Passion Pursuit: What Kind of Love Are You Making?*
- Dr. Gary and Barbara Rosberg, *The 5 Sex Needs of Men and Women*

Session 14: **Let's Fight It Out!** *(Resolving Conflict)*

BOOKS:
- Stormie Omartian, *The Power of a Praying Wife*
- John Bevere, *The Bait of Satan*
- Ken Sande, *The Peacemaker*

Sessions 15–16: **Got Kids?** *(How to Love Them!)*

BOOKS:
- Tedd Tripp, *Shepherding a Child's Heart* (Though we do not agree with all aspects of this book, we do feel it is an excellent book on parenting.)
- George Barna, *Revolutionary Parenting*

Session 18: **Clear the Clutter and Create the Comfort**
(There's No Place Like Home)

BOOKS:
- Mindy Starns Clark, *The House That Cleans Itself*
- Glynnis Whitwer, *I Used to Be So Organized*
- Karen Ehman, *The Complete Guide to Getting and Staying Organized*
- Cheryl Mendelson, *Home Comforts*
- Deborah Needleman, *The Perfectly Imperfect Home: How to Decorate and Live Well*
- Sharon Hanby-Robie, *The Simple Home: A Faith-Filled Guide to Simplicity, Peace, and Joy in Your Home*
- Karen Ehman, *A Life That Says Welcome: Simple Ways to Open Your Heart and Home to Others*

Session 19: **What's for Dinner?** *(Menus and Food Preparation)*

WEBSITES:
- www.cookinglight.com/food/in-season
- www.cookingtheseasons.com
- www.cooking4allseasons.blogspot.com
- www.webmd.com/a-to-z-guides/features/family-dinners-are-important

Session 20: **The Door Is Open, the Light Is On!** *(Hospitality)*

BOOKS:
- Pat Ennis and Lisa Tatlock, *Practicing Hospitality: The Joy of Serving Others* (great encouragement and practical ideas from a biblical perspective)
- Karen Ehman, *A Life That Says Welcome: Simple Ways to Open Your Heart and Home to Others* (great ideas for hospitality and home management)

Be Amazing

- Karen Mains, *Open Heart, Open Home* (This is an older book that really gets at the heart of sharing our homes with others. She clearly explains the difference between entertaining and hospitality. It is not filled with practical ideas so much as an outstanding foundation as to why and how to open our homes. Thought-provoking and encouraging.)
- Grace Pittman, *Hospitality with Confidence* (This is an older book yet it has wonderful practical ideas and recipes for welcoming people into your home.)
- Devi Titus and Marilyn Weiher, *The Home Experience* (This is a rather expensive hardcover book that is beautiful and filled with lots of practical ideas, beautiful colored photos, and wonderful recipes.)

Session 21: **Show Me the Money** (Finances)

WEBSITES:
- www.Christianpf.com
- www.frugalliving.about.com
- www.Financialhighway.com
- www.MyDollarPlan.com

Session 22: **Bag a Buck!** (Time and Money Saving Tips)

WEBSITES:
- www.southernsavers.com
- www.pinterest.com
- www.livingsocial.com
- www.couponmom.com

Session 23: **Behave!** (Etiquette)

BOOKS:
- Judith Martin, *Miss Manners' Guide for the Turn-of-the-Millennium*
- Peggy Post, Anna Post, Lizzie Post, and Daniel Post Senning, *Emily Post's Etiquette*

WEBSITES:
- www.elegantwoman.org
- www.emilypost.com

WEBSITES:

- http://www.72hours.org
- http://www.ready.gov/
- http://www.redcross.org
- www.freezedriedguy.com
- https://registration.weather.com/ursa/alerts/step1?initAlerts=SVR (to register for weather alerts)

Be Amazing

Notes

1. Howard Hendricks, "Strategic Nature of Leadership, Part 1," *Dynamics of Christian Leadership* class, Dallas Theological Seminary.

2. "Vital Statistics of the Self Storage Industry," *Self Storage Blog,* http://www .selfstorageblog.com/vital-statistics-of-the-self-storage-industry/.

3. James MacDonald, *Downpour* (Nashville: Broadman & Holman, 2006), 82.

4. "14 Shocking Pornography Statistics," *The United Families International Blog,* June 2, 2010, http://unitedfamiliesinternational.wordpress.com/?s=shocking+pornography+ statistics.

5. Archibald Naismith, "My Name Is Gossip," *A Treasury of Notes, Quotes, and Anecdotes for Sermon Building* (Grand Rapids, MI: Baker, 1976), 97.

6. James MacDonald and Barb Peil, *Lord, Change My Attitude* (Nashville: LifeWay Christian Resources, 2008), 88.

7. MacDonald, *Downpour,* 118.

8. Eleanor Doan, "You Tell on Yourself," quoted in Elizabeth George, *A Woman's High Calling* (Eugene, OR: Harvest House, 2001), 22.

9. Jeff Pollard, *Christian Modesty and the Public Undressing of America* (San Antonio, TX: The Vision Forum, Inc., 2001), 19.

10. Pollard, 25.

11. Reprinted with permission.

12. Adapted from Ruth E. Grosse, "Does God Care What Women Wear?" http://www .missionsrevival.org/files/Does%20God%20Care%20What%20Women%20Wear%20 -%20Dec%2008%20Revision.pdf.

13. Greek word "fruit," *Strong's Concordance,* www.blueletterbible.com.

14. "The Younger Saints," *The Bible Exposition Commentary,* vol. 2, Ephesians—Revelation (Colorado Springs, CO: Victor Books, 1989), 265.

15. Bryan Mckinley, "Paul Newman Quotes: His Top Ten Best Quotations & Sayings," *Yahoo! Voices,* January 9, 2011, http://voices.yahoo.com/paul-newman-quotes-his-top -ten-best-quotations-sayings-7572356.html.

16. *Encyclopedia of Bible Words.*

17. Stormie Omartian, *The Power of a Praying Wife* (Eugene, OR: Harvest House, 1997), 44–46.

18. John Bevere, *The Bait of Satan* (Lake Mary, FL: Charisma House, 2004), 138–139.

19. "The Apology Hotline," *House to House,* http://www.housetohouse.com/ HTHPubPage.aspx?cid=3613, accessed May 6, 2013.

20. Bevere, 157.

21. "Just a Housewife," *Chicago Tribune,* July 23, 1988.

22. John MacArthur, *The MacArthur Study Bible, NKJV* (Nashville: Word, 1997), 1886.

23. Jeanie Lerche Davis, "Family Dinners Are Important: 10 Reasons Why, and 10 Shortcuts to Help Get the Family to the Table," *WebMD,* July 17, 2007, www.webmd .com/a-to-z-guides/features/family-dinners-are-important.

24. "Benefits of Family Dinners," *The Family Dinner Project.org,* http:// thefamilydinnerproject.org/benefits-of-family-dinners/ (accessed May 13, 2013), and Davis, "Family Dinners Are Important."

25. Ray C. Stedman, "Get Smart with Money," *Treasures of the Parables* sermon series, June 22, 1969, http://www.raystedman.org/thematic-studies/treasures-of-the-parables/ get-smart-with-money.

26. Based on an article by Stephanie AuWerter of American Institute of Certified Public Accountants (AICPA), *Money Magazine,* October 2012, 27.

27. "Phyllis Theroux Quotes," *Good Reads,* http://www.goodreads.com/quotes/159520-to -send-a-letter-is-a-good-way-to-go (accessed May 13, 2013).

28. Rosa Golijan, "It's Not Just You: Facebook Envy Makes People Miserable, Studies Show," *Today Tech,* January 25, 2013, http://www.today.com/tech/ its-not-just-you-facebook-envy-makes-people-miserable-studies-1C8119557.

29. FEMA, "Ready," http://www.ready.gov.

Reflections

ABOUT BIG DREAM MINISTRIES

Big Dream Ministries exists to help people understand the Bible as God's complete and amazing story of redemption through Jesus Christ and equip them to apply Biblical truths to their lives. We do this by offering studies that drive people to the Scriptures for answers and providing tools to reinforce learning. Our vision is for people to be AMAZED by God's Word: to learn it, live it, and have it for life.

Our Collection of Bible Studies:

The Amazing Collection, The Bible, Book by Book
- Composed of 11 separate studies each teaching a section of the Bible. Together, *The Amazing Collection* covers every book of the Bible.
- Also available in Spanish (La Coleccion Maravillosa: La Biblia, Libro por Libro)

The Amazing Adventure
- An early childhood (3 – 7 years) curriculum with lessons, activities, and music to teach every book of the Bible

Be Amazing
- Based on Titus 2:3-5, this study teaches young women about godly character, healthy relationships, and managing a home.
- Also available in Portuguese (Seja Surpreendente: Estudo a luz da Biblia para a mulher surpreendente de hoje)

Invincible Love, Invisible War
- An excellent study for those who want to be prepared for spiritual battles by being armed with God's Word

The Amazing Temperaments
- This 6-week study biblically explores the strengths and weaknesses of each personality type to reach a full understanding and appreciation of yourself and others.

The Amazing Life of Jesus Christ, Part One and Part Two
- A chronological study of the Gospels that teaches about Christ's life in a deeper, more intentional way.

www.BigDreamMinistries.org

Made in the USA
Coppell, TX
08 September 2020